Linda —

I hope you find this useful.

Good luck with your projects,

[signature] 12/9/98

Building the New Enterprise

People, Processes, and Technology

Harris Kern, Randy Johnson, Stuart D. Galup, and Dennis Horgan
with Mark Cappel

Sun Microsystems Press
A Prentice Hall Title

The publisher offers discounts on this book when ordered in bulk quantities. For more information, contact Corporate Sales Department, Prentice Hall PTR, One Lake Street, Upper Saddle River, NJ 07458. Phone: 800-382-3419; FAX: 201-236-7141.
E-mail: corpsales@prenhall.com.

Editorial/production supervision: *Joe Czerwinski*
Cover designer: *M&K Design, Palo Alto, California*
Cover design director: *Jerry Votta*
Manufacturing manager: *Alexis R. Heydt*
Marketing manager: *Kaylie Smith*
Acquisitions editor: *Gregory G. Doench*
Sun Microsystems Press publisher: *Rachel Borden*

10 9 8 7 6 5 4 3 2

ISBN 0-13-079671-9

Sun Microsystems Press
A Prentice Hall Title

A. Appendix: IS job descriptions 133

Dedication

This is our fourth book in the "New Enterprise" series. Like the previous three, it is the product of many people who helped us directly and indirectly. We dedicate this book to our friends and family who supported us while researching, writing, and rewriting *Building the New Enterprise.*

Acknowledgments

To Michael Hawkins, who we recognize for his insight, vision, hard work, and dedication to the New Enterprise series. Without Michael there would be no series.

To the employees of Palm Beach County's Information Systems Services Department who had the guts to go the distance and succeed.

To Steve Mckenna for being one of our first supporters when very few understood our methodologies. Steve truly understands what it takes to manage an enterprise.

To Brad Hodges for his brilliance in designing the first-of-its-kind training manager.

To the Los Angeles Sun Microsystems sales and engineering organization (in particular Tom Swysgood, Craig Tempelton, Clark Bloom, Rick Kuhs, Mike Cirrincione, Shannon Kim, Jae Chung, Guy Nemiro, Cheryl Kolbor) for believing and supporting us.

To Howie Lyke for being a close friend and for his key contributions to this book.

To Richard Webster for his friendship and once again helping us with this book as he did with our earlier books.

To Kevin Kryzda, director of IT, Martin County-Florida for allowing us to study one of the most efficient IT infrastructures we've witnessed.

To Karin Ellison, Rachael Borden, and John Bortner for their ongoing support.

To Diolina Singca for her editing contributions.

To the IS organization at Instinet in New York lead by Brennan Carley, senior vice president, who contacted us to assist in implementing the processes required to effectively support mission-critical, client/server applications.

To Stuart's wife and daughter who suffered through the Palm Beach County transformation and this book.

Thanks to Michelle Lenham for all the editorial comments and support for this and our previous books.

To Hanny for her support.

To Arissa, Tad, and Jody.

Finally, thanks to our friends in the Southwest for their help with Chapter 7.

Foreword

Online banking and brokerage, planetary exploration, purchasing and logistics systems, electronic commerce... These and other mission-critical systems are now running on open, distributed platforms around the world. Gone are the days when UNIX was only for engineers and programmers. More businesses are retiring proprietary legacy systems and moving to client/server and Internet technology.

With the advent of the Web, many of these systems are not just running the business, they are delivering services directly to customers. When we buy a book or a CD on the Web, the reliability, performance, and ease of use of the Web page determine our experience as a customer. If the system is down we take our business elsewhere.

The computer industry has supplied us with high performance hardware and networks, while the software industry has fueled the growth of client/server with object oriented programming, rapid prototyping tools and more. Web technology makes it possible to develop and distribute new applications faster than ever. Go to any bookstore and you will find hundreds of titles on designing and programming these new applications, books on Visual Basic, books on OO analysis and design. The application developer today is well supplied with both technology and advice.

What has been left behind is the ability to manage these systems to deliver consistently high levels of reliability, availability, and serviceability. While our customers expect applications to be delivered in less time than ever before, they also depend on those applications to perform well and to be available when needed. The computer industry has responded to this challenge by delivering a confusing array of tools: OpenView, Ciscoworks, SunNet Manager, Tivoli, CA Unicenter, RMON, SNMP, the list is endless. As technologists, we are too easily seduced by technology solutions to our problems. But technology is only a small part of the solution. You cannot buy Openview (or Netview, or SunNet Manager) and call your network management problem solved.

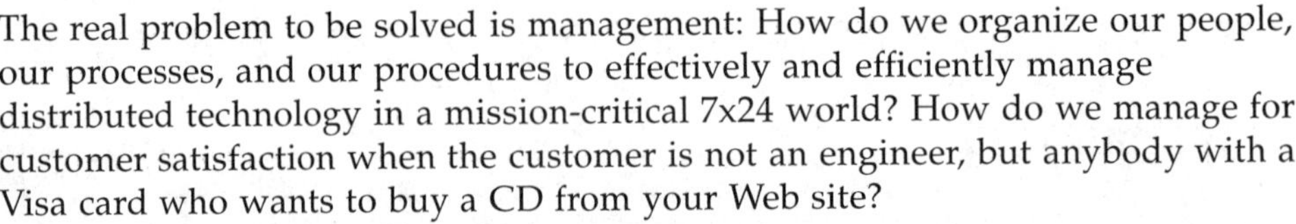

The real problem to be solved is management: How do we organize our people, our processes, and our procedures to effectively and efficiently manage distributed technology in a mission-critical 7x24 world? How do we manage for customer satisfaction when the customer is not an engineer, but anybody with a Visa card who wants to buy a CD from your Web site?

Scan the bookshelves and amid those hundreds of books on Java you will find very little to help you manage and support the steady stream of rapidly prototyped and delivered applications your users demand. You will also find many excellent books on management and leadership that leave you to make the connection between management theory and real-world application in IS.

Harris Kern and Randy Johnson, Stuart Galup, and Dennis Horgan have lived the experience, survived and learned from it. In this and their previous books, they share that experience. More important, they provide specific, actionable steps that you can take to harness the power of distributed computing while at the same time delivering high levels of service to your clients.

You won't find abstract management theories that leave the application to IS as an "exercise for the reader." This is not about five-year strategic technology plans. Harris, Randy, Stuart, and Dennis provide the nuts and bolts "basic blocking and tackling" skills that the others leave out. They walk you through the people issues, the core processes and disciplines, and show how they relate to the technologies.

You will find concrete, specific guidelines on managing the organizational issues, managing customer expectations and then managing the IS processes and disciplines to meet or exceed your customers expectations. The authors walk you through the architectural issues and the trade-offs between "buy" and "build," insourcing vs. outsourcing, so that you can make informed decisions on these critical issues. They lead you through the steps you need to take to set service level objectives, manage to those objectives, and measure your organizations performance against those objectives.

None of this is easy. In a fast-paced business environment that is dependent on distributed technology, you can't afford to get it wrong and you can't afford to learn by experience. Those experiences will cost you customers and cost you money. You need ideas and plans that you can adopt to your environment and put into effect. That's what Harris, Randy, Stuart, and Dennis deliver. This is mandatory reading for any CIO or IS manager who is moving to client/server (or has moved there and is trying to manage it.) Read it. Get copies for your staff and have them read it. Then put it into action and thrill your customers.

W. Brennan Carley
Senior VP, Information Technology
Instinet Corp.

Preface

Walk the aisles of the largest bookstores and you will see hundreds of books on management and leadership. You'll find even more on computer programming and systems design. Few explain how to organize and lead the Information Systems (IS) function in a large organization. *Building the New Enterprise* and its three predecessors (*Rightsizing the New Enterprise, Managing the New Enterprise,* and *Networking the New Enterprise*) are bridges linking business leadership and information technology. You don't need to be a hot Java programmer to understand this book. You don't need an MBA, or a degree in psychology, or organizational behavior. You do need an *interest* in all of these to grasp the leadership issues we share.

We give away the secrets to this book in its subtitle: *People, Processes, and Technology.* Not only do we reveal the key ingredients to creating a successful IS function, we also rank their relative importance.

You might think a collection of IS professionals would consider technology more important than personnel. Not us. We visited hundreds of IS shops around the world in the last few years. We found everyone running IS shops understands IS. But only one in five do a good job in managing processes. People-related problems are the No. 1 problem in the IS industry. While this has always been the case, today's complicated network computing combined with high demand for staff and increasing time pressures has brought out the worst in everyone. Coupled with the lack of efficient, non-bureaucratic processes, times are worse than ever for some IS organizations. The people issues we refer to are:

1. **Legacy and client/server personnel have different perspectives, values, and priorities**

   IS executives must forge one alloy out of the legacy and client/server worldviews. The legacy mentality is disciplined, with years of knowing how to support mission-critical applications. The high-tech, new-wave client/server perspective is more freewheeling and network-focussed. We'll show you how to harness the best of both worlds.

You *can* build an IS organization that relies on a flexible, disciplined yet non-bureaucratic and cost-efficient infrastructure, but it takes patience, dedication, specialized training, sincerity, and an investment in time and money from management. You need commitment and focus to make this happen. This could be the largest and most time-consuming project you will *ever* undertake in IS. This issue will make or break your infrastructure.

If you don't have a legacy staff to contend with don't think you're out of the woods. You will probably have a bigger problem with which to contend — teaching UNIX and NT hacks discipline. That's not the answer you wanted to hear. But there is a solution (see *Transitioning/training/mentoring staff* on page 34).

2. **The perception that the Internet is a solution, not a technology**

   The Internet craze brings a whole new set of people issues. A new breed of computer-literates are building intranet Towers of Babel. The Babelonians are more of a problem than mainframers and client/server mavens. At least these two understand the value of a disciplined environment. The new Internet jocks are so undisciplined their tools (most tools, anyway) lack version control!

3. **Communication within IS and external to IS is non-existent or poor**

   IS personnel are more decentralized than ever. It was hard enough to communicate effectively back in the 1970s within one data center. Now you may have ten network computing data centers (or what we refer to as glass closets) distributing data all over the corporate network and support personnel scattered throughout the world. There is hope, there is a process that promotes communication and we refer to it as Client Server Production Acceptance (see page 63).

4. **Organizations are not structured to properly support the new enterprise.**

   Many organizations are structured using technology silos instead of functional requirements. This causes tremendous communications barriers, poor morale, and a failure to use all available resources. The walls must come down!

5. **Politics are worse than ever. Is there an answer?**

   No, and there never will be. If you can fix items 1-4 then politics won't cripple you.

Processes, what processes?

IS must have discipline to support mission-critical distributed systems properly. Lately, we've noticed a heartening trend to embrace a disciplined approach to processes. The focus, however, is still on development and rightly so. We hear IS management say, "Get those new client/server applications out the door as quickly as possible and don't let that operational support staff slow you down!" And the most widely used quote from the user community "for every day that we don't get those applications in production we lose millions!"

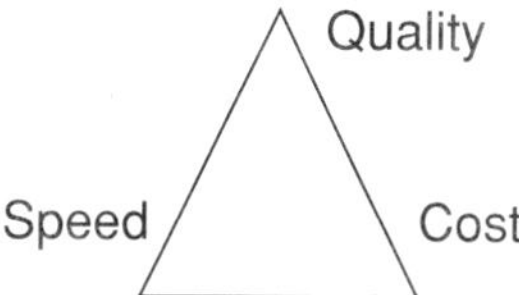

Figure 0-1 *Eldridge's Axiom: Quality, Speed, and Cost: You can have one or two, but not all three simultaneously.*

Everything, eventually, has a cost. It's expensive or impossible to support systems rushed into production that had no firm standards, guidelines, or documentation. We'll show you the streamlined, non-bureaucratic, cost-efficient way of implementing the right processes in *Client/Server Production Acceptance (CSPA)* on page 61.

The real importance of computer technology

Like sports fans identifying with with a team, IS people align themselves by their technology choices. Now that technology is more fragmented, people can be too. The right way to overcome differences between groups is to establish common beliefs, goals, and interests and work from there.

Get all factions to agree to something. Start with something as innocuous as IS's role in the future. Consider the following.

The next millennium will be dominated by digital information. Businesses will be moving too fast to wait for a report to be printed and shipped overnight mail to an overseas office.

The Internet promises to allow businesses and consumers the ability to execute transactions without paper. Once electronic cash is successfully implemented and low-end Internet appliances are affordable, the growth of digital business transactions will explode. Is your business ready?

Just look at the growth of information technology as documented by *Investor's Business Daily*[1]:

- Forrester Research Inc. expects growth of online accounts in the personal financial trading business to grow from 1.5 million in 1997 to 10 million in 2001. E-trade, an electronic trading service, is signing up 400 to 500 new accounts each day (*February 28,1997*).
- 90% of all 14.4 million college students have access to PCs and use them in one form or another (*March 12, 1997*).
- PC purchases in Latin America grew 30% to 3.1 million in 1996 (*March 12,1997*).
- Advertising on the Web topped $300 million in 1996 (*March 20, 1997*)
- Computer networks and the Internet fueled an explosion in e-mail usage, with about 1.6 trillion messages sent in 1996 (*February 18, 1997*).
- The average school district will spend $91 per student for technology in 96-97, up 3% from the year-ago period (*February 12, 1997*).
- 80 million PCs are expected to be sold in 1997. Up 17% from 1996 (*March 31, 1997*).

These statistics show a clear direction to a digital economy and the growth of the Internet.

In 1991, spending on computing and communications equipment exceeded spending on manufacturing and industrial equipment for the first time. And for those who don't believe the digital age is here now, back in 1992 the market capitalization of Microsoft exceeded that of General Motors for th first time. Today, just five years later, only General Electric has a higher market capitalization than Microsoft.

Yet, these trends show us the future and we are living in the present. This is still a time where corporate information systems are dominated by mainframe hardware and software. The future will be dominated by client/server open systems. The Internet will ensure that client/server and open systems technologies continue to grow and expand.

Our challenge is to get from the present to the future. We want to transition all the skills and disciplines we learned from the mainframe environment to the new client/server open systems environment.

This book will show you the way to the world-class IS organization can exist in the present, transition, and emerge in the future. It will hopefully enlighten you to many of the pitfalls that we the authors have witnessed in helping IS organizations move ahead.

1. http://www.investors.com

The first challenge faced by any IS organization is dealing with the universal shortage of the 1990s — time. In a recent survey in *Information Week* magazine[2], CIOs said their worst problem was not adequate budget or getting the right people, it was the lack of time. The time shortage manifests itself in both a shortage of personal time and time to market. Today, many businesses and industries are hyperevolving: merging and divesting to align with new market, challenging internal operations to employ best business practices, competing fiercely to win customers and forming new supplier alliances to reduce time to market. CIOs are expected to be participants, and increasingly, to lead the initiatives to help their companies move forward.

But IS departments everywhere are being trapped by systems that were engineered in an earlier age when businesses and their supporting technologies were largely stable. Much of tradition of data processing in American business evolved during the postwar American prosperity — a time during which business models changed slowly. And data system development followed that time schedule. For example, in the early 1950s the Sabre reservations system took nine years to implement after the initial proposal from IBM to American Airlines. Unfortunately, many businesses still wait years for new systems.

IS systems and assets once implemented were expected to last a long time. We recently talked with a project manager who was replacing a general ledger system at a large U.S. railroad. He said that the previous system had been placed in service in the mid-1960s on an IBM System 360 and had been in service with only minor modifications for 30 years. He was proud that they had made such efficient use of their IS assets.

There are many technical reasons why IS systems are slow to implement and evolve, but high on the list is that they are engineered systems. Unfortunately they are engineered on a model that any civil engineer would understand — like building a bridge. The development model for large enterprise systems, called the "waterfall" lifecycle, is one of the major barriers to innovation and speed in IS organizations.

Before you reject this analogy, we will use the construction of the Golden Gate Bridge as an example of how the process works. The Golden Gate Bridge project, one of the engineering marvels of the world, took more than 20 years. The engineers surveyed the site, and studied its geology. They produced preliminary design solutions and reduced the design to detailed engineering drawings. While design process was underway, the project champion, Louis Strauss, worked to obtain funding and approvals for the project — a process that took 14 years of

2. http://www.informationweek.com

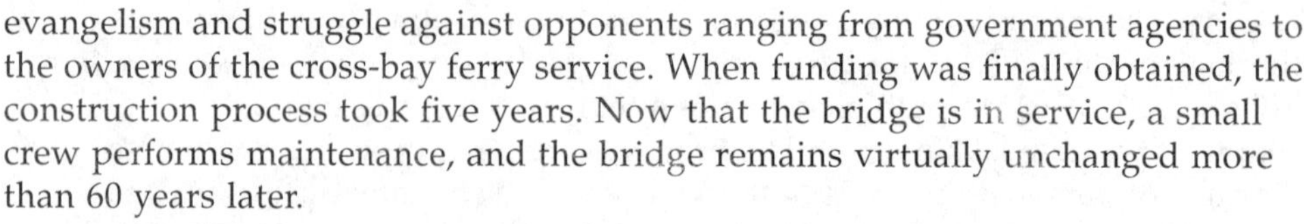

evangelism and struggle against opponents ranging from government agencies to the owners of the cross-bay ferry service. When funding was finally obtained, the construction process took five years. Now that the bridge is in service, a small crew performs maintenance, and the bridge remains virtually unchanged more than 60 years later.

Unfortunately, many data system development projects look a lot like the Golden Gate Bridge with Strauss as the CIO. The waterfall, an orderly process of requirements collection and systems analysis, design, development, and testing followed by turn on and minor maintenance is still the norm in many IS organizations. And while it may work for a bridge, the process is simply too slow to meet the needs of the modern enterprise.

Our goal for this book is to turn IS departments from civil engineers into combat engineers. Military combat engineers of the Army Corps of Engineers and the Navy Seebees have the same fundamental engineering training as their civilian counterparts, but they have the tools and methodology adapted to the hyperevolving conditions of warfare. Their goal is not to build elegant, long-lasting bridges, but instead to use adaptable technologies like pontoon bridges to move soldiers across the water and on to the next battle.

The goal of this book is to provide IS professional with the tools and methodologies so they can be flexible and responsive, and still maintain the integrity of systems and data. Just as no general would wait years for a bridge, CEOs will not wait years for a critical data system. For today's IS, agility is survival — and we will show you how to become more agile.

Ten commandments of a world-class IS infrastructure

1 

All great organizations infuse their people with elemental guidelines for proper behavior. Perhaps the oldest code of conduct is the Ten Commandments. Almost since the day Moses stumbled off Mount Sinai, people have applied the idea of condensing their groups' rules of conduct into ten, easy-to-remember sentences. Knowing a Good Thing when we see one, we've distilled our teachings on today's Information Services (IS) into Ten commandments of a world-class IS infrastructure. If you want a world-class infrastructure embrace these ideals:

1. **Treat thy network as thy data center.**

   In other words, "The network is the data center." What gives? Ask yourself: What is the most secure and reliable environment in data processing? Every IS professional can answer that one! The data center! It's your company's security blanket for essential, mission-critical, bread-and-butter, financial manufacturing, and human resource business systems.

   We can hear desktop cowboys stirring right now. Yes, there are some desktop applications that could be considered mission critical. And with client/server the desktop in general has become more important. But we agree only to a point. Desktops do not form the central nervous system of major organizations. If a desktop goes down, or even a LAN for that matter, a company *will* survive. Certainly a few people will take an unplanned break, but the WAN will keep the rest of the company actively employed. However, the desktop, file and print servers, and LANS are becoming as important, and in some cases more important, than the business applications. In this vein, the data center processes become more important when considering the whole enterprise.

   As you deploy the proper infrastructure, your objective should be to make the network as Reliable, Available, and Serviceable (RAS) as the data center. This requires processes, standards, and procedures, which leads us to our second commandment.

2. **Honor thy mainframe disciplines, and keep them holy**

   Mainframe disciplines, processes and procedures, standards and guidelines — we can't live with them and can't live without them. In the age of distributed everything to everywhere, disciplines are more important than ever. But you cannot simply transplant mainframe disciplines with all their bureaucracy on client/server technology. You need to customize and streamline these disciplines so they can manage a modern, chaotic, heterogeneous infrastructure. We grew up with these processes in the legacy environment, which included change management, capacity planning, disaster recovery, and so on. Today, we need these disciplines more than ever — but not the bureaucracy.

3. **Thou shalt keep minimum yet sufficient architectures.**

   Develop organization-wide standards for each area of the infrastructure, including the network, data center, desktops, development tools, nomadic computers, servers, and so on. You need standards for today, and clear statements of direction for your standards, environments, platforms, paradigms, or architectures (you pick the buzzword) for the future. For example, your desktops today could be Windows 3.1.1 boxes on 10BaseT. Your plan could call for NCs running on 100BaseT, or PDAs running Java nomadically.

4. **Thou shalt maintain centralized control with decentralized operations.**

   Implement the new enterprise with a mixture of centralized control and decentralized operations. Centralized control means controlling costs, developing architectures, and deploying standards and guidelines from a central location. Decentralized operations means it doesn't matter where your IS support personnel are located. They can be placed to best support networked computing in general and your customer specifically.

5. **Honor thy users and communicate with them often.**

   The failure to communicate is a big problem. Generally speaking, IS professionals would rather string cable and write code than hang out with users and listen to them. This failure is wired, as it were, into IS people, and supported by the culture of IS organizations. To make matters worse, IS itself can't seem to communicate within its own borders. Back in the mainframe days, we enjoyed a clear demarcation as to who did what to whom and when. Everyone's responsibilities were clearly defined. DBAs knew exactly where their roles started and ended. Ditto for systems programmers, and so on.

Here comes this crazy world of network computing without any clear boundaries. Everything is spread across the network. There needs to be a process that promotes and instills communication between IS and its customers, and between the different groups within IS. This process should clearly spell-out everyone's roles and responsibilities.

6. **Keep all production systems equal in the eyes of the IS staff.**

   From a hardware perspective, today's enterprise consists of mainframes, PC's, Macintoshes, workstations, servers, etc. You might be tempted to create separate support groups for each, Wrong!

   Do not build silos surrounding technologies. Your support team should be referred to as *technical support* (no more and no less) and all its staff members should be cross-trained on as many platforms as each can handle.

   Separating support along technologies results in inefficiencies, political problems, poor communications, and awful morale. These are a few problems that will occur when organizing to focus on a particular technology. Today, where everyone is doing more with less you need to get the most out of your staff. Never re-organize based on technology.

7. **Measure all; verily, you can not manage what you do not measure.**

   Think back to your legacy environment and how you were able to measure every aspect of the infrastructure. Some of the metrics that we gathered included:

   - Online system availability
   - Network availability
   - Number of trouble calls
   - Number of application amendments
   - Application response times
   - Percent of trouble calls resolved within two hours, four hours and so on.

   Ask any IS executive in the 1970s and 1980s about their system availability, and they were proud to respond with 99.5 percent, 99.8 percent, and so on. What about today's networked enterprise? Forget it. Who has the time to collect all this trivia? We're the first to agree it takes energy to establish metrics. It took time, a lot of time, to collect uptime statistics in the mainframe era, but it was one of the reasons the legacy world was so reliable. We knew the numbers. We managed because we measured.

   Crunch your uptime numbers, hold people accountable, and your people will somehow find a way to run your shop more efficiently.

8. **Thou shalt build an attractive IS service, and users will come.**

   Once you get your house in order your customers will come back. But most IS shops are far from getting their internal workings in order. In the 1980s, most of IS's customers abandoned the centralized support group to develop and deploy their own client/server applications. Centralized IS was too bureaucratic and costly.

   Today, those same customers have felt the pain of trying to support their own mini-IS operations and quite frankly are willing to give up the technology support issues. They need help, but centralized IS still must re-engineer itself to provide a better level of service.

   In our previous books *Rightsizing the New Enterprise* and *Managing the New Enterprise* we discuss a process that's a requirement in the New Enterprise. It's the foundation for your infrastructure. This process happens to be the largest piece of the puzzle, but there are many others as well. Once these processes become streamlined and cost efficient, your house (infrastructure) will support the New Enterprise. Then you need to advertise your services. Yes, services are what matters. People need business problems solved, not technology offerings to admire.

9. **Thou shalt share the good news of thy services.**

   In the before time, mainframers would meditate in data centers perched in lofty ivory towers. The only time we would interact with common users is when the help desk would beckon with an unusual problem. We operated in reactionary mode.

   Today, IS professionals need to walk with the great unwashed and communicate with customers. We need to shmooze, sell, and otherwise promote our services. In our second book *Managing the New Enterprise* we referred to it as reengineering IS.

10. **Know that success equals the change thou manages.**

    Change will not stop. In fact, we are all now running on Internet time, even if our companies do not sell products that operate on any network. Technology is evolving and shifting faster than ever. Follow the first nine methodologies in building a world-class Infrastructure and you *will* find success.

It begins with planning 2 

One of the main objectives of the New Enterprise Information Services (IS) should be to implement production-quality infrastructures for the distributed computing environment. Frequently in our travels we see organizations in which applications are deployed without regard to the services that support them. When implementing new systems or services it is essential to implement the necessary management tools and operational processes, procedures, organization, workflow, and service levels to effectively manage the more complex environment.

Although the subtitle of the book is *People, Processes, and Technology* we break down the model into the three P's.

- Planning
- People
- Process & procedures

It needs to begin with planning. Here's why:

Planning

We must first define and develop a plan for supporting the new distributed model. Many corporations plan their applications and applications architecture. With the emphasis placed on deploying new systems quickly they neglect to develop the infrastructure plan. We strongly recommend the infrastructure support plan be deemed as important and equal to the applications architecture plan. The plan should look at the current environment and provide a step-by-step approach to supporting the new.

Over the years we in the IS business spent most of our time planning, planning and more planning and then budgeting, budgeting, and more budgeting. Since IS was seen as the necessary evil and simply overhead in most corporations, we were forced to justify ourselves at every turn. We had very little ability to do things on our own without someone, usually the financial officer, questioning every activity and dollar spent. Based on this history we got to the point of being too conservative and lost the ingenuity that tended to set us apart from other disciplines within the corporation.

In the past, IS was seen as the savior of all the corporate administrative problems when we provided automated payroll and general ledger processing on the mainframe. In some cases we were allowed to delve into strategic business initiatives and develop or implement systems that supported key business requirements.

Another ageless IS problem is the Vice Grip between users who want more service and upper management, which controls the budget. We refer to this as the *IS squeeze.*

But then came the PC

The PC brought power and technology to the local department and to the desktop. Users of IS service quit coming. They implemented their own technology solutions and systems on the desktop. IS continued with the administrative systems on the mainframe while the users implemented local PC-based solutions to support their business requirements. They didn't want to use IS services because of the conservative and obnoxious nature they had grown to expect over the years. Users felt they could implement their own solutions. And, of course, we gave up on any kind of support for the PC environment. IS management wanted no part of that environment and left the users on their own to fend for themselves.

IS management thought the users would find too many technology issues awaiting them, then fail so they could say "We told you so, the mainframe is the only solution!" But the PC users didn't fail (or they just wouldn't admit it). PC users could use the local technology to support their requirements in a more timely and less costly manner. "We don't need IS anymore and it costs too much," they would say.

But then came client/server

Then came the client/server technology. This new technology provided even more power at the local level and more ability to support local departmental business issues. End-users started looking toward replacing mainframe applications and/or new business functions with client/server technology. They still felt they didn't need IS.

As these new applications were being developed, deployed and put into production, everyone in the industry started hearing those horror stories of "this stuff doesn't work," or, "development and deployment is taking longer than on the mainframe," or, "the technology isn't ready for prime-time." In reality, from our perspective, it wasn't the technology that was the problem, it was mostly because the end-users never learned what *mission-critical* meant or what it takes to support mission-critical systems.

But then came IS (again)

With the advent of client/server technology it has become more and more a requirement to support mission-critical applications at the local level or what we consider at the network level. The network (wide-area, local-area) desktop, application server and database server are becoming mission-critical and need to be supported as such, and it gets worse! Customers are demanding support for nomadic computing, PDAs and thin clients.

That's why we coined the phrase, "The network is the data center." Mission-critical means a set of standards, guidelines, processes, procedures, and management policies that were developed in the data center long ago. (The data center staff had to implement these management policies based on budget, planning, overhead, etc.) It took many years to establish mission-critical guidelines. How do we implement these processes and procedures in a network-computing environment based on all those sins of the past?

We think the time is now. It is time for IS to get back into the thick of technology support and implementation of client/server. How? It takes planning. We have to acknowledge the need for team involvement (IS and end-users), communication and planning — together. And, guess what! This isn't easy. How do we get rid of all that old baggage and come together to do things the right way for the corporation. How do we get rid of the politics that have been ingrained now these past ten to 15 years?

This is many times harder than dealing with technology. It is cultural. How do we change the IS culture and the end-user culture? We think (based on successes) that we've found the answer.

Scenario-based architectural planning

We are continually surprised and amazed at how many IS organizations are not in tune with the business model for their industry or their company. A successful architecture cannot be developed without an understanding of corporate or industry economics and business strategy. Why? Because if you don't understand what drives your business, you will never be able to design an information system that will be capable of responding to the inevitable changes.

Ask yourself these questions:

- Is your business driven by sales or manufacturing?
- Is the key to your success the ability to control costs, produce products faster than your competitors, or to innovate faster in the market?
- How easily can your products or services be imitated?
- How many competitors do you have today and how many do you expect to have in five years?
- Is your industry easy to enter or require major investments to get started?

This is an IS book, not a book on corporate strategy — but the answers to these questions have a profound effect on IS architecture.

To understand the effects of strategy on IS, ask yourself these questions:

- How fast could you separate your IS systems and restate your financial results if a division was sold suddenly?
- How fast could you merge systems if a new division was suddenly acquired?
- Are you likely to undergo a major reorganization, open or close a new facility this year?
- How many new products or services do you expect to introduce this year?
- Are there new reengineering initiatives starting or underway at your company this year?

These questions are essential for all architectural and capacity planning processes. They are also a litmus test for any CIO or senior IS manager to check out how well-connected you are with your company's business model. If you cannot answer these questions you have a research challenge ahead.

Once you have the business background, try weaving some scenarios around these futures. There is nothing remarkable about scenario-based planning. The military calls it war-gaming and has practiced it for years. These do not need to be long exercises, but you will be surprised at the results.

Try a simple scenario in the form of a "what if" analysis on disruptive changes in the business plan to see what the impacts on your IS system might be. Many managers are surprised about the results of these analyses and discover business vulnerabilities well beyond the technical issues with which we normally deal.

The lesson from these architectural exercises is the need for flexibility. But too many managers forget the challenges of flexible design and instead create the illusion of flexibility with their customers by "complexifying" their data systems and then attempting to hide the complexities from their customers. We call this IS "water ballet." Water ballet looks graceful and smooth to the spectators, but when seen from underneath the water, there is a lot of frantic paddling and breath holding going on.

So it is with IS organizations that say *yes* without an architecture to support them. They can hide their deficiencies from their customers, but in the end they either overwork themselves and their staffs or blow their budgets on consultants, hardware, and software trying to keep up with the promises they've made.

What to do? We recommend some basic processes and technologies to help simplify and create flexible architectures that customers will support.

People

The second *P* (but probably the most important piece of the puzzle) in our New Enterprise IS services model is people. Now that we have provided the planning, we must focus on the people issues to complete the model. The New Enterprise IS must first be positioned as a service organization and focus on these issues just as any service vendor would do.

The best way to look at this is to think of the requirements of a service provider that you would contract to supplement your services. If you contract for services you expect the vendor to provide the expertise. This should be no different in the New Enterprise IS. The key asset for any services organization is the people and addressing the people issues is the most important issue. Remember: it is not *technology* that matters; it's *people*. Here are the most important areas to address.

- Organization
- Staffing
- Roles and responsibilities
- Mentoring
- Training/Transitioning
- Human Resources
- Metrics
- Cultural differences

 2

Principles of organizational design

3 

The glass closet in context

In the United States, modern business enterprises started to develop after the Civil War. Since then two major milestones transpired in organizational design. The distinguishing of management from ownership between 1895 and 1905 was the first major shift in power and knowledge.

Approximately 20 years later the second major evolution took place. It is what we have grown to expect as the typical organization structure. This shift occurred when Pierre S. Du Pont restructured the family business in the early 1920s. It continued with Alfred P. Slone's introduction of command and control procedures that allowed for a decentralized organizational structure with centralized staff functions.

In the first two decades of this century, Frederick W. Taylor's scientific management established a framework that advanced the total system of management. He introduced a new and influential technology, which focused on the subdivision of tasks into manageable and controllable units. This lead the way to the division of labor as exemplified by Ford Motor Company's assembly line manufacture of automobiles.

Following World War II, a second management method, participative management, introduced the human side of management. Participative management greatly lessened the dominance that scientific management had controlled up to that point. The concept that performance was driven by motivational factors, and not the division of functions, partially displaced scientific management.

Alfred P. Sloan, chief executive officer of General Motors, followed Pierre S. Du Pont a few years later by taking Taylor's work one step further. He created the divisional corporation. Du Pont, as well as Henry Ford and others of that time, had created large organizations that had grown beyond the capabilities of general management. Sloan divided General Motors into divisions to allow his management group to control and organize business activities. This defined how large multinational corporations were structured for several decades.

The information age is a new period of change. A shift from command and control organizations, the organization of departments and divisions, to an information-based organization.

Why is the history of organizational design important? The "glass house" is designed using Taylor and Sloan's definition of best practices for organization design. We often refer to this organizational design as a *stovepipe.* IS groups are structured into divisions, department, groups, etc., with a clear division of labor and resources.

As we move to the information age, it is increasingly important to evaluate the organizational design of our IS groups and to determine if change is needed. We must eliminate waste and increase production. We must face global competition with efficiencies and quality. But most importantly, we must look at the changes in our organization and we must adjust the IS group to best fit the needs of the new organization.

More and more organizations are reviewing their business processes and evaluating the need for changes to improve efficiency and quality. It is increasingly apparent that improved business processes necessitate improved information flows supported by information technologies. For example, if all members of a manufacturing process are involved in the design and development of the product, less design flaws are found and less rework is required. This yields a higher quality product at a substantially cheaper production cost.

It's challenging to view the organization as a series of processes and translate them into accepted business norms is a challenge. It's even harder to modify existing stovepipe information systems to allow data movement across organizational borders.

Often the challenge is not the technology, but the IS group's organizational design. Many IS groups cannot support the development of information systems that support business processes that transverse multiple divisions. The IS group is divided into multiple sub-groups that support the organization's sub-groups. Teaming is the only approach that will allow cross-organizational business processes supported by integrated information systems to work.

We are not advocating matrix management. But, to develop information systems that support cross-organizational business processes, you must use cross-functional teams. We define a business process as all tasks and sub-processes, wherever they may exist, that result in the creation of a service or product. For example, an auto maker requires sales, marketing, engineering, manufacturing, administration, etc. It is a total process that creates the car and prepares it for sale to motorists.

If the organization is based on vertical division lines, stovepipe information systems are fundamental component of the information architecture. If the organization decides to restructure to compete in a global economy and to survive in the information age, it must modify its business processes and organizational structure as required. The IS group needs to evaluate its contribution to this change and also restructure as required. IS must walk-the-talk.

We have three suggestions for IS groups ready for change:

1. **Draw many maps**

   Analyzing the organization's business processes. Diagram the process flows. Map the data and applications that support these tasks and sub-processes (fundamental information engineering practices). Map the IS resources needed to support the business processes.

   The result is a cross-functional IS team that can build and maintain the information system that supports the business processes. Remember, the information system is now horizontal in nature, not vertical. This may seem simple, but it is a difficult concept for mainframe and client/server developers to accept.

2. **Find owners**

   You must have a process owner at the organization level and at the IS group level. Yes, this sounds like matrix management. It is very close. You can still have traditional lines of authority with one boss, and participate as a team member. The key is cultural change in the IS group. The difference is that a process is almost forever and a project ends. The IS process owner manages the technical issues and the IS area manager (network administration, applications development, etc.) manages the people. Performance reviews are prepared jointly and the IS process owner's vote is worth more that the IS area manager's vote. Remember, results are the bottom line!

3. **Develop processes for getting essential tasks completed on time**

   To make this all work you must have a fully functional customer request/problem report project management system. Remember, if you are going to focus on processes for the organization, you must develop internal IS group processes for getting work done. The work must be done right the first time and on time. If the IS organization is defined as processes, it can execute customer requests quickly and correctly because all the members of the team know what their job is and how to get it done. How many times have you requested a PC installation and find out that the unit is operational and the ID wasn't registered or the IP address is in use by another device on the network? These mistakes are a result of stovepipe IS services.

The right organizational design for an IS group is one that parallels the organization. If the organization is a vertical structure with hierarchical management layers, than the IS organization should be structured in a similar way and will most likely be dominated by host-based systems (no client/server). If the organization is a formal hierarchical structure, but uses information technology in a way that employees can communicate freely without pre-established management layer boarders, we recommend cross-functional teams to development and maintain cross-organizational information systems.

There are very few flat organization structures. Formal hierarchy are still required for most organizations to function. The use of information technology within the IS group and throughout the organization can start to eliminate the borders.

Organizational issues

All the finest processes in the world won't help if the organization is not structured to support any technology. So, the IS group must structure for success. Success in this case is supporting the legacy and client/server environments while technologies and people integrate.

How do we get there? We start by looking at the balance of people, process and technology in mathematical terms:

> Technical change + resources and time for implementation = learning + economic benefits to the firm + benefits to the worker.

The balance between technology, resources, and time, and the benefits that the combination of these ingredients can generate will result in a successful transformation.

First, realize that all the information technologies you purchase are important and must be managed in a consistent manner (i.e., enterprise-wide application development standards). Second, realize that your staff, no matter what technology platform they work on, must be treated the same. We know that this is sometimes hard. We all have biases, but the only way to unify an IS organization is to treat everyone equally. Third, realize that a merger of legacy and client/server staffs is a restructure and will take time. It will take time because you're merging two different cultures.

Culture is the single most important issue to manage during the transformation. Since most IS organizations are divided into sub-cultures, usually legacy and client/server, the job gets more difficult. Sub-cultures will show themselves and often in very negative and self-serving ways.

We found the client/server sub-culture to be very anti-establishment, and for good reason. During the 198's, the PC programmers, who evolved into today's client/server technologists, were not treated equally by IS management. As a result, many IS organizations are now experiencing a reverse discrimination by the client/server employees towards the mainframe employees. We've witnessed IS organizations where the client/server employees banned together and refused to allow the systems support staff (networks and operating systems) to manage the development environment. They did their own cabling and set up their own servers. The group developed fantastic client/server systems that failed miserably when migrated to a production WAN environment. Trust between the two groups just wasn't there!

The one thing we found most often was poor project management tools and methodologies. If you plan to integrate legacy and client/server environments, you must update the internal information technologies used by the information systems professional. Standard software tools, such as, project management, customer request, system performance measurement, electronic mail, etc. are required for the two groups to work together. Shared disciplines and tools force everyone to work together.

We recommend human resource practices that re-enforce the integration of legacy and client/server employees. This means not having the same old job descriptions based on the platform. There should be one job description for a Systems Programmer across all platforms (i.e., UNIX, and mainframe).

There should also be curriculums and programs which instill and promote teamwork. It is crucial that UNIX, NT, and mainframe people work on projects together. Cross-train wherever possible. Establish a common test area. The New Enterprise IS must be organized to support customers and the network computing model.

Global infrastructures

Thinking globally and working locally, as it is often stated, is not a simple act when you are standardizing on IS tool and processes. For example, using an authority hierarchy for signature approval of completed work can cause great difficulty from one culture to another.

Nothing should change. The people issues and processes we talk about should be flexible enough to adapt to regional locations as well as corporate headquarters. The key word is *adapt* not build something new. If not the consequences are obvious. Costs will continue to skyrocket and RAS will continue to deteriorate.

Decentralized staff

IS staff now reside at their customer sites and in many cases report right into their business units. The intent is that they will work closely with the customer, respond in a timely manner based on their specific needs, and therefore develop a more acceptable or polished finished product. This is a very positive way to build quality IS systems and cultivate customer relations.

The down side is that many IS professionals that are assigned to customer sites or report into the divisions wane from the central policies and procedures of the central IS organization. Although everyone says it's better to standardize for the good of the company but that's just corporate lip service. No one wants to cooperate. Decentralized IS staff do things their way for the good of their customers only. So, how do you overcome this? Using a set of governance policies allows the de-centralized staff to play a role in the development of the enterprise's IS standards. Having a voice makes a big difference and getting input from the de-centralized staff creates a more robust set of standards.

Where can you find out more about governance policies? We have included a copy that we obtained from a county government policy board in south Florida. We also recommend that you read Paul Strassmann's *Politics of Information Management*. (See

In conjunction with the governance policies between the centralized and de-centralized IS staffs there's also a process which we refer to as the CSPA. This is the process that builds the bridge and just like the Golden Gate Bridge in San Francisco, which is continuously being painted all year round, the CSPA promotes ongoing communication between centralized and decentralized organizations. It actually forces people to adhere to a minimum set of standards and guidelines and work together daily.

Roles and responsibilities

Defining everyone's roles and responsibilities is essential in a network environment. Demarcation between organizations is fading.

Single job descriptions for similar technologies (MVS & UNIX)

One of the simplest and most unused approaches to unifying the IS organization during the merger of the mainframe and client/server staffs is job classifications. Most organizations continue to divide their staffs by using job descriptions that are germane to the mainframe or client/server environments. For example, client/server developers are sometimes classified as micro-system analysts as opposed to their counterparts on the mainframe that are called systems analysts.

We recommend that you use the same titles and diversify the skill sets of both groups. This allows the team to emerge naturally and everyone feel that they are first-class citizens.

Here are some job classifications that we've written detailed job descriptions for in *Appendix: IS job descriptions* on page 133:

Planning and Research Services

- Senior Technology Architect
- Technology Architect III

Software Engineering Services

- Senior Software Engineer
- Software Engineer III
- Software Engineer II
- Software Engineer I

Network Administration Services

- Senior Network Engineer
- Network Engineer III
- Network Engineer II
- Network Engineer I

Server Administration Services

- Senior Server Administrator
- Server Administrator III
- Server Administrator II
- Server Administrator I

Database Administration Services

- Senior Database Administrator
- Database Administrator III
- Database Administrator II
- Database Administrator I

Each position group (i.e., Senior, III, II, etc.) share a similar pay range. This promotes cross training and stops the exodus from one technical area to another when hot technologies drive the cost of technical talent through the roof. It establishes clarity to the organization structure and skills become the issue of discussion, not the differences or perceived differences in job titles.

Responsibilities by application

Thanks to network computing, support requirements need to be defined for each production application deployed on your network. Part of the CSPA process (described *Client/Server Production Acceptance (CSPA)* on page 61) is to clearly define who does what to whom and when. Each application has different requirements and needs special attention.

Staffing

Staffing should be based on the organizational structure and the new IS model of doing more with less. We must provide equal or better levels of service at lower costs to be effective. To accomplish this daunting task we recommend implementing the processes and systems management model, then automate, automate, automate! The best ways to control costs and provide effective service is to standardize and invest in tools and provide the right staffing to meet the new service model.

Key areas to focus on are systems administration, networking, database administration, and production control. *Production control* is probably one of the most important. In the past, companies tended to staff the other functions but leave out production control. This is especially the case in organizations without mainframe experience.

To be effective, the New Enterprise IS must define and implement a production control function.

We like to define production as any system, network, application, or database that requires RAS (reliability, availability and serviceability) as identified in our systems management model. Once you define your scope of production in the new model, there must be a group accountable for delivery and ownership of the production environment. We call it production control. Production control resides within the technical support group in the data center organization or infrastructure support group (see *Organizing for the next millennium* on page 43 for a detailed description of the organizational structure).

Mentoring

We define mentoring as specialized hand-holding and guidance in building a very flexible and cost-effective infrastructure. Mentoring helps people helps them learn and overcome biases.

Evangelize that a production system is a production system is a production system. Use mentoring to teach that legacy people are equal to client/server support staff and vice-versa.

Unfortunately, mentoring takes time. It is critical to the overall structure of the organization. Mentoring is also about having the right expertise in the new-wave stuff.

Many organizations go into the client/server distributed model without any in-house expertise. In most cases they have read a lot of computer trade press indicating that new applications can be implemented without expertise in UNIX, the RDBMS, and operations. In fact, some IS organizations have cut their operations staff (or outsourced them) because they were told the functions were no longer required. Wrong! You must have the expertise internally to succeed.

We recommend implementing a mentoring program to help bring your staff forward. If you do not have the expertise internally, there are consulting firms that can provide mentoring programs. The ideal scenario is to have staff with experience in legacy disciplines of running a mission-critical environment and the new-wave thinking of networks computing. It would be great to have this type of mind set to implement the proper infrastructure. Unfortunately most companies don't have this type of expertise. Read more about this in *Transitioning/training/mentoring staff* on page 34.

Training/transitioning

One of most important functions of any service organization is training. To provide effective levels of service and be active in supporting the environment, the New Enterprise IS must invest and provide training for the staff. For some reason, we have continually pushed off training because there is no budget (or the budget gets cut) or we simply do not make the time.

We expect any other service vendor we do business with to have the expertise we are buying, why not ourselves? You must focus on training and have training programs in place to move forward. You can teach old dogs new tricks. We always recommend training the existing staff. Why? They understand your business! See *The politics of people, process, and technology* on page 23 for a detailed look at transitioning your staff.

Metrics

What metrics? And what's that got to do with people issues? It's quite simple but we cannot underestimate its importance.

Track every class taken, technical seminar attended, projects completed, books read, homework assignments completed, and so on. It's tedious and boring but it's a must.

Cultural differences

One of the biggest problems in the industry today! In our previous books this subject rears its ugly head. Simply stated legacy people and client/server people come from two different planets. This relationship was never meant to be but the best infrastructures will be built with both mind sets working together as one unit. The outcome will be a highly Reliable, Available, and Serviceable environment that's streamlined without the bureaucracy of the past. See *Transitioning/training/mentoring staff* on page 34 for a more detailed discussion on transitioning your staff.

The leader

What will destroy the move to a unified IS organization? *Inertia.* The general tendency of any large group of people during a time of change is to wait and see.

How do you over come this? It really depends.

First, is your CIO a leader that is a hands-on person or does the CIO work through a network of management layers? The closer the CIO is to the action, and therefore the technologists doing the work, the better chance the IS organization has of unifying.

When a CIO is knowledgeable of day-to-day issues, it allows him/her to step in and lead when the staff deviates from the stated goal. Deviating from the goal is common and can be dealt with easily. It just requires extra effort.

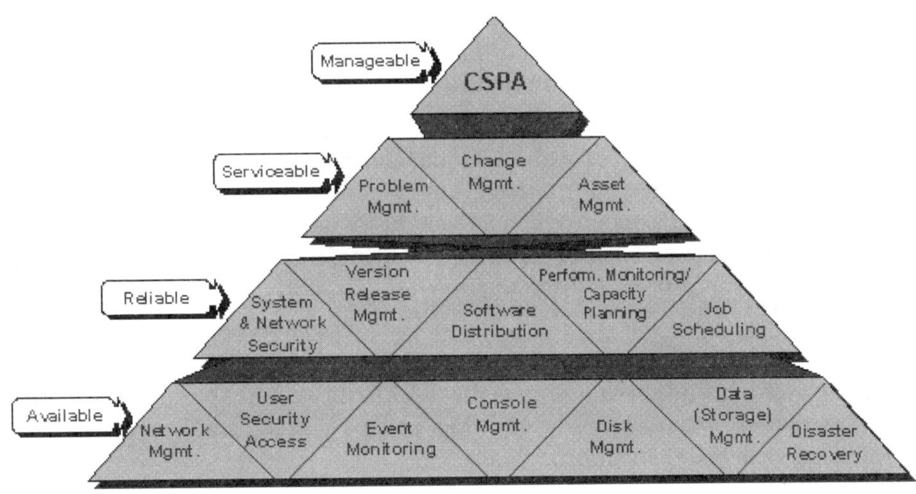

Figure 3-1 *Systems Management Implementation Model*

Processes and procedures

The New Enterprise IS service model's second section is centered on processes and procedures.

We have depicted the appropriate set of processes and procedures in our Systems Management Implementation model shown in *Systems Management Implementation Model* on page 21. Continuing the operations support role, we recommend implementation of the processes and procedures that support high Reliability, Availability, Serviceability, and Manageability in the new network enterprise. Each function is broken into groups according to the service level it provides. The CSPA (Client/Server Production Acceptance) process is at the top of the pyramid because it is the umbrella for establishing communication and management of the entire infrastructure.

Once the planning is complete and the process and procedures are defined, it becomes necessary to begin implementation of the tools, standards, and support infrastructure for the open distributed environment. Another important component in distributed computing is automating the environment through systems management tools. You must first define the process (all processes were defined in detail in chapter 8 of our second book *Managing the New Enterprise*), then automate with software tools. Why define the processes first? Because the tools are only as good as the processes behind them. But you must automate. To support your enterprise and be active you must automate the environment (detailed discussion of automation is in our third book *Networking the New Enterprise*)! And there are many tools available now. You'll probably need scalable heterogeneous tools that can grow with the environment and there are many to choose from to meet your needs.

During our extensive training/transitioning/mentoring program (for staff) we were discussing how all of our curriculums were based on "hands-on" assignments. We documented which classes, homework assignments, and projects that were completed by each of our staff. That information would be noted into our monthly status report. These metrics were tracked very closely by our entire IS organization. Why?

Training metrics are important for several reasons. First is the need to make sure that your training budget is going to the most critical skill shortages. We are always surprised to find how the training budget is being used in ways that are not aligned with the institutional goals.

Second is the need to ensure equity in training and to avoid politics. Some individuals and departments always seem to be masters at getting more than their share of the training budget and this issue must be managed.

Finally, training metrics are an important part of any modern HR plan. Career development is important in this age of the "all-volunteer workforce" as both a motivator and an invaluable tool for employee retention. Training can also protect the organization if downsizing becomes necessary, since up-to-date skills make the employee more marketable.

Look beyond technology

Technology can do ill as easily as good. The *only* way you can take full advantage of technology is by resolving people and process issues. We're not saying to slow down or stop implementing new goodies. On the contrary. Things will never slow down! Just give the two P's (people issues and processes) a chance.

The politics of people, process, and technology 4

Office and organizational politics will never go away. But you can overcome the more unproductive aspects of politics. Even the most difficult situation can be overcome if you create a quality, effective product that's priced right and delivered with a smile.

Selling it to the CIO

CIOs don't have time to learn what it takes to implement and support the New Enterprise. They have other issues competing for their attention, and most are more immediate than your organization's computational plumbing.

Start with the CIO. Without the support of the CIO any project attempted will fail. Start a pilot project with a friendly customer, and allow them to help you with it. You may need the credibility of a major win, and a pilot customer can give it to you.

Don't try to take on the entire organization at once. Get some early wins with your user community and then have them sell for you. Customers listen to each other, and will always place more trust in a peer.

Smart CIOs listen to customers. With credibility in place, remind customers, prospects, and management that additional successes with today's technology will come at a price. Recount how difficult it was to exchange one mainframe operating system for another. Remind everyone of the months of planning and testing to move the organization from, essentially, one railroad track to another. Then remind them that going from the mainframe to a distributed computing environment is like having a fleet of trucks replace the old iron horse. (How quickly people forget the three decades it took to establish the procedures that form the foundation for a secure and reliable data center.)

Executives and users are demanding and impatient, spurred on by competition and oftentimes glowing accounts in trade magazines of client/server bliss. They often fail to recognize that not only is a small system change tough under ideal conditions, establishing the New Enterprise means making many large changes and adopting a computing system with double or perhaps triple the number of variables.

Both executives and users need to understand that today's network-based computing paradigm implies wide-ranging organizational changes far beyond Microsoft's plan for selling Windows 98 to hoi polloi and Windows NT to more demanding users. By change, we mean establishing a new, fast-moving, flexible organization where information is available promptly to those who need to make decisions.

Satisfying the customer

One of the great revolutions in American business that began in the 1980s (and is still underway) is the ascendancy of the customer. It is now much more than a cliche that the customer is king. And today this is as true for internal customers as it is for external customers. The rise of packaged enterprise systems and the rapid growth of outsourcing means that IS customers have more choices than ever, and our experience is that they will use them if they are dissatisfied. Yet we still find many IS departments that are not focusing on customer satisfaction and are using their institutional position to control their customers. But over time, by not satisfying their customers they are putting their budgets and continued employment at risk. We are going to discuss some of the principles of customer satisfaction and offer suggestions for getting and staying in tune with your customers.

Satisfaction is important because it is a lagging indicator of service quality. If customers are dissatisfied, it is probably because their needs have not been met for some time. When customers become vocally dissatisfied about IS performance, it suggests a systemic failure to communicate and properly set expectations with them.

Watch for telltale signs of dissatisfied customers. Here is a brief customer satisfaction quiz:

1. What's the size of your service request backlog in number and in time to complete?
2. Are customers resisting serving on your review boards and committees?
3. Do customers control their share of your IS budget or does IS dictate priorities and project funding?
4. Does the customer have a choice of service levels, and are there auditable metrics on the quality of service?

5. Are customers going around IS departments by setting up local mini-IS functions?
6. Are you having trouble getting support for your initiatives and budget requests?
7. When you implement a new system, does the complaining die away in days, weeks, months or never?
8. How often do you have a major system outages of multiple hours or even days in duration?

If you answered yes to some or all of these questions we can guarantee you have dissatisfied customers even if they are not complaining to you directly. In fact, if they are not communicating, you are in big trouble. In our experience, when customers stop publicly griping it may be the calm before the storm.

What can be done to improve satisfaction? Here are some simple steps to making customers more satisfied:

1. **Meet their expectations**

   This is so important that we've devoted the next section to this subject. A customer who expects more that they are receiving will be dissatisfied no matter what the absolute quality of the service. If your department has a reputation of giving customers happy talk, or future promises to keep them at bay — watch out!

2. **Believe their complaints, not their vision**

   As we discuss in *Technology: Software* on page 95, customers are not necessarily the best determiners of technology choices. They tend to define their needs based on what they know, not what is possible. However, if you offer them options, they are able to select among them and to articulate flaws. Customers are best able to help correct flaws in interfaces, usability issues, and functional deficiencies. These flaws should not be criticized, but listened to and corrected as soon as possible.

   Customers are notoriously bad at helping define directions for system development or in helping define an architecture. There are some exceptions to this rule — people who have had training in reengineering are a possibility — but *IS* needs to be the keeper of the IS vision, not customers.

3. **Empower customers**

   A common complaint we hear from IS is that customers are setting up their own shadow IS departments and are not using the institutional systems. This is particularly true in high-tech organizations where there is an abundance of computer literate staff who are often frustrated at the slow pace of change and the lack of control over the systems they use daily.

   There are two solutions to this problem. One is to become an IS dictator. Refuse to allow your customers the freedom to move forward on their own. The other is to empower the customers by giving them some control setting their priorities.

4. **Involve customers**

   Customer involvement is essential for the success of any system. This axiom has never been truer. We still meet IS managers who believe that they can work with the customers through a requirements definition process, create a design document, and then turn it over to their developers for delivery. Wrong!

   Customers must be involved at each step through techniques such as functional walk-throughs, conference room pilots, and frequent discussions about business plans and future needs. IS must assume every system will change throughout its life cycle.

5. **Don't ask customers technical questions. That's your job.**

   In a recent meeting, discussion turned to the uptime requirement for a new customer-management system under development. The project manager was trying to decide if the project needed a high-availability server with automatic fail-over or if an inexpensive, off-the-shelf server would suffice. She said her customers told her 99 percent uptime would be fine and that they would put it in writing in the specification document. Therefore, she could safely buy a standard, single server. Wrong answer!

   This project manager had fallen into a common trap. She had asked her customers for a technical answer, and even worse, she was going to try to hold them to it. Do the math! Ninety-nine percent uptime for a 12x5 system implies total outages of about three days per year, which is unlikely to be acceptable to anyone, especially for a customer-management system. Having a signed document saying that 99 percent is okay will not save you when the complaining starts.

6. **Measure the quality of your service, and communicate it with your customers**

   Independently verifiable performance metrics are essential in satisfying the customer. Good IS shops measure all aspects of their performance and regularly communicate the quality of their work. There are several important impacts of metrics. First, everyone knows the quality of the work, and often can use the metrics to prevent problems from becoming critical.

   Second, metrics become the basis of objective discussions with customers about the acceptability of service, and the cost of making it better. Customers will not support your efforts to improve service unless you can objectively demonstrate what they receive and why.

7. **Test yourself against the outsourcers — your customers are**

   Every IS department should regularly benchmark itself against the standards of IS best practices and be prepared to act on the findings. There are many ways to do such a benchmark exercise. Compare yourself against the many surveys conducted in the trade press such as *CIO* magazine or *Information Week*. Consulting organizations such as the Big 6 or industry watchers such as Gartner Group maintain databases of best practices and standards of productivity and efficiency.

   Conduct benchmark discussions with your peers in other companies. As long as your benchmark partners are not direct competitors, most companies are eager to share ideas. One good source of benchmark data is suppliers who are often eager to share ideas that may help improve your commercial relationship with them.

   Good candidates for benchmarks are your internal service bureaus, such as help desk, or data center operations, or customer service functions, such as system administration or training. If your results are seriously out of line with industry practice, begin improving them right away. Your customers are continually being approached by outsourcing and consulting companies anxious to demonstrate their capabilities. There are a lot of outsourcing companies who prey like wolves on weakly performing IS organizations. Compete and control your destiny or someone else will. For more on this subject read the section on *Cost of Service Methodology*.

8. **Keep your attitude positive and your frustrations in check.**

   IS management is not primarily a technical function. It's a services business. When you become frustrated with your customers remember that you are in your job because they have theirs. We see frustrated IS managers who wish for a better class of customers. "Why can't my customers be more technically literate and trainable?" Dream on. Take your customers as you find them.

If you become frustrated and lose your poise you will lose your ability to communicate. You "push back" instead of listen. Your customers will become dissatisfied with your service. Maintaining a positive attitude is the key to customer satisfaction (and indeed many other things in life). We talk more about this in the next section.

Managing expectations

Each year *Information Week* takes a poll of its readers on the top issues affecting CIOs and IS departments. Each year the issue of aligning IS to the business is at or near the top of the list. Key to the issue of aligning IS is the ability to maintain credibility with which requires properly managing customer expectations.

We have watched many IS organizations struggle to gain and maintain credibility with their customers. We hear the frustrations on both sides — IS managers frustrated at the pressure and lack of appreciation from their customers, and customers frustrated at the slow pace of systems implementation and poor quality of service. These disconnects are disappointing but are often understandable given how IS professionals are often unable to effectively manage their role as service providers by aligning their customers expectations with their department's ability to deliver services. Here are four lessons we have learned in working with IS departments and our own customers.

Attitude

Attitude is everything in business and in life, and there are hundreds of books available on how to build and maintain a success-oriented attitude. We will not duplicate that literature, nor is it our place to help you feel good about yourself. Managing your customers is essential to your success, however, so we need to cover a few basics.

IS professionals often disconnect with customers early by not having the right perspective. IS professionals consider themselves computer scientists rather than business people or service providers. We are in the service business, not the science business. Your customers care as much about computer technology as automobile drivers care about combustion technology. It's your job to align yourself with your customer's needs, and explain your services in *their* terms, not yours.

 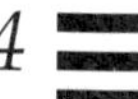

The second attitude disconnect is to not understand the basic human psychology of expectation and satisfaction. *Keep commitments.* If you promise five widgets and deliver six, the customer is happy. If you promise five and deliver four, they're disappointed. They may get over their disappointment and adjust to the reality, but you won't get full credit for your hard work.

Resist the temptation to alleviate short-term stress by over-promising future products.

Planning

In managing expectations, planning means the art of anticipating your customers' next moves. Woe to the IS manager who is blindsided by a key customer who announces one day he is going to consolidate 12 warehouses into three during the next six months, or is doubling the size of his organization in the next 60 days. We are continually amazed by the number of IS managers and CIOs who have no idea where their business is headed or how to respond when it takes a sharp turn. This is a recipe for disaster, because the last thing you want to be is on the critical path to business success. The pressures and "assistance" from upper management, can ruin even the best IS shop.

How can you prevent these kind of disasters?

Understand your business and your industry. Read the trade press and understand the forces that are acting on your industry. Listen to your internal customers, learn their plans and concerns, and find what keeps them up at night. This sounds sophomoric and preachy, but it seems that many companies do not involve their IS departments as an element of their business planning. Without integrating IS, IS can become a bottleneck. Through planning you can meet customer expectations and become strategically valuable to your business.

Communicate, communicate, and communicate

You cannot manage expectations without communication. (In fact, you cannot manage *anything* without communication). If some is good, more is better. The customer continually needs to know how you are making progress on their problems, what you will deliver, and what you need. Don't let daily pressures crowd out the continuing dialog that is essential for success.

Communications cannot always be clear, so communicate frequently. If you communicate often, you can make the myriad mid-course adjustments needed for success.

Don't confuse customer contracts with communication. Having a signed requirements document and an approved budget is only the beginning of communication not the end. Never let your team wander off in a vacuum to "do their thing" and deliver when the product is ready. Insist on frequent short deliverables from your team, and insist on customer involvement at each delivery however small. Without continuing discussions, IS inevitably diverges from customer wishes and leads to the traditional IS complaint, "We gave them just what they asked for, but it wasn't what they wanted!"

Communication forces alignment at two levels — the IS professionals with their customers, and just as important, the customers with themselves. Customers almost never have a clear idea of the details of what they want, and if they get it, they will change their minds.

As much as IS managers complain about indecisive and demanding customers, there are sound reasons for this behavior. First, people almost always interpret their needs in terms of what they know. They are often best able to define their needs in terms of what they don't like rather than what they do like. The old saw "I'll know it when I see it" is literally true.

It would appear that the best approach to satisfying the customer is to allow them to shop for the best answer. But IS managers are co-developing new systems and introducing new technologies, and don't have the time or budget to allow their customers to follow this approach. We see time and again IS departments that are chewed up by customers who demand to see the final product, critique it, and then discard what they don't like. This process is a recipe for delay, budget overruns, and frustration. By negotiating continually over the features, functions, priorities, and acceptance of a new system, the IS manager can manage customer expectations to ensure timely completion within budget.

Communication is the biggest problem within IS today. IS simply doesn't know how to effectively communicate with their customers nor do they effectively communicate within their own organization. Communication is not very high on the priority list, and effective communication takes time!

Speed

Long-term IS projects are the exception rather than the rule, and one sure way to disconnect with customers is to begin a long-term, monolithic project developed on the traditional "waterfall" life cycle. Such a process assumes the product is a point solution that once specified can be developed in a vacuum, which is never true. Successful IS systems must evolve with the enterprise, which means that we assume that they will change continuously to meet customer's evolving needs. If this is true, customers will be happiest if the product is a continuous string of small incremental deliverables, developed quickly enough that the customers cannot become dissatisfied. This implies that systems are always under construction, and that the development process involves constant rework. With older technologies this was not possible, but with modern objects, messaging, and multi-tiered architectures, it is possible.

Two examples to prove our point: one a success and one a failure. One of the best client/server system developers we know set a standard with his customers that his development team would make any customer-requested change of a minor nature in two weeks. Major revisions would happen at three month intervals. He would meet with the customer, learn of their complaints, and offer them a prototype solution in a week. If they liked it, he would put the change in production in another week. Customers never had time to be dissatisfied. His was the most successful system in the department, although the CIO was frustrated because it was never "finished."

By contrast, we learned recently of a large utility that spent five years and tens of millions developing a new customer information system — including a year just to test it. The slow pace of development meant that by the time the system was completed the business environment for the utility had changed. Deregulation is eminent and the system is not capable of accommodating the new reality without extensive rework. Customers are demanding major changes and large portions of the system are now being rebuilt at great expense.

The project managers and CIO should have *never* agreed to spend so much time in development.

Working with limited resources

Information technology is cheap and abundant but expertise is neither. IS departments are tasked to do more with less because IS's customers are. Is this realistic? Perhaps not, but shareholders demand a return on their investments. How can you do more with less? Make your staff smarter through structured and informal training. Yes, this takes time, but we've found no better alternative.

Why train?

Training is an integral part of a healthy IS team. Training is important not only because it keeps skills up to date, but it also sends powerful cultural messages throughout the organization. Some of the most dysfunctional IS organizations we've worked with are those that take the position that they will buy the skills they need and discard people when they make a technology shift. The result of this lack of people orientation is that employees are more disloyal, politics are more vicious, and costs are higher.

But training is not driven by altruism alone. You can't afford to hire or contract for a different person for every type of technology your organization supports. You need to get more out of your existing staff than ever before. Therein lies a compelling reason why IS should never organize itself by technology. You need to encourage your people to learn many things, which will help with you resource constraints *and* make them more valuable.

Show compassion when broaching the subject of training, especially to more personally conservative, long-tenure team members. Distributed servers, thin clients, networks, HTTP, TCP/IP, and Java are overwhelming to some people accustomed to life with the mainframe safe in the glass house. Some may be frightened that they'll be left behind, or that they may be too old to learn new tricks. Walk in their shoes, and understand their frustration and fear. But as manager, you can only do so much. Some staff may choose to leave rather than change technologies. We find most computer professionals will jump at the chance to learn new technologies. They know new skills keep them from getting stale and becoming unemployable.

Training is critical but IS does not always have the luxury of sending people to classes during the day. Training programs must be flexible and require personal investment from the employees. In some instances training needs to be done during off-hours. Everyone has their normal jobs to perform during the day — how badly do you want to learn the new technology? Times are tough, technology is evolving faster than ever before. Network computing technology is speeding down the track at 150 MPH— how badly do you want to catch it? Sure we all work 50- to 80-hour work weeks just to maintain. But learning is crucial to success. Unfortunately some of it has to be on your own time. IS managers must put together an effective training plan and budget, then sell the need to their executives. In the past most training budgets were cut drastically or eliminated all together. One of the most important goals of IS now must be to provide and support training. And it must be a mixture of classroom and self-taught. IS managers must provide the time and support for continuous education.

Hiring technical staff

Always hire people possessing skills spanning several technologies *and* customer relations. Well, easier said than done. Do the best you can by finding people with deep skills in one area who have also supported mission-critical applications. As the desktop is becoming more mission-critical, organizations are realizing the importance of applying disciplines throughout the enterprise. It's easy to teach a technical person a new technology, but it's a hair-pulling experience trying to teach someone mainframe-style discipline.

Look for these three attributes in your candidates:

- Disciplined background (supported mission-critical environments)
- Interpersonal skills (customer-oriented people skills)
- Technology.

In that order!

Dictators vs. cowboys

With the introduction of client/server and the infusion of heterogeneity into that mainframe-bred "glass-house," friction and skepticism run rampant. The legacy system counter-revolutionaries believe it impossible to maintain acceptable levels of RAS with UNIX, NT, and NetWare, mainly due to a lack of disciplines. The client/server angry young men and women decry legacy practices as too bureaucratic, reactionary, and (the unkindest cut of all) tired. How can we get both factions working together?

A Hollywood staple is the "buddy movie." Buddy movies, as you know, pair two seemingly incompatible characters in a difficult situation the two must solve together. One character is usually straight-laced, and often crotchety. The other is more carefree, and even silly. Mayhem, in the form of comedy or violence, always follows these characters as they stumble their way through the film.

IS managers direct their own buddy movies today. Representing the prototypical "Clint Eastwood" characters are the dyed-in-the-wool mainframers. The prototypical "Jim Careys" in IS are the UNIX, NT, and NetWare experts. No one, but no one understands the meaning of *mission-critical* better than Clint Eastwood. And no one understands free-form network computing better than Jim Carey (so to speak).

You need to find a happy medium! Clint needs to ease up a bit and Jim needs to acquire some discipline. This is, of course, easier said than done. Clint and Jim are as different as night and day. If you can combine the best of both and harness their collective power your chances for implementing the proper infrastructure are much greater. The proper infrastructure implies and creates a very flexible, streamlined, and cost-efficient environment.

It starts by getting Clint and Jim working together. We just don't mean under the same boss, we mean physically located in the same set of offices. They need to interact on a daily basis. They need to feel as if they are on the same team. Clint and Jim need to attend the same staff meetings and even hang around the coffee machine together. (We'll revisit Jim and Clint later in this chapter.)

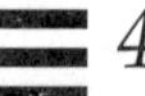 4

Transitioning/training/mentoring staff

Alas, about two-thirds of the organizations we visit still have walls between legacy and client/server staff. They're organized by technology instead of functionality, which is a direct violation of chapter one's sixth commandment (*Keep all production systems equal in the eyes of the IS staff*). Everything should be treated equally. The quicker you embrace this throughout your organization the smoother the transition will be. The walls must come down. Many executives argue they cannot disrupt the companies most mission-critical systems on those mainframes. "The legacy staff is already busy — what's the point of reorganizing to mesh the organizations if no one can take advantage of it?"

Make the opportunity for everyone to learn the new and exciting technology. At the same time, let it be known that much of this training needs to be done on their own time. If you exclude anyone you will suffer morale problems. In most organizations, the mainframe isn't going away soon. You'd be surprised as to how many mainframers will actually work more hours to take advantage of learning something new. Let them make that decision.

Locate functional groups together (i.e., mainframe and client/server DBAs, or systems programming and systems administration).

One of the most important ingredients and biggest challenges in transitioning to client/server distributed computing is motivating the mainframe professionals to adopt and adapt to the client/server environment. They need to be involved in the planning and implementation of your new distributed computing environment while maintaining RAS in the legacy environment.

There are several reasons why mainframers are important. Mainframe staff are trained and disciplined in supporting a controlled and managed environment. It's easier to teach mainframe staff a new technology than it is to teach client/server technical staff discipline.

Mainframe staffers know your business.

You also want to sustain morale. If you separate the new and the legacy you've inviting:

- Finger-pointing
- Duplication of efforts for processes and enterprise-wide system management tools
- Poor or no communication
- Resource constraints

It takes everyone working together to make this transition successful. Providing the organization with at least the opportunity to learn is important. The ones with the initiative and drive will take advantage of these programs. The ones that won't will have nothing to complain about as long as they were provided the chance. It is imperative that you use training programs to break the mindset barriers between the legacy and newer distributed environments. You may want to consider the following programs:

1. **Get acquainted with the hardware**

   Mainframers are not taking this UNIX or NT stuff seriously, at least not for replacing the companies mission-critical systems. Mainframers are okay with this technology for the desktop or non-mission-critical systems. They should be embracing it but are not. They talk like they do and make occasional half-hearted attempts at it but their minds equate mission-critical with mainframe and mainframe with mission-critical—nothing else will do.

   A program consisting of a half-day classroom session to understand and familiarize themselves with the hardware i.e., this is the CPU board, memory, disk, etc. The second half of the class should be hands-on in the data center (their home turf) in which teams of three to five students will take apart new servers then put them back together again. This does wonders for the mindset and promotes the fact that a production system is a production system is a production system regardless of the box.

2. **Professional technical training**

   Pick a minimum set of classes for a particular organization. For data center personnel pick at least three courses. Make sure you include classes on systems administration and shell programming. Provide this minimal set to all data center employees, including computer operations.

   As an inexpensive approach to acquire quality training look at your local university for fundamental training, such as SQL basics.

3. **Automate and streamline bureaucratic processes**

   Shell programming is included in the equation because you just don't send people to training without having them involved in real projects. Shell script writing and editing are essential skills for UNIX systems management and development. Require several other essential courses for senior technical staff members including C++ programming, advanced systems administration, operating systems Internals, etc.

Look at all the manual processes you have in place today. Put your UNIX system administrators and mainframe system programmers on projects together to create shell scripts to eliminate as much of the bureaucracy as possible. We recommend locating them physically together if at all possible.

4. **Train the trainer**

   Have your lead MVS systems programmer be the first person to go through your training programs. Once he or she completes the program, the rest of your mainframes will follow suit. They have to be convinced that you are committed to the programs. To make sure the programs are the right ones for retraining mainframes for UNIX, who better but your best and most respected systems programmer will be able to help you along the right track and lead the others down the path of distributed computing. It is essential that this person display initiative and drive.

5. **Brown bag lunchtime seminars**

   This newly trained individual could also hold weekly lunchtime sessions on different topics. Each topic should have homework assignments that are to be done on staff's own time. Establish a special lab containing servers where students would complete their assignments, which varies from reconfiguring hardware to modifying the operating system.

6. **Books**

   Provide them with a list of books to read on their own time. Pick the top two or three books on networking, database administration, system administration, and so on. Maintain a current book list.

7. **Vendor-sponsored events on technology trends in the marketplace**

   Things are moving more quickly than ever. Use your hardware or software vendor to share those trends with your organization on a monthly basis. Legacy types have been doing the same type of things for 30 years. Many of them are just plain afraid of the unknown, so they back off. Your vendor has system or field engineers that would love to come brag about their latest widget and gadget. Make this mandatory for your staff and keep track of who attends the sessions.

8. **Metrics**

   There needs to be management commitment and oversight. Track the students' performance. Include the students' progress through the retraining courses each month in your status report to management. So, if an employee has a performance problem — as determined through other human resources-sanctioned evaluations — you could easily see if the cause was insufficient training.

9. **Job descriptions**

   Establish *one* generic job description for each function, which include all technologies. As part of the training, the employees get business-related projects to pilot test their new skills. For example, we did three-tier client/server training and had the staff develop some small internal ISS systems that they would eventually use. This gave them some low-pressure projects.

Projects can promote teamwork

You can't just talk about teamwork. You need to establish programs that instill it. We recommend establishing a hands-on curricula. In the olden days (whoops, it still continues today) mainframers, especially system programmers, used to develop nifty little clists to help streamline and automate the production environment. Combine the old with the new, and develop some shell scripts to manage a non-bureaucratic enterprise.

Look at your current processes. Surely there could be something that needs improvement. Look at simple processes to start with, and then move to something more complex. A good example of a simple yet bureaucratic legacy process might be something us old mainframers refer to as shift turnover. In a 24x7 (24 hours a day, 7 days a week) computing environment, we have a simple process of trading information between the three shifts (day, swing, and grave). What we had before was a piece of paper on a clipboard that passed between the shifts. This paper contained special requests for that night's processing (i.e., backups, batch runs, report distribution, etc.). Anything out of the ordinary was highlighted for the operations staff on different shifts. Then these forms would be stored in a file cabinet for later reference. The shift turnover document represents an effective yet cumbersome and bureaucratic process.

Jim Carey may mock this process while Clint Eastwood insists it's the way things must be. Remember never trash mainframe disciplines. Modify and streamline them to effectively manage the new enterprise, since they may not work in their present state.

You need to toss your collective Clint and Jim into this project. We call it `shiftT`. Clint and Jim need to write a script, or series of scripts that allow managers to fill out all shift turnover requirements online. `shiftT` e-mails a report to the appropriate people on all shifts, then archives the report in a database for auditing. It appears we found a happy medium. Clint eased up some and Jim learned a thing or two about discipline. There are dozens of these types of processes that need to be modified for the New Enterprise.

You need a unified team. But you also need to make reliability, availability, and serviceability goals a part of both Clint and Jim's performance evaluations. These sound like major commitments on the part of management they are but the alternatives are morale problems and an environment that cannot effectively support mission-critical applications.

IS's unlucky 13 organizational problems

This all came about when executives would ask for help in implementing the right processes to make their shops more efficient. It was difficult to break the sad news to them: it's impossible to implement processes without understanding and resolving the people issues first. That always starts with the organization structure. Another problem these executives were facing was the lack of clear-cut support responsibilities. With every client/server application they were deploying on their corporate network it was getting more and more difficult to understand who did what to whom and when. They were discovering how complex this new network era has become. Their only savior is to make the organization structure as simple and efficient as possible.

The 13 most common problems are:

1. **Organizing by technology**

   Many shops organize to focus on a particular technology i.e., mainframe, NT, or UNIX. This is done primarily to make sure there is no degradation of service to the corporation's legacy environment and that's usually the mainframe. This causes finger-pointing, poor morale, duplication of processes, duplication of efforts for the analysis/implementation of system management tools, lack of enterprise-wide initiatives, poor communication and lack of resources.

2. **Not having an architecture/planning function at the CIO level.**

   At some organizations, this function would be buried in the development or support organization. This always causes preferential treatment with the organization they report to.

3. **Architecture/planning function becoming too large**

   At some organizations, this group would start developing and implementing the latest and greatest with the intent of turning it over to applications development or operational support. But all development efforts usually occur in a vacuum without involving either group until the system is already in a production status.

4. **Architecture/planning function not focusing on their original mission**

   This group needs to have one ear to the business, one ear to the infrastructure, one ear to technology, and one ear to similar businesses.

5. **Having multiple executives responsible for global support**

   This causes major headaches and problems when adhering to corporate architecture, standards, and guidelines. They will do whatever makes sense for their region. The political atmosphere really heats up and in most instances all these executives care about is pleasing their own customers in whatever manner makes them look good.

6. **The help desk not properly organized at the enterprise level**

   Many times this function is buried within the LAN, desktop, data center, operations support, or network groups. Once again this causes preferential treatment (better service) to the group it reports into.

7. **IS not aligned with the business**

   It's just in it's own little world still operating as if it was in the mainframe days. This causes poor communications.

8. **Infrastructure support group poorly organized**

   Each infrastructure assessment starts out by interviewing key personnel to determine the most critical issues. One of the most common complaints was the lack of resources. Most of the time this cry comes from IS shops that are organized to focus on particular technologies. It's hard to find and retain good technical help but many times we overlook the obvious. Problem management is not well defined to support the enterprise. Is second-level support well defined?

   A common problem in the industry today is that technical problems come directly from the operations area or the help desk right to the senior technical staff. These highly paid technicians are getting bogged down with that daily fire-fighting routine. There's no time to plan and build a streamlined and more "lights-out" environment.

9. **Confusion on how to effectively structure desktop and LAN support**

   Should they be combined or kept separate? What about the LAN? Should The WAN and LAN be combined?

10. **Production control not defined to support the Enterprise**

    This group evolved from the legacy world. They're still around but unfortunately they haven't changed with the times. For some of our younger readers that don't quite understand what this function does—its primary role is to schedule resources, own change control, act as second-level support for mainframe types of problems.

11. **Confusion as to where to organize the database administration function**

    Many IS shops structure this function under applications development while some are aligned with operations support. In the world of network computing it's critical to have this function in the right area.

12. **Find a home for applications support**

    Should there be a separate applications support function for distributed computing or should this function reside with the applications development function? The problem is in most shops the applications support person is the same person doing the coding. This could potentially cause delays in systems development.

13. **Where should disaster recovery reside?**

    This function has been shuffled around in more places than any other function yet is one of the most critical.

You *cannot* implement effective processes until you resolve organizational issues.

Reorganizing IS to meet the challenge of a new technology

Never reorganize purely for technical reasons. Only rarely does a technology come along that changes, in a profound way, the way people work or the way the IS organization fulfills its mission. Remember when client/server hit the front pages? Decentralization of IS services was the common theme. How many millions (of dollars, lost hours, torn hair follicles, antacid tablets, you name it!) have organizations wasted due to the effects of wanton decentralization? It is not only nearly impossible, but it is, as many organizations have found, extraordinarily expensive to decentralize mission-critical computing services. You cannot hope to establish full-service computing centers in each department worldwide and provide local computing services with on-site personnel. Indeed, we strenuously argue that a decentralized IS is IS in chaos. What is the answer?

We have found only one answer: centralized control with a twist of decentralized operations. To control costs by deploying standards and disciplines throughout your enterprise you must maintain centralized control! Over the past half dozen years we have seen hundreds of organizations founder in computer anarchy because no one was willing or able to control the organization's computer environment. The model that works re-engineers business processes and deploys new client/server applications to support them. The need of the user wags the IS dog's tail, not the other way around.

Organizing for the next millennium

5

The organizational chart below presents our model for the new IS. It may not be exactly right for your organization, but as a general design it works. It empowers the right people with the right responsibilities and right place in the enterprise.

A balance between the data center and the business units is paramount. Corporate policy establishes the roles of each group and where each has control. The data center must control the network and must establish programming and data administration standards. Business units must provide local services without harm to the network. Business units have autonomy yet follow rules of good conduct that benefit all.

The CIO

One person, the chief information officer (CIO), needs responsibility for all of IS. The title and reporting relationships make a difference — we can usually understand how important IS is to the success of the enterprise by where the head of IS fits in the overall organization and their respective title. The CIO must be empowered and committed to make decrees, understand technology, and enforce the new service model throughout the enterprise.

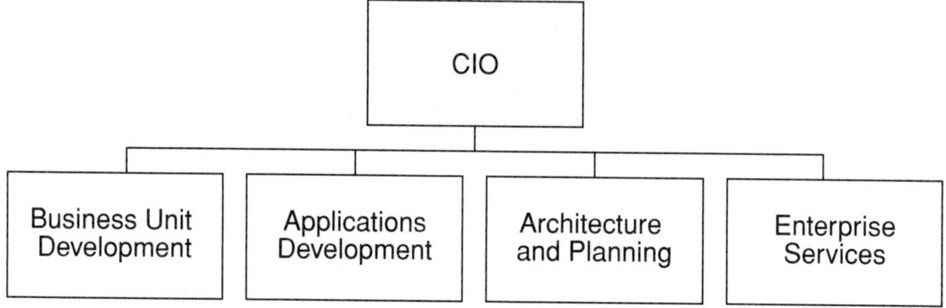

Figure 5-1 The organization chart for the new IS

Business unit IS

We refer to departments, agencies, and other subsections in an organization as "business units." IS is responsible for business-unit applications. In large organizations, each business unit has different systems requirements to fulfill their missions. Groups should be defined to meet those specific needs. Defining an IS function for each allows them to focus on those particular needs. In the new IS, this allows each business unit to have control of systems and application requirements. Each is responsible for maintaining their own set of priorities and backlogs, and can make changes accordingly based on their budget. They can change the priorities and reduce or increase the backlog without negotiating with some large, centralized bureaucracy that never satisfies anyone.

The business unit IS manager or director must report directly to the CIO and has a direct relationship with the business unit's general manager or key executive. While serving more than one master is not recommended for most positions, it is necessary in this case to seal a high-level relationship between the new IS and its customer. The business unit group within IS should include both applications development and applications support and maintenance.

We recommend the support and maintenance function be aligned with the business unit, not a large, centralized function, so each can determine their maintenance and support priorities and backlog. The development and support organizations should be separate but report to the same business unit IS manager. Again, business unit development must be owned by IS so that the CIO can understand and own the total cost of IS and implement standards where possible, such as enterprise-wide application development methodologies and tools (a decree). Also, by reporting to the CIO, they can be charged to focus on business systems, not technology. (Architects handle the technology.)

Architects

Although the CIO must be conversant with new technologies, it is impossible for one person to understand innovations and details sufficiently to implement them in the new IS. That's why, we recommend a small group of technology architects.

Architects are full-time technologists who critically examine new technologies, talk with business units to introduce new technologies and discover how they might meet their computing needs, and define the three- to five-year strategic plans for IS to meet critical business needs. We should note that the plans are really targets. Technology changes so fast that the architectures must be flexible.

Architects cannot be prima donnas or be perceived as being "in the ivory tower." They must work effectively as a team with the development organization(s) and the infrastructure operational units (networking, data center, and desktop support). They must produce a "minimum and sufficient" architecture that has the support of the rest of IS and the CIO.

Architects act as checks and balances. In the old IS, when a customer came to us with a need for something different or new, we simply said, "No, you must follow the standards that we support," or, as in the case of LANs, "No, we don't support that, but you can do it yourself."

Today we still define and publish standards. The difference is that if a customer comes to us with a new technology that is not part of our supported standards, architects get involved and see if it should be part of IS's arsenal. Architects determine whether it should be part of the service model, and determine the additional costs and training for IS to support it. Being an IS architect is a full-time job, and we recommend it be staffed from the current operations organization. Why? Because they understand your business!

Corporate applications development

There have always been enterprise-wide business applications for human resources, finance, and payroll. In the new IS, there should be a small, centralized group of developers for these systems. The new IS must have a focus on these applications for architecture and overall cost. Think of those instances when each department or business unit tries to solve its own issues related to these types of applications. Think of the cost of trying to interface them from a corporate perspective!

For smaller organizations with an IS staff of 50 or less, the corporate applications group has responsibility for all applications. As always, do not separate development of new applications on new technology, such as going from mainframe to client/server, into a new group.

Enterprise services

Enterprise services is the infrastructure implementation and operational support function for the new IS. Infrastructure includes "utility" services such as networking (LAN and WAN), data center(s), desktop (user) support, database administration, and centralized third-party software. The infrastructure is where most of the total cost of IS resides and should be centrally controlled and managed. In the new distributed enterprise, there needs to be controls and standards down to, and including, the desktop. The desktop is becoming mission-critical and must be managed by IS. In the old enterprise, desktop support reported to business units. In the new enterprise we want business units to focus on business requirements, not technology.

There should be only one enterprise services leader. If you are a global company you *cannot* have multiple bosses—one for each region or territory. We see many companies with one boss for Asia, one for Europe, and one for the Americas. They all report into the CIO. This is a huge mistake. We see duplication of efforts everywhere, no one adhering to corporate standards, and politics running rampant. Your infrastructure costs will double because everyone will do whatever is necessary to make their customers happy. They rarely look at the entire picture. Don't count on the CIO to keep the regional chiefs in line — you know very well that he or she is too busy fretting about getting new systems deployed as quickly as possible to meet business requirements. If you must organize by region or territory due to the size of the organization then each area should have a lieutenant reporting into an infrastructure chief and *not* into the CIO.

Software development

In the new IS, there should be a centralized function, as part of enterprise

Figure 5-2 The organization chart for the new IS in greater detail.

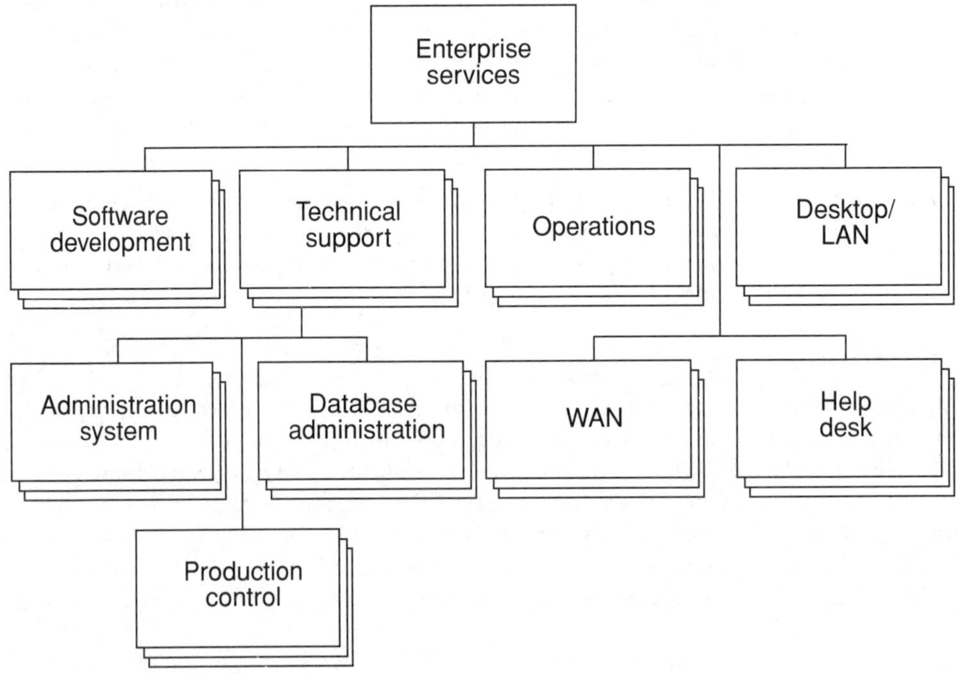

services, that is responsible for customized third-party software for the entire organization. We define third-party software as desktop tools and applications like spreadsheets, desktop publishing, middleware, and so on. The other focus of this group is to build automation into the infrastructure. Design simplicity into every product. A good example of this is what we recommend developing is a crude gauge of customer satisfaction.

We recommend a standard menu of tools that provide solutions for each of the functions required, because different people need different tools. There should be no decrees in this area.

You can help reduce the cost of desktop productivity suites by providing corporate licenses through centralized software services. This group should work closely with a purchasing function to negotiate site-licensing agreements. This goes a long way in helping reduce the total cost of IS. Any new version of the third-party software is delivered to the group from the vendor. They are then chartered to test and quality assure the new version before going on the network file server or desktop. This is yet another example of IS dealing with the technology issues rather than having the user or business unit license, install, and qualify software.

Operations

Operations is still operations. This is the traditional glass-house support (but in the network now) with on-site, 24-hour, seven-day-per-week computer operator coverage. Employ a minimal set of operators. Operators are tape librarians, print distribution clerks, and support to system administrators production controllers. Operators should *not* monitor systems. Systems should be monitored using tools such as SunNet Manager, HP OpenView, Tivoli, and Unicenter. These tools should automatically page the appropriate staff (or take automated corrective action) when difficulties arise. The career path from operations should be into production control.

Technical support

Technical support is the bread-and-butter for building a new, streamlined heterogeneous infrastructure. Remember how you relied so heavily on your system programmers and database administrators in the mainframe years? Nothing's changed. They're the ones that will implement the processes, system and database management tools, and keep databases and operating systems humming like finely tuned race engines.

Technical support designs and builds an efficient and cost-effective infrastructure with as much automation as possible. Do not expect to implement a truly "lights-out" environment. In *Networking the New Enterprise* we define what lights-out could be. But it's time to put this fallacy to rest. There is no such thing as lights-out, but you can get close. Technical support could build scripts to monitor and automate most of the manual processes used today in production environments — given enough time.

It becomes technical support's responsibility to maintain a production server once it is running in the data center. Accordingly, technical support evaluates, develops, and implements utilities that support servers and applications in the production environment. Technical support ensures RAS. With that responsibility also comes ownership. Technical support in the data center is the only group with full access (root) privileges to the systems and to manage all security, including authorization of users.

Technical support is responsible for data backups and tape management, filesystem checks, and monitoring of disk space usage.

Give your system administrators, system programmers, and database administrators the time to automate routine operations. You'll see dividends in happier operations staff, more satisfied customers, and more uptime. Technical support should include the following functions.

Database administration (DBA)

Should database staff report into technical support or at the enterprise services level? It depends on the size of your shop. For larger organization, DBA should report to technical support. If you have a small shop the DBAs can certainly report into enterprise services.

Another issue that comes up in many of our discussions is whether the DBA group should report into applications development or operation. We prefer operational support, which we also refer to as enterprise services. If the DBA reported into the applications development arena the focus would always be on the latest and greatest applications. If they were located in operations the focus would be on ongoing maintenance, performance, and tuning, which are critical.

System administration (for 24X7 support)

System administrators are today's equivalent of yesterday's system programmers. We distinguish system administrators from desktop and LAN systems administration because system administrators provide 24x7, mission-critical support. You can also refer to system administrators as system programers to set them apart from LAN administrators.

Systems administration works with customers to install, configure, and connect the network to production servers in the data center, as well as install peripherals and arrange a preventive maintenance check for all hardware coming into the data center. Once the equipment is in place, system administrators then partitions the disks and installs the operating system on the servers. The OS kernel is configured so that root is the owner of all system files (shell scripts, `fstab`, `printcap`, and `crontab`, for example). System administrators apply patches and other modifications to the operating system as necessary and according to IS standards and practices.

They also work with database administrators to install and configure databases and database management systems. Plus, provide and maintain the various networking services, including information systems (NIS), distributed filesystems (NFS), domain-name resolution (DNS), and mainframe connectivity (MVS to NFS).

The system administration function will also install third-party software on servers, as specified by the customer and execute plans and processes to remove antiquated servers and applications from the production environment.

System administrators restore backed up files, as needed, and apply software patches to the operating system to fix bugs, enhance security, and boost performance. Technical support also actively monitors the performance and availability of servers in the production environment. Working with applications support groups and operations, technical support monitors daily processing, capacity, performance, and usage. They also are responsible for job scheduling, starting, restarting, and stopping applications, and for the development and scheduling of automated processes (`cron` jobs).

Production control

Production control has a new role today. In the legacy world, production control handled scheduling, resolved nightly production problems, provided second-level production support, and owned change control.

Production control is more than production ownership. Production controllers are the junior administrators for the senior system administrators and database administrators.

Most of the cries for resources comes from system and database administrators, and legitimately so. Servers are popping up everywhere. New technologies are evolving by the hour. Production controllers should take some of the workload from the senior technical staff. They should help with operating system installation and maintenance, hardware implementations, and third party tools support.

The career path from production control is to system or database administration.

Here's a handy summary of the roles of system administration, database administration, and production control:

System administration

- Third-level operating system support.
- enterprise system management tool ownership and support.
- Operating system installation and maintenance
- Security
- Performance and tuning
- Disaster recovery

Database administration

- Performance and tuning
- Database installation
- General database administration
- Third-level support
- Security planning and implementation
- Provide design support to application development
- Disaster recovery

Production control

- Scheduling
- Client/Server Production Acceptance (CSPA) gatekeeper
- Second-level system and database administration support
- Owns change control
- Disaster recovery
- Availability metrics
- Security administration

Keeping the rules

To ensure that the rules are followed, your organizations internal auditor should work with central IS to review the application of information technology by business units. It is also imperative that each business unit IS group have a say in the development of corporate IS policies and procedures.

One of the best ways to accomplish this is to use a set of governance policies. These are rules, akin to a Constitution, that define the roles of the central IS and business unit IS organizations.The separation between the central IS and the business unit IS are clearly defined.

Governance documents explain the rules of network connectivity and the balance of power between the central and business unit IS organizations. For example, the business unit IS organization can run their information systems autonomously, yet once these systems connect to the WAN, they must play by the rules established by central IS.

Internal support agreements (ISAs)

With applications running wild over WANs and LANs, it's not easy to pinpoint trouble and figure out which group is responsible for solving it. Users know that when a process goes awry they should notify IS— which's the easy part. Pity the poor help desk person who must find the right group or groups from whom they can obtain solutions to these problems. The Internal Support Agreement (ISA) is used for defining these types of support roles and responsibilities.

Although we preach the same organizational methodology as we once had with centralized control in the legacy world, today (in most companies) IS support people are scattered throughout divisions where they once were cloistered in the same building. Wasn't it difficult enough to support the production and development environments and interact between the centralized IS staff? It is a nightmare now in the complex world of distributed computing with decentralized support organizations.

In most of the companies we visit, the applications development staff is located at the division- or business unit-level. Unfortunately, the support groups reside in different buildings. How does a centralized IS support group help scattered corporate developers? These issues should be clearly defined in the ISA.

An ISA between applications development and technical support

Of all of the battles inside of IS none have been uglier than those between applications development function and the operational support function. Even when development and operations were centralized under one organization, there was always finger-pointing.

Most of the issues were always around implementation and support of mission-critical applications. Development would blame operations for messing up a restart to an "abend," or operations would blame development for lack of QA or support. There were many other issues of this nature.

In most shops today applications development is located within the business unit or division for business reasons. This is good in that it helps assure developers meet business requirements, but now there's long-distance finger pointing.

Like in the mainframe era, developers still want the centralized IS staff to support development servers in a limited way for such mundane tasks as backups and restores. But today's development servers are a problem for both the development group and operations. Developers want top-level, "root" or full administrative access to their development machines. This is a problem, because owners of root passwords can bypass normal safeguards and unwittingly destabilize a machine in seconds.

On the other hand, developers do need unlimited access to a machine occasionally. Denying them access makes their jobs more difficult than necessary, or impossible. What to do?

We devised "joint root authority." The data center the two most senior developers will own root access. If developers abuse root privileges technical support will no longer support development servers.

The most important piece of this puzzle was to put together a Service Level Agreement (SLA) internally between the centralized IS data center support staff and de-centralized development staff.

Below are some of the key categories documented in the ISA:

1. **Root authority**

   Root access will be given to Mr. A and Ms. B to support servers AD0001 and AD0002. Mr. A and Ms. B are to support and backup each other (i.e., illness or vacation). If they're both unavailable contact technical support (within the data center).

   All changes to root will be audited to provide a trace of activity from the root user. These activities are to be done by technical support upon request:

   - Kernel changes
   - Disk reconfigurations
   - Modifying the root user environment
   - Installation of any binary into the system directory structure
   - Modification to any network-related configuration files
   - The modification of any system daemon that is run as root
   - Changes to the `/etc/rc*` files

   The following activities (but not limited to) may be done by the applications development root owners:

- Change `/etc/exports` for mount directories
- Change `/etc/fstab`
- Add users/groups

2. **Server availability hours**
    - 00:00 - 23:59 Monday, Tuesday, Wednesday, Thursday, and Sunday
    - 00:00 - 23:00 Friday
    - 03:01 - 23:59 Saturday
    - 20:00 - 23:59 (Once a month for system maintenance/upgrade/testing, all will be posted through change control)
3. **Backups**
    - Full system backups start at 23:00 every Friday, downtime is four hours.
    - Incremental backups start at 20:00 (approximately 30 min. Monday through Thursday)
4. **Support responsibility**

Table 5-1 Who's responsible for what

Services	Group	Type of service	Hours
Systems software	Technical support	Solaris, Sybase, installation, upgrade, maintenance	00:00-23:59
Systems hardware	Workstation support	Hardware, server, monitor, workstation, installation, maintenance	00:00-23:59
Application	Application development	Set-up application demos, project files access	08:00-18:00

5. **Function of each server**
    a. **Server: AD01**

    This server will be the primary development machine to carry the more CPU-intensive workload. Free temporary disk space is available on this machine via UNIX automount. Disk quota will be set up for each project. Disk space availability will be determined by the scope of the project.

    b. **Solaris X.X**
    - DNS and NIS (YP) slave server host name, IP address, aliases,

- Data base server (For example: `/home/sybase`)
- "free hog" disk space via automount (For example: `/home/common`)

c. **Server: AD02**

This machine will be used as the Pre-Production (PREP) server.

- Solaris X.X
- Project files, data, databases (For example: `/home/hrproj`)
- Clients personal files (For example: `/home/username`)
- Support sun4 clients

6. **Special requests**

These are different categories of special requests and their estimated completion times. These changes include investigating whether the proposed change affects other applications on the server. Technical support will notify the requestor if the request takes longer than the estimated completion time.

i. **Emergency backups and restores:** processed within four hours

ii. **File Maintenance:** processed within eight hours

- Change `/etc/exports` for mount directories
- Change `/etc/fstab`
- Add users/groups
- Modifications to `fstab`, group, add user, permission change

iii. **Operational Request:** up to two working days

- Backup and restore for UNIX files only

iv. **Solaris kernel:** up to five working days for

- software that requires kernel modification

v. **Database change:** up to five working days

vi. **Hardware configuring:** up to five working days

With the Internal Support Agreement in place, there are few headaches and finger-pointing.

Reliability, availability, and supportability 6

Many organizations allow business units to implement LAN-based applications without the support of the traditional IS department. This is very similar to the way in which they were allowed to implement, manage, and support PCs and Local Area Networks (LANs), which meant there was no reliability, availability, and supportability (RAS) goals defined. In IS terminology, business units pay attention to day-one issues (implementation), and little or no attention to day-two issues (ongoing maintenance and support).

Business units rarely have any idea what RAS procedures are or what mission-critical support means. We in IS deal with RAS and mission-critical services every day. We know what the processes for support RAS are, how to implement them, and what the ramifications are if we don't. IS is paid to know RAS! And IS has improved these processes over the past 30 years. Why stop using them just because we change some of the technology and structure of how applications are delivered? RAS processes must move into the network environment.

It is mostly IS's fault for not educating their customers on what mission-critical support and RAS means. We never explained what change control, configuration management, problem management, backup and restore processes were and how they must be in place to effectively support the environment.

It's worth a major effort by the New Enterprise IS to educate customers on the need and importance of RAS and to market and sell them on the idea that IS should be the group to implement and support RAS for network-based applications including PCs and LANs. To understand where and when RAS processes must be implemented we must first define what we call the "scope of production."

Defining the scope of production

As these locally grown and network-based computing services become more important (and perhaps mission-critical) you need to "RAS" the service. First, we must define the "scope of production" using a teamwork approach. The team should consist of key people from IS including networking, data center, database administration, desktop support, and LAN support, plus some key users of IS services (preferably someone who is planning to or has implemented LAN-, WAN-, or desktop-based applications).

The first thing the team must agree on is one very important assumption: *Any component defined in the scope of production must be RASed.* This agreement must be achieved before moving forward to the next step, otherwise the remaining activities are a waste of time. In many enterprises this is a very difficult bridge to cross but once over it many pieces of the overall service puzzle fall into place.

Secondly, the team should then look at what the total enterprise network-computing environment is that could be considered part of the scope of production. Figure 1 provides an example of the potential total scope for the enterprise-computing environment.

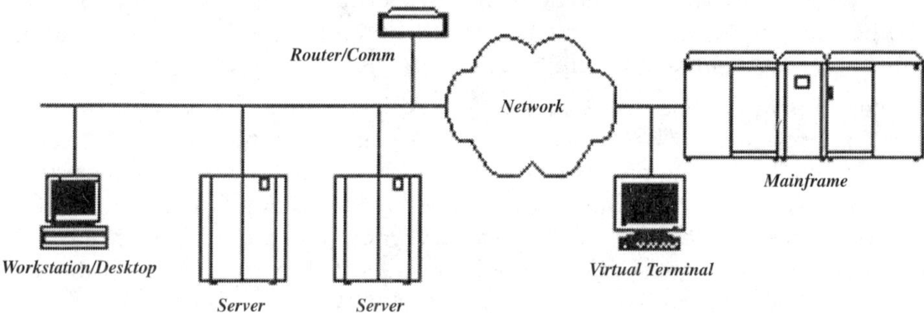

Figure 6-1 Example of the potential scope of production in the Enterprise

To start, present a view of your enterprise environment to the team such as the one above. Then have the team answer the following questions:

- Is the mainframe part of our scope of production?
- Is the network (WAN) part of our scope of production?
- Is the network router part of our scope of production?
- Is the LAN part of our scope of production?
- Is the server part of our scope of production?
- Is the PC/workstation part of our scope of production?

The team must answer all questions and agree on each answer. What you are really doing here is identifying what pieces, parts, and components of your total network should (or eventually will) be considered mission-critical. Review this list during regularly scheduled team meetings. The environment will certainly change and so will the scope. Also, on the first pass, you may not be able to consider all components part of the scope of production just because of the daunting task. The next step is to define the Reliability, Availability, and Serviceability requirements for all *Yes* answers.

Implementing Reliability, Availability, and Serviceability

Now that your team has identified the scope of production it is time to define and plan the implementation of the RAS processes to support it. This is a huge effort and can take a long time, but must be done (i.e., you can pay now or pay later). The returns can be seen in improved service, availability, productivity and reduced costs. However, it does take an up-front investment in time, money, tools, and outside assistance.

The first step is to define a priority list of the RAS processes to implement. Since there are many in the total list (included at the end of this section) it usually makes sense to start with the top five or ten that are currently causing the most pain in your environment. We normally do not provide a generally recommended top-ten list because it depends on enterprise's unique environment, the scope of production and, probably most importantly, the corporate culture. However, from process implementation engagements we have been involved with plus case studies over the past two years we are providing a list you can use as a place to start. (We have found that the first three are the most important and recommend implementing them as a minimum.) They are:

1. Change control
2. Problem management
3. Production acceptance
4. Test and release
5. Performance and tuning
6. Capacity planning
7. Metrics
8. Security
9. Software distribution
10. System management

To get started it may be easiest to identify a simple implementation. For example, a minimum and sufficient implementation of change management would be to:

1. Identify a change coordinator
2. Define a Change Review Board (CRB)
3. Develop a simple e-mail change control form
4. Publish the process, how to retrieve and complete the form and where to send it
5. Schedule regular change control meetings (i.e., once a week)
6. Determine approval criteria
7. Schedule approved changes (to be made by the requestor)
8. Publish approved changes, the schedule and potential impacts (i.e., once a week)
9. Review the process

That wasn't so hard! Now identify the implementation criteria for the next one on your list, and so on. Once the list is complete, make another list until all the processes have been defined and implemented. Along the way, you may want the team to review the completed processes including how well they are working, how effective they are, if they are making a difference and if improvements are required.

Remember this is an evolving procedure, and can take a lot of time and investment. (We included the process definition for metrics on our list because we always recommend developing internal IS measurements.) These measurements should tell us how well we are doing and if we are getting any better. They are not metrics intended for our customer. Remember, you manage what you measure!

Once the processes are in place and effective, you should look for a tool to automate them. There are many tools available from many different vendors. The important factor here is that tools are only as good as the processes and standards that support them!

Finally, make sure you define an owner of these processes. No owner means no accountability. To be effective there must be accountability. We usually recommend the data center organization (if there is one) as the owner since they maintained ownership of mainframe RAS processes.

RAS processes defined

Here is a fairly comprehensive list of all the processes that support RAS in the enterprise. Note that they are not listed in any particular order.

- Production acceptance (deployment process)

- Problem management
- Change management
- Asset management
- System and network security
- Version/release management (including test and release)
- Software distribution
- Performance monitoring and tuning
- Capacity planning
- Job scheduling (workload balancing)
- Network management
- User access
- Event management
- Console monitoring/management (single view)
- Disk management
- Storage management (backup, restore, archive)
- Disaster recovery
- Database administration/management

Client/server failure

Client/server technology is a quantum leap forward for information systems. Many IS professionals may not have looked closely enough at this advancement, but as the Internet, extranet, and intranet expand and electronic commerce becomes a mainstay, client/server technology will become commonplace.

The cousin to client/server technology is process re-engineering. We're not talking about radical change necessarily. Radical change or business process re-engineering as made popular by Michael Hammer and James Champy (1993) is appropriate in certain situations. Just as TQM is appropriate in other situations. The key is whether you need to dramatically alter the existing processes or simply adjust incrementally.

We like Thomas Davenport's (1993) description of process innovation and process improvements. We agree that both approaches are valid and at times it may be necessary to make radical changes and then continue to improve them over time until they become obsolete and radical change is required again.

What most IS practitioners don't concentrate enough time on when building client/server information systems are the associated processes that use the information systems. Client/server developers often re-automate existing business procedures that single-tier (legacy) information systems captured years ago. They leave customers with a fancy system that basically performs the same functions as the previous single-tier information system.

The new client/server system looks good, and it should since it cost a lot to develop, but the full advantage of the technology isn't realized and operating costs do not shrink. This is really a sad situation for the information systems group and the organization in general.

How do you succeed with client/server technology? How do you really sell it to upper management as a long-term strategy? Develop your information systems plan with business process re-engineering as a major part of the joint application planning and joint application design process. Your already taking the time to learn the business, otherwise you can't really develop the best system. So, step over the wall and help them redefine their business processes. Learn the new technology and that you read a few books on process innovation and process improvement.

Planning for the integration of business processes and client/server information systems can produce the results you expect for your efforts.

Client/Server Production Acceptance (CSPA)

7 

What do you do with distributed systems on Day 2? Sure, it's fun to develop and customize new applications (which we refer to as "Day 1"), showing off the bells and whistles that were lacking from the legacy world. Few get passionate about operations, but we do.

You need a single process that's streamlined and non-bureaucratic — this process should promote, instill, and maintain IS and customer dialogue as you deploy and harden mission-critical applications. Communicating effectively in these distributed times is more important than ever. Our Client/Server Production Acceptance (CSPA) process and philosophy is a bible for deploying and supporting mission critical distributed applications. The CSPA is a process that guarantees RAS by ensuring:

1. **Continuous communications**

   The world's number one problem needs top billing. The CSPA was designed not as an afterthought to combat communications problems, but as the primary focus. We needed a process to promote communications everyday. What's closer to the customer than their application and all the daily issues that surround it? Everyone talks about communication problems but no one (until now) has ever developed a process to tackle it.

2. **Standards and guidelines**

   The CSPA is the traffic cop ensuring that applications are following the rules.

3. **Quality assurance**

   Quality must be high to ensure customers' trust. There should be no exceptions to the process. We're not dictating — the process was developed with flexibility in mind.

4. **Roles and responsibilities are clearly defined**

   This spells-out exactly who does what to whom and when for each application. Distributed computing is much more complex than host-based computing it's critical you define all roles and responsibilities during application deployment (i.e., application developers, user-owners, the production support staff, help desk, and so on). This also determines who has update authority, how remote servers are supported, and so on.

5. **Resources are scheduled properly**

   Establish a Runbook. This is an old mainframe process we still need with modern technology. A Runbook spelled out the operational support requirements for each application (i.e., scheduling dependencies, special backups, print distribution, and so on).

6. **Service-level agreements**

   You do not need a separate document. The CSPA process caters to your customer's requirements and expectations. From this point on the term *SLA* is stricken from MIS's past. The CSPA is the total package. Anytime there is a revision to an application the CSPA is updated, which includes the SLA. One of the biggest problems with SLAs in the past is that once developed and approved by IS and the customer the SLA would just gather dust. The CSPA documents are not static.

7. **Operations involvement**

   Operations is involved from the very beginning of the development/deployment cycle with no surprises nor hidden agendas. After all, they're the ones providing 99.9 percent online availability.

8. **Customer satisfaction**

   This is an almost-forgotten phrase. It's time we use it instead of "paradigm shift," "disintermediation," and "Internet time." The CSPA reminds us who is important to us — our customers. We can't forget them because we interact with them continuously. The CSPA makes us meet the needs and requirements of individual users (i.e., backup times, disaster recovery requirements, maintenance schedule, hardware selection, etc.) Most users are different and have different requirements to run their business to be productive and profitable. The CSPA is flexible and treats every customer uniquely. That's what we expect from our vendors — shouldn't *your* customers expect the same?

9. **Visibility for all**

   Operations used to hide things from development, and development didn't about operations. Things have changed with the CSPA. Developers, project leaders, systems analysts, operations, etc.) have visibility to it all from application development and deployment to post-production support. There is no more finger-pointing — it's on an intranet server for all to see. That doesn't mean that everyone can muck with it. Update authority can only be given to one group and we define that group as production control, which we will discuss later in more detail.

10. **One document (the bible)**

    The CSPA details pre- and post-support requirements. Place it on your intranet server.

11. **Disciplines**

    Change and configuration management are adhered to in a very streamlined, non-bureaucratic manner.

12. **Include a deployment checklist**

    This is set of questions to answer, including where will the server be located, the number of users, where are they located, where is the data coming from and going to, etc. Design your set of questions, a minimum yet sufficient amount. Ideally you want to keep it under 50 — aim for 25.

13. **The product**

    Today we talk about marketing and selling practices. The CSPA becomes your product to market and sell. But don't go and sell something before its time.When you think you have a good product to sell find a friendly place to pilot it. Make sure they've got an application that's not mission-critical. Get this process as streamlined and cost-effective as possible. Once you get them sold then have them help you sell it to the rest of the company.

Too good to be true? No, it's taken us many years to develop a product that's flexible and cost-effective. It is the #1 priority for implementing and supporting mission-critical applications throughout the enterprise. It should be used for any application for any platform — even mainframes. It's the umbrella or glue ensuring all disciplines are followed. It's what makes up a RAS-disciplined, mission-critical, production computing infrastructure.

How the CSPA works

Phase 1—notification

A customer of IS services or an application development person (more so the latter on behalf of the customer) will notify the production support organization that they are designing/developing a new mission-critical production application. The notification should be established using an e-mail alias. At this time the CSPA questionnaire is returned to the developer. This questionnaire contains information about the project, including the application name, the names of the project team, team owner, a description of the application, if it needs a database, what type of hardware it will use, if it requires continuous support, where users are located, whether users need front-end or remote login access and help desk support, and expected target dates for server installation, alpha and beta tests, production freeze, software distribution, CSPA sign-off, a production implementation date, disaster recovery requirements, data dependencies, etc. The questionnaire is the first step in developing the CSPA process for each system.

The questionnaire will then evolve into the CSPA deployment checklist, which includes technical and operational support details for the application. The checklist usually addresses many issues (averages about three dozen) from how and when data is transferred to training the help desk personnel.

Phase II—resource planning/communications

A production analyst (who could be the data center operations analyst) assigned to the project reviews the questionnaire and, based on the application's needs, formulates an appropriate CSPA team. The operations analyst works with the technical support staff (consisting of systems programming and production control) to define data center space, equipment, and costs to support the project. The operations analyst also works on the CSPA template with the application's project leader. The project leader orders needed equipment during Phase II.

The CSPA team could consist of a project lead, user owner, data base administrator, systems programmer, and operations analyst (production control). The role of production control has expanded to take on ownership of the CSPA by coordinating meetings, inviting the appropriate team members when required. You don't want to invite everyone to all the meetings. Their role is to invite the appropriate people at select phases.

For example you may want a networking person in the beginning of the process but not the help desk representative until later meetings. Attending meetings is not a full-time assignment (maybe 1 to 2 hours a week) but an assignment that promotes and instills communication between the organizations. It forces people to work together towards a common goal — instill the highest level of RAS in every mission-critical application.

Also during Phase II, technical support personnel installs the necessary hardware, software, and all supporting utilities on the server. The tape librarian is instructed to create tapes with labels and to install the appropriate Unix backup procedures. The data center's database administration people work with the application's developers to prepare the supporting database (if needed), and then relay disk partition information and database creation scripts for installation and execution by technical support.

Phase III—implementation period

Appropriate system management and data center support tools are implemented, the application and all data center support systems are brought on-line and tested on subnets (consisting of rigorous stress testing) for as long as it takes to ensure that the application can run reliably in a production environment. Once the application is considered production, the CSPA is signed-off by the team and then placed on the intranet server for all to use.

Once fully completed, an application's CSPA is maintained by the data center organization. Database administration maintains and upgrades the database and software, making any needed system changes such as adding dump devices, increasing database sizes, and analyzing and reconciling maintenance errors. Production control manages job scheduling, restarts applications, and makes `crontab` changes. Tech support maintains the operating system software and hardware, and formats and repartitions disks, installs unbundled software, and maintains, and configures system security and network services.

Phase IV—maintenance and support

Each time there is a new release of an application, the production control group assures that the CSPA is adhered to and updated.

Now let's take it one step further — put it on-line (on an intranet server) for developers, users, operations support, and everyone else involved to use as their new bible for implementing and supporting mission-critical, client/server applications.

This may sound like a bunch of bureaucracy brought over with the legacy systems. You cannot disparage those time-tested disciplines —just streamline them by eliminating the bureaucracy. We've done just that and called it CSPA.

The economics of client/server and process engineering 8

The economics of client/server computing rests in the balance of IS and business process engineering. Many organizations try to address business issues with IS or organizational quick fixes. To use electrical engineering terms, this results in an impedance mismatch between IS and the business.

It is interesting that we continually see this issue discussed and yet never fixed. The answer is simple. Applying the answer is not. Follow these two steps:

1. **Align information technology with the business by understanding the business's mission, operations, and strategic direction.**
2. **Make your organization a team.**

A bit of a cliché to be sure, but misaligned, fighting, and apathetic employees can scuttle the best plans, processes, and technology.

We see economic gain when client/server technologies are aligned with business processes. You can find economics of scale, scope, learning, experience, and sharing.

Economies of scale are the decline of average costs per unit of production due to increases in production volume per unit of time.

Economies of scope are the reduction of average costs per unit of production by the addition of another product to the product portfolio.

Economies of learning and experience are the decline in average costs per unit of production sue to improved quality, excellence, or design of product by virtue of learning and experience.

Economies of sharing are the decline in average cost per unit due to increased efficiencies of reuse. Efficiencies are achieved by reducing the consumed units of production rather than the cost per unit.

How does this relate to your enterprise? The alignment of business processes with information technologies allows you to realize these economic principles.

The sharing of data entered once (single source) and distributed to remote locations as needed enables an organization to save the duplicated costs of entry. It also reduces errors and increases quality. If we share single-source data, we gain economies of scale by reducing per-unit data costs. Data entered once and used many times saves money. Single-source data enables us to metamorphosis the data into numerous information products do to the fact that we have purer data. We gain economies of scope.

Economies of learning and experience are gained because the single source allows organization-wide exposure of a single data source. A single data source means that the employee needs to learn where the database is once, and how to view or extract the data once. Data sharing is one of the critical success factors to the alignment of business processes and information technology.

Once data sharing is in place, viewing the organization as a value chain with a series of sub-processes enables the organization to determine where employees need information. At these points, information systems are required. Correctly placing information where and when the employees needs it results in streamlined operations.

You may say that older single-tier software such as CICS-COBOL and VSAM can allow the sharing of data. The difference between single-tier and client/server (two-tier or *n*-tier) is that client/server applications can more easily access data from multiple heterogeneous database management systems. Thus, data sharing can be realized without changing to a single database engine or a single server platform. Client-side presentation logic can perform data requests to servers anywhere in the organization's network or via the Internet and direct network access. This flexibility and ease of access is what can give an organization a competitive edge.

To outsource or not to outsource

A decision to outsource is one that must not be taken lightly. CIOs face increased cost pressures and the demand for better service. To address this situation many managers (including CEOs) suggest an outsourcing provider can solve all problems.

In addition, purveyors of client/server applications promise to reduce the need for in-house IS services. This suggests to some executives that the remaining IS functions could be handled by a third party.

Why consider outsourcing?

IS is under scrutiny. Executives, who don't consider IS to be a competitive advantage, are concerned about the Return on Investment (ROI). They ask, "We spend millions on IS. Is IS a competitive advantage for our organization?" With the advent of client/server, distributed applications, and network computing the

 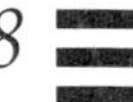

users of IS services are even wondering if there should be an IS function. Outsourcing is a business decision that must fit your organization's business model. Is the ROI acceptable? Does outsourcing meet our business objectives?

Of course, outsourcing has been around for many years. And there are several major corporations that are very successful in this business.

We have visited hundreds of organizations in the last four years and have seen an entire spectrum from outsourcing some components of IS (which we call selective outsourcing), to completely outsourcing the entire IS, to keeping all IS within the company. What is right for some is not for others. Some may think that outsourcing is the answer to all the problems. There are five facts IS executives should look at before deciding for or against outsourcing:

1. Define the IS service model
2. Determine the total cost of service
3. Determine the core competencies in the organization and outsourcing firm
4. Determine if outsourcing fits the corporate culture
5. Determine if selective or total outsourcing is best

Define the IS service model

The first thing that the IS organization should do (regardless of the consideration for outsourcing) is define the service model. "The sins of the past," combined with the new distributed-computing model, demand we reconsider what services should be provided. IS cannot be all things to all people. There are some services that can and should be provided effectively.

These include planning, process, and people. The plan should understand who the customer is and include the services provided. The process will define how the services are supported. The most important piece is how we organize, train, and retain the IS staff. (Oh, those people issues!) The service model should be defined, documented, marketed, and sold to users of IS services regardless of whether or not you may be considering outsourcing. And if you are considering outsourcing this will really help in preparation of a Request for Proposal (RFP).

Define the total cost of service

Defining the total cost of service can only be defined after you have defined the service model. As part of the service model, IS must engage customers and (again) market and sell their services. What better way to be operative than to provide them with a menu of services and associated costs.

A word of caution — don't start selling until you know you can deliver! There is a fee for services rendered. Any customer who asks for services from a vendor should understand that they need to pay for services. We do this in our every day lives, why can't we do it with IS? The big thing is making sure we deliver effective levels of services for the fees. As part of the menu of services provided, IS should show comparison costs to other vendors of the same services. This gives the customer a view of the total costs and potential added value. As an example, we are providing a look at the desktop support functions, what the services might be and what the costs would be for those services. Cost-of-service doesn't need to be sophisticated or lengthy, keep it simple.

We should then develop the same set of cost structures for all IS functions including wide-area network, local-area networks, data centers, etc. If you haven't already done so, document the service levels available at the cost. These two things (cost and service level) will probably be the two most important items when you benchmark your costs and developing a contract with potential third-party service providers. If a contract is signed with a vendor, understanding what services are provided in the contract, for the cost, will ultimately determine the success of transition. We won't want our service providers saying to our customer that the service they are asking for is not part of the contract and will be billed separately. We have found this to happen in many cases because the outsourcing contract was done without a complete understanding of the services provided.

Competitiveness is essential to IS survival, but a word of caution. In determining the cost of service include all costs. Do not allow customers to ignore the monetized cost of all the "futzing" they do with their PCs.

Many people are amateur PC experts. They install their own systems, perform minor repairs, do their own backups, and so on. We visit many companies where the cost of doing minor PC service is never tallied. It's a hidden cost.

For example, in one department of a large public agency, departmental administrators are responsible for maintaining Novell NetWare file and print servers. They performed maintenance and backups on the servers as added duties to their regular jobs. There were two problems. Few administrators had training on Novell systems so the quality of service was erratic. Second, the costs of providing these services were unknown. As a result, these "shadow" IS services were never counted as a cost to the organization. The IS department could never get funding to do the job in a professional manner since the cost was seen as a budget increase. When the organization finally did need to outsource the job became much more difficult because no department believed that these costs needed to be paid. This caused friction with the outsourcer.

Determine the core competencies

One of the main things we in IS seem to have forgotten lately is to look at what things we do right. Since we've been reacting instead of acting, we have not taken the time to publicize our successes. We should take the time to tout our successes not only to show that we can do well but to help morale. This is a very important step when looking at a potential outsourcing scenario. (It will really help when you benchmark your services.)

Should you outsource everything in IS? Should we keep the functions that we do well or better than anyone else?

The best way to get started is to ask questions. Is the network a core competency? Is the desktop support function a core competency? Do we manage data centers as well as anyone? Once you have answered these questions you need to get customer opinions.

Hopefully, you are competent at things customers care about, but perhaps not. If there are holes in your skill base, these become services to be considered as outsourcing possibilities. Another consideration is to align your skills with the strategic considerations of the business. Which services are commodities that are not strategic to your business? Examples might be payroll or benefits systems. They are important, but hardly strategic. Areas that may be strategic are customer service systems, purchasing or supply-chain systems, where your company may want to differentiate itself from the competition in superior customer service.

Gray areas may be purchasing or general accounting functions, particularly if the companies business model is relatively stable. Strategic alignment is essential — there is no faster way for IS professionals to be seen as self-serving propellerheads than to be spending time and resources on things their internal customers don't care about.

Will outsourcing fit my corporate culture?

A major factor that IS needs to consider (and many times doesn't) relates to the corporate culture. Many have asked us over the years to provide a set of standard guidelines for our methodologies, processes and procedures. We would surely like to be able to give a cookie cutter approach, but it's impossible due to differences in culture. The successful IS will always know its customers and the surrounding culture. In many cases IS will have the most impact on culture! And how we deal with culture usually determines our success.

Outsourcing changes corporate culture. Depending on the outsourcing vendor and depending on the transition plan the transition itself can be seamless with no impact on service. Have we measured the impact on the culture? Probably not. The impact on culture also depends on the agreement with the vendor and how we treat the vendor. In some cases the vendor is seen as a "partner" and becomes the IS department. If the vendor does not have experience with the culture, it may take several months before the impact on service goes down (i.e., how the "new" IS responds to service issues, the customer, what services are included in the contract, and which aren't). In other cases where the service vendor has had more experience with similar cultures the impact can be less.

What are some of the cultural alerts in evaluating outsourcing. First consider that outsourcing is a contract with an outside company. As a result, the service delivery will be open and above board, but governed by a legal arrangement. As one CIO put it, "Before we outsourced, I had no visibility into anything, but complete control of everything. Now I have complete visibility into everything, but no control over anything."

This implies that if your culture is collegial and your IS team regularly helps out and bonds with your customers, outsourcing will end that relationship. On the other hand, if your organization is more formal, and accepting of internal contracts, the outsourcing approach will be more easily accepted. Don't be casual about the impact these changes can have within an organization. And consider the consequences carefully before you invest in an outsourcing contract.

Selective vs. total

Once there has been a determination to look at outsourcing and the core competencies have been defined, the next step will be to look at selective vs. total outsourcing. With either event we must first define some basic objectives and goals to be accomplished from outsourcing. Some examples are;

- Provide a better levels of service
- Reduce the total cost of IS by 20 percent
- Provide an increase in potential career opportunities for the IS staff

Next we look at the core competencies. If there are services provided by IS that are considered company strategic then we always recommend they should automatically be eliminated from consideration. This is where selective vs. total is determined. If there are no particular core competencies then we may just consider total outsourcing (many use the term facilities management). If there are, we then would consider selective outsourcing. Selective means that we outsource particular functions within IS that are currently not being done very well, reduce cost and more easily accomplished by vendors who specialize in those functions. Examples include:

- Desktop support
- Help desk

- Network management
- Telecommunications support (adds, moves and changes)
- Wiring and cabling

During this time it is probably a good idea to send out a Request For Information (RFI) to potential service vendors. The results of the RFI can provide valuable information about the vendors. Once you determine which vendors to consider, the next step is to develop and send the Request For Proposal (RFP). The response to the RFP should be a very detailed response from the selected vendors containing their proposed solutions and costs to meet your objectives.

The RFP is very important! We recommend that technical managers be involved in preparation of the RFP to make sure all the current and potential services are defined. We have seen many RFPs developed at the executive level and many important services and service levels were not included. This can cause some potentially extreme cost exposures because service vendors will charge different rates for any service outside the scope of the contract. We have also seen this reduce the service levels because there is no one chartered to provide the service (i.e., the IS department thinks that the service is within scope of contract while the service vendor indicates it is outside the scope and can only support the service after an agreement to pay).

The preparation of the RFP is critical. It must contain a very detailed description of the current services that are to be considered for outsourcing and the objectives and goals of the services as a result of an outsourcing engagement. Who better to prepare this than those who currently manage the service? Based on the responses we can then make a business decision to outsource. Remember to never lose site of the goals and objectives. They can be pushed aside or forgotten during heavy negotiations!

If a decision has been made to look at total outsourcing this should not mean that the IS function goes away. The IS function is still important and a part of the corporation, it is just that you have chosen a third party to provide the IS services. There must still be key company managers that manage the vendor and it's services. The key thing to remember is that they are providing a service to the organization, not a partnership, and need to be managed as such. IS employees (of the organization) should be the interface between the service provider and the customer (user of IS services). IS must continue to manage customer expectations and service.

Another consideration in evaluating outsourcing is the term of the agreement with the outsourcer. It is extremely important that the term of the contract be matched to the anticipated changes in the business model. Don't sign a 10-year contract if you anticipate significant changes in your business model through merger, radically different changes in production processes or the anticipated creation of new lines of business. We regularly see organizations that have signed 10-year IS outsourcing contracts, but the company subsequently has merged or divested a significant portion of its business. Without careful planning, the contract terms can make it difficult to quickly change directions.

An example is the recent merger of two large aerospace companies. One of the partners has internally managed IS, and the other is heavily dependent on outsourced services. The integration of these two organizations is significantly more difficult than it would be without the added complication of an outsourcing contract. This is not necessary, but it does require careful planning to ensure the desired result.

Another consideration is an exit strategy if at some future time IS needs to be returned. After you have fully outsourced and sent your employees to work for the outsourcer, will you be able to pull them back into the organization. Also, in a complete facilities management environment, what are the terms for repurchasing equipment and systems from the outsourcer?

The bottom line—your poor customer

We've seen many horrible examples of outsourcing. Those who suffer the most are your customer. Outsourcing is not conducive to promoting customer satisfaction. A service provider does exactly what they're paid to — exactly what's in black and white. If you want them to sick around an extra 15 minutes out of the goodness of their heart to help you solve a critical problem with your desktop — forget it unless you pay overtime. In most cases your own company employee would help in a heartbeat.

Another problem is most companies do not outsource their entire computing environment and that adds another layer of bureaucracy for your poor customer To whom do they turn for help? No one clearly owns the infrastructure and this is something that cannot be shared.

And yet another big problem in the industry is CFOs generally outsource because they're fed up with the cost of IS. Outsourcing always costs more money in the end. And don't that think just by outsourcing you'll resolve your infrastructure problems. In most cases the people you outsource aren't going anywhere, they just changed company badges. Avoid outsourcing where you can.

Cost-of-service

Cost-of-service encompasses:

- Knowing your customer

- Services and costs
- Service levels
- Metrics
- Benchmark the infrastructure
- Charge-back

Just as IS bundles change management, problem management, performance management, and so on into the category of disciplines, we've combined these into a new category we call cost-of-service. For IS to be cost-effective and customer satisfaction-oriented we need to focus on this methodology.

With outsourcing being hot, we think cost-of-service will become the de facto buzzword through the turn of the century.

Cost-of-service simply means IS needs to understand:

- Its customers
- Its standard and non-standard services
- The cost of its services
- Its customers' expectations
- The metrics to measure these areas
- The competition

Sounds like a whole new department with resources and added costs for IS. No, you need to keep it simple—no bureaucracy. For IS to survive outsourcing threats from the CFO revolts from customers IS must dedicate time and resources to implement and effective cost-of-service methodology. We describe this methodology below.

Know thy customer

Everyone *says* know the users of their services. The truth is we really know *some* of them — the ones who call the help desk and the nerds who embrace every new computer gadget and like to hang-out with the IS staff. That's a pretty skewed snapshot of most organizations, however.

Cost-of-service should be the catalyst to get you acquainted with all of your users in a hurry. Being *operative* is critical. *Being operative* is IS terminology we've borrowed from the past. It refers to the problem management process. What better way to be operative than to provide users with a menu of services and associated costs? But don't do this unless you've got your act together first.

Whenever anyone sees a bill for the very first time, well, you know the reaction. But if you provide someone a bill for services *and* give them a higher bill for the same types of services from another vendor then you've made a friend.

Services and costs

Let's take a look at desktop support and list the services you would provide — it doesn't need to be sophisticated nor lengthy. Keep things simple:

Table 8-1 Brief list of services and their costs per person

Services and costs — $12/day/person	
Standard services $6/day/person	**Resources/equipment $6/day/person**
System administration	Client servers
System security	Network servers
Hardware installation	Disk use
Telecommunications	Home directories
Local network services	Mail
Selected optional software	Miscellaneous
Systems analysis	
Disaster recovery	
Desktop application	
Software distribution	
User training	
Software configuration	
Database administration	
Performance and tuning	

Customers understand this list. Customer will not bother looking elsewhere nor will they want to perform these functions on their own if you present the cost of your services in this manner. Why should they if you are that efficient? Customers are feeling much pain trying to support their own environment — come in with the right product and they're yours for the taking.

What are your network costs, data center costs, desktop, how much does it cost to support mission critical client/server applications? You must know those numbers. But most companies make the mistake of stopping there. Wrong! Once you get those numbers compare them to those outsourcing vendors like EDS, CSC, etc. Beat your CFO to the punch.

Service levels

Shouldn't it read Service Level Agreements (SLA)? We no longer recommend separate Service Level Agreements. We still believe in the time-tested SLA, but not as a separate document and process. You can either combine it as part of the CSPA or cost-of-service methodology. The SLA as a separate process wasn't very effective. It started out with good intentions, an agreement with customers outlining their expectations. Once these expectations have been agreed upon everyone involved signed it A very good process with only one flaw. Everyone was too busy or the bi-annual reorganization occurred or new management appeared on the scene. So much for the SLA. SLAs are only effective if it's imbedded within a process such as the CSPA or cost-of-service methodology where it's part of a check-list to bring continuous focus and visibility to the customer.

Metrics (if you can't measure it you cannot manage it)

In the New Enterprise metrics are more important than ever before. When things were simple your entire company's computing infrastructure was under one glass house. In the legacy world we used to track and measure everything and then some including:

- Availability
- Response times
- abends (An abnormal end to a program's operation.)
- Reports not printed by 08:00
- Batch jobs not completed by 08:00
- Number users: highwater mark
- Number users: throughout the day
- Number of application transactions
    - < 1-second response
    - > 3-second response
- Total number of production jobs

- Number of production reports
- CPU utilization
- Network availability

If you don't know the numbers in your area then who does? Measure everything!

We've been telling people for years that the reason mainframe computing was so reliable was not because of the box but because of the surrounding disciplines. Metrics are a major part of disciplines.

Few client/server environments are managed properly. With the complexity of client/server, metrics are more important than ever!

Benchmark your infrastructure

Don't just document your services and costs and hand a bill to your users. Go out and compare. Compare the cost of help desk support, or desktop support. Tear your infrastructure apart in pieces. Then go out and benchmark against the top competition. Ask them what they would charge to run your help desk, network and so on.

Show your customer a complete package, including services, costs, service levels, metrics, and benchmark data. If you want to implement charge-back — *no problem*—as long as your benchmark data is better than your competition's.

Charge back

Charge back? Yuk! Do we have to? We dislike talking about this subject just as much as you do—but guess what? Charge back is an important issue. Everyone we talk to still asks about it so it must be important. How does IS implement charge back in the new client/server environment? In the mainframe environment we are used to at least two different methodologies: utilization billing or allocation. We will concentrate on the not-for-profit entities (i.e., net-to-zero), since most IS organizations fall into this category.

However, the processes could also apply to the for-profit IS organizations.

Utilization billing

The utilization billing methodology bills for actual computing resources consumed like: disk space, CPU, network connect, network usage, and printing. There are software systems in place implemented like any other major business system. Daily utilization is captured, merged, and then taken through an intricate set of computations for billing, usually once a month. There are a lot of third-party software tools to do the function. We found that issues tend to arise on the amount of resources required to implement, maintain, and support such an application (i.e., people, CPU cycles, and disk space). The costs seem to outweigh the requirements and end-users couldn't understand the complex algorithms for calculating a charge like:

> Disk charge is equal to disk space times 1.125 + disk I/O's times 3.315 plus the loose change in your pocket!

Business units could never understand utilization and always felt they were charged too much. To alleviate this difficult nightmare, IS and finance people devised the allocation method.

Allocate, smallocate

Allocation is simple and usually handled by accountants. Each month-end close the bean counters would divide the total IS expense by the number of using departments and charge each that amount. In a more "calculated" approach, they (the bean counters) would break down the percentage of utilization into using departments and "allocate" that percentage of IS costs back. For example, if Department A used 30% of the IS resources, the calculation would be:

> Total IS expense X .30 = Department A charge

The biggest problem in this scenario is determining that Department A actually used 30 percent of the resources. This has always been a controversy because departments felt they were still being over-charged! There seems to be no right way but we do recommend keeping it simple.

Getting started

The first and probably most important charge back issue is dealing with the capital budget on the front side. We found that by first giving some capital costs for IS infrastructure back to the business units, it was easier to deal with business units and meet their requirements. Let them justify the capital requirements for new business systems (hardware, software, and support). This way they determine the real cost/benefit of a new system and if it meets their business needs. IS does not "shove" systems down business unit throats; business units determine their own systems needs. We also recommend that the business units justify (and have capital authority for) such infrastructure components as: desktop, desktop upgrades, application servers, plus printers, modems, plotters, etc.

Once installed, the asset is transferred to IS, who owns the expense budget (a key issue here is insuring that Business Unit Capital budgets are kept in line with IS expense budgets. This requires ongoing, effective communication—especially during the budget cycle. If the CIO budget is reduced, then it is up to the CEO to get corresponding business unit capital budget reductions). Now there is no real contention between business units and IS because the business units "own" the capital and justification for IS spending based on business requirements. This also requires continuous communications between the parties involved. And this cannot be over-stressed—communicate, communicate, and communicate! The CIO must keep an open, direct dialogue with business unit management and business unit IS functions.

IS piece of the pie

Business units get some of the capital requirements for IS infrastructure, not all! We recommend that the CIO maintain capital requirements for infrastructures such as: networking, telephones, and other utility functions that are provided to the organization. He or she must also have expense budget authority for people like system administration (desktop support), data center staff, and network support staff. For infrastructure, there should also be some directives from the CEO level, like: "Our company will have an effective enterprise-wide, global network that will help us become a competitive advantage." The CEO has then given the CIO authority to 'spend' on the network. If these directives don't occur then there will still be cost issues between IS and the business units— guaranteed! So, now that we've established the budget methodologies, how do we charge back?

KIS method

It's always best to keep things simple, even in charge back methodology. We've spent time identifying new ways to deal with capital and expense budgets; now let's look at a simple method of charge back. For networking, determine the network charge. This consists of all network-related expenses such as: labor, leased lines, equipment, software, etc. Divide the total network charge by the number of employees.

This becomes the "network charge" (and can be monthly or quarterly). Do the same for desktop, telephone, voice mail, etc. Add these figures together for the total desktop charge. Bill the using department this charge times the total number of employees in the department/division. For the data center, define the total data center charge including hardware, labor, software licensing, maintenance, etc. Divide the total data center charge by the number of applications/servers supported to obtain a per application charge. Bill the business unit an application/server charge for each of their owned applications. For application developers/support, the charge is direct to the business unit for their development function since the development/support people report (dotted line) to the business unit.

This not only keeps the charge simple, but it also prevents customers from micromanaging their charges to the detriment of the institution. We recently visited a government laboratory that was moving to chargeback and divided down its costs into microscopic service bundles with separate charges to have a name in the directory, an e-mail account, a security token, etc. Users then tried to save money by not having their names in the directory or forgoing e-mail service. This is clearly not acceptable to the organization and a struggle ensued over mandatory versus discretionary services. Far better to have a package of basic services and every employee is signed-up automatically.

The business unit now has direct control of their development costs, priorities, and backlog since they have their own development resource. Billing IS's charges back to the business units is then accomplished by set internal standards like through general ledger.

We developed the "invoice" inside IS, and sent it to a using department server where they viewed the invoice on-line (no need for paper).

Some might say this is another allocation method. It certainly seems that way but at least now there is a way to compare costs. On an ongoing basis we would compare the cost of our internal IS service to those provided by outside vendors and provide that information to our customers. One example would be networking. Since we know our network cost we could compare that to value-added networks and provide the results.

Business unit could then weigh the cost of IS providing the service versus getting that service from someone else (We did not dictate they use our service). This way we were able to show that we provide effective service for the cost.

Charge back has always been a serious issue because business units were never satisfied with the cost or the level of service. Utilization billing became the norm because of that, but guess what—it still didn't solve the issue. We recommend re-engineering IS to become more active with business units and be perceived as a help, not a hindrance. With that re-engineering we also recommend re-alignment of the budgets as outlined earlier. By doing this you attack the problem, not put up more roadblocks.

Charge back can become a simple methodology, not a cumbersome headache.

Cost-of-service case study 9

Below is a case study with a very simple cost-of-service methodology we piloted for the IS department at the county government at Martin County, Florida. Martin County is in the southeast portion of Florida. Its largest city is Stuart. In 1998, the population of Martin County was approximately 24,000, making it a small county in Florida. Martin County's IS department consists of 30 full-time staff members, one part-time employee, and two regular contractors. The IS department is responsible for the 300 desktop computers, 20 servers, and 20 mobile laptops drawing sustenance from the County's network.

The County's IS department guarantees the following service to the County's 700+ employees:

- The Martin County computer network must operate 7 days a week, 24 hours a day.
- The network can never intentionally be brought down Monday through Friday, 8 AM to 5 PM.
- Any intentional downtime (installations, maintenance and repair) must be announced to the users at least 24 hours prior to the outage.
- Any unplanned network outage occurring Monday through Friday between 8 AM and 5 PM will be corrected within 4 hours.
- Any unplanned network outage occurring any other time will be corrected by noon the following scheduled workday.
- Excluding planned network outages, the network must be available 99.9 percent in any 28-day period.
- All open help desk problems attributed to the network service are handled in accordance with the general help desk service level.

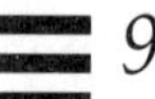 9

The network

The most important performance metric for a network is availability. Availability measures the aggregate users ability to connect anywhere in the network at any moment, measured as the percentage of time a connection is possible compared to time that a connection is supposed to be possible.

The metric can be measured by tracking network downtime as reported to the help desk (see below). For example, if a network has 1,600 physical connections (ports), and somewhere in that network a 16-port concentrator fails, that network is for the moment only 99 percent available. (One percent is unavailable). If the outage lasts 8 hours, then for a 24 hour reporting period, the network was 8/24ths of 1 percent unavailable, which is 99.67 percent availability:

```
100 - ((16/1600) * (8/24)
```

The County's IS department has designed, implemented, and maintains a state-of-the-art WAN. This network consists of a 100-megabit fiber backbone and a 10-megabit LAN and 100-megabit switches. It is installed at the main administration building and seven remote locations. These remote locations have LANs that are connected via ISDN and Frame Relay to the main LAN. Users not at the county administration building or one of the seven networked facilities can dial into the network via modem.

Network components (cabling, routers, hubs, switches, and terminal servers) are state-of-the-art and were manufactured by Bay Networks. Older devices from other manufactures are scheduled for replacement. The County's IS department also provides the voice network to multiple county facilities, currently supporting more than 1,200 telephone numbers.

Infrastructure costs

The cost of service analysis will only consider the computer network; the voice network is not included in the following numbers. The size of the physical network is best defined by the number of network ports (device connection points) and the speed of these ports (measured in megabits per second).

Port type	Quantity
10 megabit	986
10 or 100 megabit	192
dial-in	144
Total	**1,322**

Table 9-1 Inventory of Martin County, Florida's network ports.

The Martin County network has approximately 300 devices (PC, workstations and servers) connected to the available ports.

The fixed costs for maintaining this network are:

Description	Cost
Telecommunications service (ISDN, Frame Relay)	$230,000
Hardware repair & maintenance	$116,000
Salary of telecommunications manager (60%)	$30,000
Salary of a computer network specialist (60%)	$27,000
Salary of PC support technicians (10%)	$6,000
Salary of system administrator (5%)	$2,000
Total	$411,000

Table 9-2 Martin County, Florida's annual cost of its network.

This yields a cost of approximately $309 per port per year to maintain the physical network. Another way to view the cost is per user, which works out to $1,363 per connected user. The rule-of-thumb in the computing community is that a WAN-connected PC incurs between $1,150 and $2,000 in annual maintenance costs. Martin County is at the low end of this range. Since the Martin County physical network is only at approximately 25 percent of capacity, this indicates the efficiency with which the ISD delivers network services. Many more devices may be accommodated with minimal impact on costs, thereby driving this number even lower.

Technology: Design & hardware

10

In building the new enterprise, we have emphasized the three-legged stool, *people*, *processes*, and (last *and* least difficult challenge) *technology*. Since this is a book written (in effect) in the long past, we cannot know the details of the rapidly evolving technology landscape you see today, We can share our experience in changing hardware and software technology from older centralized systems to newer, more distributed client/server systems. In particular, we want to warn managers that your roles will change with these new technologies. Many of the management practices that served us in the past are actually preventing us from taking full advantage of these new technologies.

The worst thing any IS manager can do to his or her department and career is to be a barnacle on the ship of progress. If there is any overriding theme the new enterprise revolution, it is that we all must "feel the need for speed." We must all adapt to ensure that we deploy these new technologies to take full advantage of their speed and flexibility. The next three chapters offer an overview of new technologies and some guiding principles so that you can lead the new wave instead of being dragged by it.

The roadmap for this section is simple. We first take you through a discussion of architectural issues in the new enterprise. Then we discuss infrastructure, what it is, how to build a good one, and how to keep it from consuming your entire budget. Then we discuss software. The world is moving quickly toward packaged applications, and we offer our thoughts on selecting and living with packaged applications. You are not likely to be able to buy all your software, so we discuss some of the current issues in software development. Finally, the impact of the World Wide Web affects all aspects of IS, so we have given it its own space.

Architecture

IS architecture means different things to different people, but for our purposes, we mean the rules that govern the interaction of all of the component pieces of an IS system. The purpose of an architecture is to provide a template for the development and evolution of the IS environment. An effective architecture will naturally help all IS functions keep aligned with each other, and do so in a non-constraining way. That is, if the architecture is effective, individual service and application providers will be able to go about their business and by referring to the architecture specifications will be able to make their activities work together seamlessly. This is a tall order, to be sure, but a well designed architecture can be tremendously empowering to IS organizations and have benefits in productivity and group dynamics well outside the obvious benefits of interoperability and cost minimization. The challenge to IS architects is growing greater, since as IS complexity grows, the need for well designed architectures grows as well.

We think computer systems architecture is important. To paraphrase the late Vince Lombardi, legendary coach of the Green Bay Packers "architecture isn't everything, it's the only thing." Or to twist another old saw "computer applications come and go, but bad architecture is timeless." We came by this attitude by watching many IS departments struggle with confused high-maintenance architectures that cannot be changed quickly enough to support modern hyperevolving business models, nor can they even be efficiently maintained.

We regularly visit IS departments of large companies using more than 250 applications, multiple mainframes, hundreds of servers, six (or more) operating systems, several network protocols, and hardware from a half-dozen vendors. The managers usually ask us why their systems cost so much, are so hard to change and upgrade, are often unreliable, and provide poor customer service. They blame their vendors and their staffs. The truth is that given the complexity and confusion in these systems, we are surprised they work at all.

Although many IS managers blame the lack of responsiveness of their systems on budget ("if only we had more money...") or technology ("the financial system just won't support that new feature...") the real truth is that many corporate information systems do not have an underlying architecture that will allow change or responsiveness. Many systems are designed around a series of "point solutions" in response to customer need or complaint. If this process carries on long enough, the architecture looks like San Jose, California's famous Winchester Mystery House. We call it the "topsy" architecture — it just grew. This type of reactive approach leads to the inevitable consequences of inflexibility and confusion.

Computer architecture in the 1990s is not for the compulsive or rigid. We have all seen IS departments that think the way to control their architecture is through the rigid use of standards enforced by various forms of customer control. Occasionally, we find these departments are successful because of their corporate cultures or their particular business model. Often we find either their customers are plotting their overthrow or we detect leakage of applications around the ends

 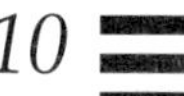

of IS control. Customers are creative, and we often find "pirate" applications and departmentally oriented "computer undergrounds" springing up around the rigidity of the formal processes.

On the other hand, compliant CIOs who pile one application on top of another soon find they have a mess. What do we suggest?

Build a standards-based architecture organized around the requirements of the enterprise model. We will make these buzzwords clear as we move through the process as follows.

Focus on the *Big Rules*

Architectural principles must flow from the top to the bottom, that is, from the high level principles, to the fine-grained detail of how the elements of the IS systems interact. Too often, we see IS organizations try to agree on the lower level specifications and protocols ("We will use Ethernet") before the management has agreed on the "Big Rules." What are Big Rules? They are the basic agreements by which people in the organization agree to work out their issues and differences relative to the architecture.

The First Rule — Consensus

If an architecture is to be followed, there must be trust between all those who live within the architectural framework. If there is to be trust, then there should be no surprises — the first Big Rule. No surprises means that within the IS organization preferential access to information cannot be used as a means of control. How often have you walked into a meeting to be surprised by a change of direction or some new piece of information that has not been shared. Following the no surprises philosophy, all information should be shared with those affected by the information, and if there is a decision to be made, there must be an active solicitation of opinion and individuals must be given adequate time to respond. To do otherwise is to breakdown the trust level between the parties. Mistrust is a powerful incentive for people to go off and "do their thing" by building shadow systems of otherwise breaking the architecture.

The Second Rule — Consistency

No one is allowed to break the architecture. Waivers can be granted if needed, but everyone must agree in advance that the architecture cannot be ignored. If this rule is not enforced, chaos will result. But at the same time, there must always be an appeal mechanism. Architecture is not a club to be used by one IS activity against another, so senior management must be sensitive to user concerns and respond appropriately.

The Third Rule — Create a written history

The third big rule is that the architecture must be written down, and those affected must have input into it. Oral architectures are a tradition in some organizations, but in our experience, unless there is a simple and clear architecture document, and every supervisor and program developer has a copy, the opportunity for missed communication with attendant misunderstandings and ill feelings, is far too great.

The Fourth Rule — Collective action

No one within the IS organization is allowed to say "not my job." Everyone must participate and no one can abrogate his or her responsibility to the success of the enterprise by passing the buck to someone else. This is a statement of esprit de corps and individual responsibility, but it is also a critical value that is essential to architectural success. If the staff of an IS organization do not have a sense of engagement and understanding of the benefits of collective action to serve customers, the organization will not be successful long term.

IS is a team sport, and cowboys need to understand the rules by which the organization functions. An IS organization with a strong architecture is better able to accommodate the cowboys and entrepreneurs, because it is able to clearly articulate the boundary conditions on all activities.

Simplify your network architecture as much as possible before deployment

We regularly see IS departments that have not moved to a single network protocol and are trying to support multiple protocols. One company we recently visited had TCP/IP, DecNet, AppleTalk, IPX, and SNA, running over Ethernet, Token Ring, FDDI, and ATM. And they complained their networks were unreliable and expensive to maintain.

Simplify down to TCP/IP, put IP stacks in your machines as you upgrade them and get rid of the older proprietary protocols. IP is even available for older mainframes, so there is no excuse for excessive complexity in your networks.

Treat architecture as a Lego set — examine the building blocks of your systems carefully

The architectural Holy Grail is to have systems that can be built like Lego blocks — each element can be replaced without affecting the whole design. This is not easy to achieve in practice, but don't give up. If your systems support standard protocols and provide APIs, you can glue the blocks together in ways that can more easily be torn apart.

Get good at glue

To follow our credo of open architecture, your development department will change its function. Instead of writing applications from scratch, they will be working to assemble functions from component parts. As a result, your development team needs to be schooled on protocols, writing and writing to APIs, and object technology.

The trends are clear. In the 1970s programmers in demand were those who were literate in 3GLs and managed file-based data systems. In the 1980s it was relational technology and PC systems. In the 1990s it is client/server. In 2000 it will be glue, objects, and Java. Make sure your people are ready.

One application per server vs. many on one

How many applications can I put on my new mainframe like server? Is it better to put one application per server? Can I shove as many applications as I can on my new server just like I used to do on my mainframe aren't they just as powerful today as those large mainframes are besides fewer boxes are easier and more cost efficient to maintain right—less floor space?

It would be more cost-efficient to treat these giant servers as mainframes, but we do not recommend it. Put one application on one box. Size the application to a box for flexibility!

Isn't it harder to manage more servers? No, if the processes and system management tools are implemented properly to manage to a more "lights-out" type of environment it shouldn't matter how many servers you support. The only drawback of course is back to the cost for data center floor space and licensing for those system management tools. But again customer productivity and satisfaction comes first.

Data warehouses are a service not an architecture

For many companies, data warehouses are a bug not a feature. We see IS departments claim data warehouses are needed to provide new and better services to their internal customers. Often, however, these warehouses compensate for the inflexibility and lack of information access in legacy systems. We understand the technical issues in warehouses, and we don't disagree with the need for such systems. Just don't use them as architectural Bondo to fill in the holes in an architecture that is in need of an overhaul. If you are considering the long-term implications of a warehouse system, hold it to the same architectural standards as other new system decisions. Warehouses grow (often quickly) and must be maintained like any other system.

Regulate architecture through an internal economy (if you can't twist arms)

In *Charge back* on page 78, we outline the importance and management of charge back. Empowering users and managing the flow of services through user fees is extremely important. The architectural benefits are more subtle but equally important. An effective architecture can be put in place by assigning fees in ways that encourage openness, standardization, and simplicity. Allowing users choices and charging for the differential cost is greatly preferable to imposing standards and then fighting with users to keep them from going off on their own. If you have a chargeback system consider using it to reward preferred behavior, such as using preferred tools or applications, rather than having to impose mandates on customers.

Build your applications architecture from a service-based foundation

Services come first, not applications. IS departments who let their architecture be dictated by any particular application are vulnerable to falling prey to vendor bias and proprietary traps that may be expensive to change later. This kind of application—centric focus is like selecting a house based on the interior furnishings rather than the number of rooms or its structural integrity.

For example, we talked with a CIO recently who was not happy with the cost of his desktop infrastructure and was looking for ways to defer an expensive upgrade. However, during our discussion, he said that he had to run Microsoft Office natively on his desktops, which meant that he had to upgrade his OS to Windows 95 which meant that he had to buy new Pentiums, which meant he had to ask for the large budget increase he knew his CEO wouldn't support. We suggested that he either reconsider his system requirements or look for a new job, since he clearly had painted himself into a corner.

Notice he violated two rules — his choices were not open, and his architecture was not standards based. He fell into the IS trap of the killer app with customers demanding "get me a box to run this application." That may make your customers happy in the short run, but when the customers turn fickle and want the "next big thing" what will you do?

Build around open standards

We are shameless advocates of open standards, although we freely admit that there are many happy CIOs who have given themselves to single-vendor, closed standards. Proprietary standards are often appealing because they are embedded in the products and do not require customer attention. Monogamous customers won't be happy at all if their vendor has troubles, or if they have to change their

systems or integrate third party software. Proprietary systems can be easy and convenient, but they can also be seductive and can result in a great loss of flexibility.

Open standards do not mean the core technology is non-proprietary, but it does mean that the means of interchanging information between applications, or between applications and the operating and network systems conforms to standard protocols and interfaces. This can be a challenge for managers, since open standards imply that some proprietary may only work on one side of an interface and can't be carried to all applications. Customers can be seduced by one vendor's functionality and may pressure management to support a vendor's unique functionality. Be sure to consider the impact on your architecture before you give in. A proprietary standard or feature can end up being the tail that wags the architectural dog.

A simple example is e-mail. Simple Mail Transport Protocol (SMTP) is a well-supported Internet standard. However, SMTP does not support such features as labeling messages as *urgent*. In proprietary systems, such as cc:Mail, you can mark a message as urgent and it will appear in the recipients in-box marked in red. One IS manager we know faced a small revolt from his users because his proposed move to an SMTP-based mail system ignored the availability of popular features such as these.

Courageous CIOs, who are able to take the heat, can move to open systems with attendant savings. Others who may not have sufficient depth of customer support must carefully weigh the advantages of proprietary features with the lower cost and universality of standards.

Control interfaces and APIs not tools or applications

Two essential questions govern any architectural interface — can I write to it, and can I transfer information across it? Beyond those essential questions, try to give the users as much freedom as possible to use the tools and platforms they want. We have watched IS managers needlessly expend their credibility with customers in order to enforce standard applications or platforms. We often hear "we only allow Excel here" (or Lotus 1-2-3 or whatever). Overcontrolling your customers will only make it harder to get their support when you need it most. If their tools can interoperate (Microsoft Word can write WordPerfect files, for example). Let them use the tools they like. If not, guide their decisions through the use of interfaces and APIs. For example, in the e-mail example discussed above, virtually all e-mail vendors provide gateways that transfer their native protocols to those of other vendors.

This open approach is being extended to larger enterprise systems as well. In many industries, vertically oriented applications dominate, largely to support a traditional stovepipe business model. For example, in health care, separate applications can be purchased to manage pharmacies, patient admitting, patient billing, and so on. These applications often didn't have open interfaces and as a result, even today, health care providers have problems with data synchronicity and multiple data entry.

Don't do business to a vendor who attempts to impose proprietary products, and doesn't support the move to open interfaces and published APIs.

Build an interoperability foundation if the vendors haven't supplied one

Mainframe application and interface inflexibility is the subject of continuing IS manager complaint. However it is easy to create the same inflexibility in client/server systems if you are not careful. For *N* servers to communicate with each other requires N2 - N connections. *N* does not have to be large before the system becomes just as unwieldy as a mainframe.

The N2 - N problem can be attacked by using technologies such as publish and subscribe to produce a "data highway." In this approach, events occurring on one server are published on the network and a software agent on the receiving servers will accept the information if it applies to them. In this way, changes can be made to one server independent of all the others.

The software that enables this technology provides an interoperability foundation for information transport. Similarly standard conversion and management tools can put your distributed systems on a common footing that will allow them to more easily exchange data and enable them to be collectively managed.

Technology: Software 11

IS's mission is to produce useful business applications by all means necessary. There are many tools and flexible software architectures that will make the job easier, more bug free and your programmers more productive. But there is a new dimension to the software development challenge. Packaged software is reaching the level of maturity that no IS manager can dismiss as a source of highly functional, easy-to-maintain applications. Long gone are the days when a manager can casually dismiss packaged applications just because "we'd rather develop our own." Large application-software vendor may have 500 programmers working on a financial application. How many programmers do you have on your staff available to develop your own financial system?

We divide this section into two parts. The first is a discussion of working with packaged application software, including selecting, implementing, and managing off-the-shelf applications. The second part is a discussion of what to do when you can't find a suitable package and need to develop your own. More IS managers have gone on the rocks by failing to bring internal development programs to completion on time and on budget than any other cause. We hope to give you some tips that will help you avoid being one of the casualties.

Make vs. buy

For many years following the introduction of computers to business in the 1950s, corporate IS departments assumed they would write most of their business software. Larger corporations would have programmers on staff to write corporate information systems, and smaller companies that could not afford staffs of their own used consultants to create data systems. Gradually, packaged software emerged first to perform standard corporate functions including accounting and payroll, and later to do other standardized functions such as purchasing, human resources, and manufacturing. As technology has improved, the packages have become more flexible so they can be adapted to individual businesses and packaged software is assumed to be suitable for most core business functions.

With the arrival of integrated enterprise data systems such as SAP R/3, many IS managers assume their data architecture can be built entirely around off-the-shelf software, and in-house capabilities can be abandoned or outsourced. Before you drop your IS capabilities, consider some of the issues in the use of purchased software and the implications for your business. Otherwise you may discover you have let your programming team go, and it will be too late to undo your error if the package doesn't meet your needs and you do need to "roll your own."

When packages make sense

Packaged software works best for commodity functions that are slow to change and are not strategic to your business. The best example is basic accounting. No one writes accounting software any more — GAAP requires that virtually all publicly traded (and many privately held) companies do their accounting within a common framework. Virtually all packages have the correct core functionality built in. No business should have difficulty finding an off-the-shelf accounting solution that will meet it's needs, except for organizations that are institutionally unique in their accounting practices.

There are many other business functions that lend themselves to packaged solutions. For example, payroll packages require continuous updating of tax information, and the package suppliers can maintain the tax experts on staff much more cheaply than all but the largest companies.

However, if you believe that a function is strategic, or that your business model is unique, beware the packaged solution. Many companies have suffered trying to force fit inappropriate packages into their operations.

When is a business function strategic? When it is a part of a process used to gain competitive advantage. If your company does some part of its business uniquely to be able to produce or deliver its products or services better or cheaper than its competitors, be careful of packaged solutions. For example, Federal Express developed the Powership system to allow customers to quickly prepare their goods for shipment, and to quickly track packages through out Federal Expresses system. FedEx spent millions developing a unique shipping system, both because there was no comparable system available for purchase, and Powership gave Federal Express a competitive advantage over UPS. If you are using a packaged solution, the business practices embedded in that package will be available to any competitor.

Another reason to be cautious of purchased solutions is if your industry or business model are either uncommon, or rapidly changing. Commercial software packages attempt to capture best business practices in their solutions, but they must also keep one eye on their legacy customers and on the practices common to the vertical industries they serve. As a result, if you want to move aggressively ahead in implementing a new technology or business practice, you need to either carefully select a package that will enable that practice, or be prepared to write your own solution.

Another reason to consider a software package is that it could be an important part of a strategy to use the package to energize business practice improvement in the organization. Ernst & Young, a leading consulting firm, calls this approach "package-enabled reengineering." The principles are simple — find the software package that comes closest to the business practices you want to implement and then use the package to force the operating business unit to change its processes to fit the package's requirements.

For example, a large distribution company was incurring large inventory costs because the warehouses located throughout the world did not use a common parts numbering system. As a result, they could not share inventory to reduce costs and improve customer service. Management estimated the excess cost of these deficiencies to be $50 million per year. By committing to SAP R/3, and using it as the enabler of a reengineering program to standardize parts numbering, management was able to accomplish goals that would have been more difficult to achieve otherwise.

Evaluating packages

Selecting enterprise packaged software is a difficult and time-consuming task. It is not uncommon for companies to assemble task forces that will spend months on a package selection, or to hire a consulting firm and spend $100,000 to pick a package. This selection briefly discusses some of the processes and selection criteria needed for a successful package selection.

Selection criteria

Every company needs to develop its own requirements for the selection of an enterprise software package. But many of the issues in selecting a package are common to everyone. This list will seem sophomoric, but we have seen many horror stories of companies that were naive in their purchases and paid a heavy price in implementation.

These issues include:

Cost

Purchase cost must be carefully evaluated since software vendors have different pricing models. Some vendors price by connected user, others price by named user (even if not connected). Some price by platform with installs on MVS mainframes priced higher than systems on NT, even if the number of users is the same. Also, be sure to ask for the total cost of the software from pilot to full deployment or you may be in for a shock.

One colleague was comparing two financial packages and found that for the first phase of the project the license cost was about the same for both vendors at $2.5 million. But when the number of users was increased as the system was expanded across the company, the cost for one vendor doubled to $5 million, but for the other, the cost soared to $20 million. The choice and the warning is clear — evaluate the total project cost.

Your cost must include annual maintenance and support fees, anticipated during the life of the system. These recurring fees must also include anticipated one-time upgrade charges if applicable. The price of development and maintenance tools must be considered, if not packaged, with the software.

If you are considering buying a total enterprise solution, carefully consider the cost of other modules you may want in the future. If you are buying a general ledger will you also want a cost-accounting or purchasing package from the same vendor.

And don't forget the cost of consulting and support. Packages that are hot in the market can drain their talent pool dry and it may be difficult for you to find affordable help to implement or maintain a package (or to keep the talent you have). When SAP R/3 caught fire in the market in 1995, it became very difficult to find affordable talent since the scarcity of R/3-trained people bid-up consulting fees.

Speed and ease of installation

It is hard to quantify the costs of speed and flexibility, but they are very real and worthy of due diligence with any prospective software vendor. Depending on the sophistication of your IS organization, there can be significant differences in the ease and speed of installing different packages. Some are tightly integrated in their functionality, while others can be more easily installed in modules. Some packages have better GUI-based tools to ease setup and maintenance. Some require learning a proprietary language or database. Others may have particularly long training periods. Talking with recent customers and reading the literature can be helpful in bringing these issues to the surface.

Functionality

We will discuss the process of matching functionality to your organization in the next section, but the old KISS rule is still the best — keep the package as simple as needed to do the job. Some packages have limited flexibility while others have every feature you may ever want. But remember that all those features that make your customers say "gee whiz" must all be maintained, users must be trained, hardware must be sized to accommodate the features. A colleague recently installed a new financial package in a division of a large natural resource company. He picked a fairly basic package, with simple functionality. At the same time, another division selected a more complex and feature-rich package from a competing vendor. The simpler package was installed in two-thirds the time for half the price.

Technical and architectural issues

Packaged software vendors have different approaches to their architecture, and you need to be sure their architecture is compatible with yours. Some vendors provide APIs that will allow you to bolt on specialized or legacy systems. Others provide proprietary languages to customize the screens or functionality. Recently, some vendors have built their systems with object layers to enable higher levels of flexibility between modules or between their systems and other vendors. Many of these issues are discussed in the Chapter 11, but here is a quick checklist of issues to discuss with every prospective package vendor:

- Support for open standards, popular operating systems, and hardware
- Development tools for modifying the data structures and input screens
- APIs to connect other packages or home-grown systems
- Support for popular system management tools such as CA Unicenter or Tivoli
- Utilities for backup, performance management, and system administration
- Integration among modules for enterprise packages, and the coherence of the upgrade strategy among modules

Selection process

Force-fitting a package into a reluctant customer organization is often a Pyrrhic victory. You may win the battle, but lose the mindshare war with your customer.

The essential challenge is to involve the functional customer groups to gain their buy-in, while not confusing them with technical issues. More importantly, you need to keep your credibility and customer focus so that you can counteract the impact of "gee whiz" features and clever vendor selling. This process can be daunting and time consuming. However, if you don't have the time, but have some money in your budget, every major consulting firm has a package-selection practice and can help you and your customers buy wisely. If you want to do it yourself, the following is a simple roadmap of the steps in package selection:

Initial requirements setting

Setting functional and performance goals for any new data system is the most difficult task. It is axiomatic that customers always interpret their needs in terms of what they know, and we have seen customers drive decisions toward packages that look just like their existing systems but with the rough edges knocked off. It quickly becomes IS's job to intervene to be sure that the enterprises needs are being met and that the new system has the functionality and flexibility to be integrated into the corporate architecture.

In setting requirements, be sure that all participants understand the reasons for shopping for a new package. Are their functional deficiencies that will no longer support the business model? Is the existing system too old and cost too much to maintain? If you are replacing a package, is it because the existing vendor is failing to keep up with evolving technology? Each of these reasons can lead to a different selection criterion and different level of customer satisfaction. Functional issues often must be reengineered into the customer organization, while technical issues can often be left to specialists.

Selection of candidates

When the requirements have been decided, a *Consumer Reports*-style chart should be produced for each candidate vendor summarizing how well each vendor's capabilities maps into your requirements. At this step, disqualify any vendor that has clear deficiencies. Don't be swayed by vendors selling futures or spreading FUD. Your goals are to reduce the number of packages to two or three candidates worthy of serious consideration. The more you let into the competition the harder the evaluation and selection process will be. Complexity grows exponentially with the number of vendors. Now is the time to be tough. Weed out weak or inappropriate vendors early.

Scripted functional demonstrations

Scripted demos have become a popular way to allow your functional customers to become familiar with the capabilities of the package, while learning more about their own needs as well. Scripting, the act of creating a roadmap for the demo is essential. Scripting captures the requirements of the customers and inhibits the vendors' natural inclination to play to their strengths and avoid discussion of weak or missing features. Every customer has a wish list of needs. But as they run through the scripted demos customers begin to learn the trade-offs vendors have made, and they will also learn which features are "must haves" and which features they can live without.

 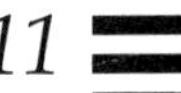

This is also the time for you to begin learning about the vendors. You are going to be making a long-term commitment to the vendor's people and organization as well as their product, so now is the time to find out how knowledgeable is their support staff, how responsive are they to issues that arise, how technically sound is their product. This discussion even goes to chemistry issues. Do they approach problems the way your organization does. Are their people empowered. Do you have access to management when you need it? If they don't impress you now, they won't likely impress you later.

Technical evaluation

While the functional customers are going through the demonstrations discussed above, a technical team needs to carefully evaluate the package architecture using the criteria discussed above. The goal of this process is straightforward — determine whether you can live with the package in light of your architecture and technical vision. If not, don't touch it.

Business discussion

In deciding on a package to become a part of your enterprise computing decision, remember that you are not buying a point solution, you are buying a long-term relationship. Be sure you clearly understand purchase costs, maintenance fees in future years, training costs, upgrade costs, technical support costs, and what insurance you have in the contract to enable you to control those costs. Get all the costs on the table, including upgrades to your infrastructure, before you decide. Going back to management with a bunch of gotchas later is not career enhancing.

Decision

Once the decision is made, check to see how loud the screaming is from those in your organization. If people are comfortable with the decision and anxious to move ahead, the decision is right. If you are going to have to drag some departments kicking and screaming, then either ensure their support, the willingness of the executive sponsors to push with you, or don't move forward. If you are out too far in front of your organization on the issue, you might think about investing more in helping your customers prepare for the future. IS management is hard enough without dragging your customers too.

Living with packages

Packaged software is advertised as the low-cost, simple, solution, but there are collateral issues that need to be considered. First, the package vendor now controls the introduction of new functionality. If internal customers request changes to a package function, they may have to wait or if the requested feature is not in the vendor's product plans, do without.

Second, do not underestimate the requirements for upgrades and maintenance. A major revision to a package can take days or weeks. Some vendors do not (or may not) use common data formats between releases. The result is that data may need reformatting and file structures completely rebuilt. Most vendors will supply conversion tools, but the job can be time consuming and in the case of large enterprise systems like SAP R/3, considerable advance planning is required for a successful upgrade or conversion.

The final issue of living with packages is that you must assume the business risk of the package vendor. If the vendor goes into decline or bankruptcy, or is merged or sold, how will you maintain and improve the package and at what cost? Several large software vendors that had good reputations have struggled in moving to client/server, and as a result, their products may no longer be competitive. This risk can be mitigated but never eliminated.

Technology infrastructure 12

What is infrastructure? It is the nothing more than collection of building blocks required to make an enterprise information system function. It consists of the desktop PCs (or terminals), the servers that contain the data and applications, the network that binds all of theses computing hosts together, and the software that manages all of these systems. In our definition, infrastructure is the civil engineering of IS. It is the foundation for the applications on which the enterprise depends.

What is our goal for infrastructure? We need to make it a flexible, cheap, and reliable as possible. We want it to accommodate the avalanche of new technologies and applications with minimal extra cost and disruption. We want it to be highly reliable. Computing infrastructure today needs to rival the continuity of service of the best electric and gas utilities. And always it needs to be as inexpensive as possible, to allow us to spend more of our budget on new systems and functions.

Technology infrastructure consists of services that support your internal corporation: networking, data center(s), and desktop (end-user) support. Recalling our model of centralized control, the New Enterprise IS should own and provide these services as well as develop the architecture and standards for them. Base types of standards and guidelines are on your corporate culture allowing for some diversity—how much depends on that culture.

The network

The network is the key infrastructure supporting our model of network-based computing and applications. In our vision, you must first implement the enterprise-wide network, and design it for high availability. Keep the user's perspective in mind: Applications are located on the network, and users shouldn't care where the server actually resides. Think in terms of an investment where you are spend money to save money. Investing in a standardized, world-class network will help reduce overall support costs.

We've seen the proof: One organization built an enterprise-wide network that grew from eight locations to more than 100 without increasing network support staff. If you use a metric consisting of network hubs per network support engineer, you can see the drastic productivity improvement for this company.

Many vendors, suppliers, and partners that make your business a success need access to your critical applications and data. We think an appropriate solution is the Internet. Just imagine having one of your major business systems connected to the Internet (highly secure of course) accessible by your suppliers, vendors, partners, and even customers while keeping your organization's internal operations private. Providing this kind of functionality will attract the best in the business and improve your competitive advantage. Now that's service and partnership!

The application platform

The next key piece, the application platform, is a critical service issue in the New Enterprise IS. The platform must be flexible enough to provide an environment that will support most of the business requirements when implementing a network computing model. Flexibility gives customers control over their applications. The platform must support applications (purchased or built) the department needs to support its business model. Otherwise, customers will feel that IS is not providing the right services, and they will want to "do their own thing" once again. There must be standards, however. The standards must be aligned with your company's culture, diversity model, and support requirements/costs.

Since you already have existing platforms that have new or legacy applications running on them such as MVS, VM, VMS, and others, the next step is to define the application platform architecture for the future.

If you pick a network application platform like UNIX, then most of the department diversity issues can be addressed. Studies have indicated that up to 40 percent of all new business applications are being developed for UNIX. If your strategy is to buy versus build, and your platform is UNIX, most of the business problems can be solved.

You may, on the other hand, end up with chaos if you let the departments pick the platform. And big problems will consequently arise in the network computing model. Complications will come when you are asked to manage, support, and integrate the environment. How will you support operational policies like backup and recovery, job scheduling, change control, disaster/recovery, and operating system maintenance?

And just wait until one department needs to integrate applications and/or data with another. You'll be spending a lot of time and money on the middleware to support this integration.

If you have the ability to define this standard architecture up front you'll keep IS costs in line and support the new IS services model. If required, market and sell the concepts to your end-users. It does work...eventually.

The desktop

This is probably going to be the toughest sell you'll have in implementing your New Enterprise network computing model. Standard desktop environments are tough to implement, especially with users in control. Remember, the desktop should be seen as a corporate asset and must be treated as such. Desktops are for business productivity improvements, not games!

Start by using IS as the test environment. Set with a model that defines the desktop configurations by job function. Define the standard desktop and desktop operating environment whether it be Windows, NT, DOS or UNIX. Build a software server environment that provides standard versions of supported desktop software and then put in the processes to support them. This involves change control, automated software distribution, and help desk support. Once you have built this environment and learn how to support it, it becomes easier to sell to others.

Why do you need standard desktops? Again, it goes back to our network computing model. If you are deploying client/server-based applications in the network, concentrate on the interface between the client and the server. Each different operating environment at the desktop will require a separate interface to the application server (i.e., one for Windows, one for NT, and one for UNIX). Testing, deployment, and support becomes more difficult. If this kind of interface is required, you'll also need to set up what we call "a one-of-a-kind network." It includes one of every operating environment deployed in your company.

This is required to effectively test, quality assure, and deploy new or revised applications. If this testing effort delays the deployment life cycle, then IS gets the blame for "not providing effective service."

But they'll say the same thing if you deploy an application in "production," and it breaks because you haven't tested that particular desktop environment.

So standardize as much as possible and sell it to your users. Be patient. It can take a year or two to get everyone converted because of the need to retire existing assets and the need to market and sell the concept. Remember, if you build it, they will come!

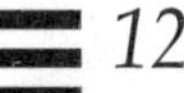 12

The network becomes the data center

People ask skeptically, "How can this be, *The network is the data center*? Shouldn't it be, *The network is the computer*?" Both are true. The network is the key component in distributed, client/server computing. Starting with a sturdy enterprise network makes deployment of distributed systems a business, and not a technical issue.

It's up to the shepherds tending an enterprise's data center and supporting mission-critical applications to provide high Reliability, Availability, and Serviceability (RAS) regardless of the operating system and hardware used.

A few old-hands in the MIS game have suggested to us the notion that if users insist on client/server applications, they should expect less RAS. After all, the reasoning goes, since business needs change faster and applications are deployed quicker, the whole structure will be more fragile. If the levels of service are less than they were, guess what the end-user blames? You got it! The new technology!

As we transition from mainframes to client/server computing, our top priority is to provide the same RAS we did as a mainframe shop. Users expect this, and since their apps and data are just as important as before, they deserve top-notch treatment.

We sell our department's disciplines to the business units constantly: "We can help. We know technology and know how to apply it to a business solution. We know support and the importance of RAS." We point out that it took the information technology industry 30 years to get data center processes right, so why ignore something that works?

What does "The network is the data center" mean? We use the same processes and procedures on every distributed, production business system server, regardless of its location, as if it were located in our data center. These processes must be automated and standardized so the same staff can support the new distributed system.

We developed these processes and tools for use on every production server. (We've identified these tools and processes in our columns before). You can't just add more work to your staff's agenda, you must automate the way you do things. And, by the way, the end-user doesn't know these processes are running. They feel they have control of their environment but we have processes in place "behind the scenes" to support our RAS goals.

You might think of this as extending the glass house around the wide-area network. The data center will go away in this new distributed environment. By agreeing with this assumption then we can now define how to make distributed data centers work. We have the glass house (central data center) for central, mission-critical applications, and now we add the glass closet (remote server rooms) for distributed, mission-critical applications.

The glass closet

A glass closet is simply a server room, attached to the WAN, that can house mission-critical applications. Production servers do not belong in offices, rather in server rooms. It may not have special environmental controls or raised floor, but it is secure and owned by our system administration function that reports to central IS.

Business units chose which server room the distributed application servers are placed. We do not dictate where a server is located. If a server room has production, mission-critical application servers inside, then it can be designated a glass closet.

Central data center staff support each glass closet. Conversely, the central staff may contract with local system administrators when we'd like to run one of our production jobs in one of their glass closets. We'll work out an agreement for the local staff to provide backups and hardware support, for example.

Supporting the glass closet

How in the world do we support remote glass closets with our central staff? Remember, we recommend the separation of desktop tool support from mission critical application support. System administration support desktop tools (i.e., spreadsheets, desktop publishing, and licensed, third-party tools), and the data center supports mission-critical applications.

Why? The data center staff knows what disciplines are required and how to provide high RAS, that's what they are paid to do! The process (or methodology) for supporting mission-critical applications in both the glass house and closet is the Client/Sever Production Acceptance (CSPA) process. This is the essential methodology we developed for successful transition from centralized mainframe to fully distributed without adding data center head count.

The glass closet design offers business units a measure of control over their servers. Managers can observe, feel, and even smell their equipment if they desire. They can upgrade their system to meet their ever-changing business needs. Last and least (from their perspective) they view our central staff as a help and not a hindrance.

Glass closets are flexible

To be successful in the 1990s we in IS need to expect and support change. Re-engineering business process requires re-engineering IS. Just as we're installing ever more flexible computing systems, we need to improve customer service and satisfaction at lower cost.

This started happening as we moved from a central mainframe environment (where we were perceived as cranky, lethargic, and domineering) to a fully distributed model (where we are perceived as helpful and flexible) while still maintaining the disciplines we learned over the last three decades. We made it happen by implementing automated software tools and the new production acceptance methodology, which also helped us to re-engineer ourselves.

The Internet

Since 1993, the Internet exploded onto the IS scene. In only a few months it went from being an academic curiosity to a household word. At one level it is connecting individuals and companies together in ways that were not previously possible. But it is also pioneering new ways of designing information systems. We see the effect of this redesign in the IS trade press every day. A new language is being invented — Internets, intranets, extranets — *nets* everywhere. Underneath the jargon is a paradigm shift in how enterprises think about developing and deploying software. The Web has shown that development and maintenance costs can be substantially reduced and the flexibility of the software is greatly increased by developing with the Web paradigm as an integral part of the enterprise architecture.

The Web has shown that developing with the Web paradigm as an integral part of the enterprise architecture can substantially reduce development and maintenance costs.

However, our goal is not to sing the praises of the Internet, but rather to pick out the underlying technologies and offer ideas that will help you accelerate your development productivity, and customer satisfaction. Moving your organization from a desktop to a "Webtop" environment, can make all the difference in creating a flexible, responsive environment that will delight our customers.

Web-centered development

The basic architecture of the Web is a simple publishing model. A client requests a "page" of information identified by a URL (Universal Resource Locator). The request is routed over the Web to the server that serves up the page formatted in HTML (Hyper Text Markup Language) and delivers it to the client using the

HTTP (Hyper Text Transfer Protocol). The browser (Netscape or Microsoft Internet Explorer are two of the most popular) is the engine that manages the requests and displays the result to the user.

What makes this architecture so appealing is that even in its simplest form it solves a number of ongoing IS challenges. First, a huge number of internal client/server communications are of the simple Web server form. *Give me a page* becomes *Give me a report*, or *Give me a page from the company policy manual*, etc. Thus without any modification, companies are realizing huge savings by putting their manuals, procedures, and other documentation onto internal Web servers.

Second, the use of the browser to ensure ubiquity of client interface. With the arrival of Mosaic and later Netscape, custom client programs became unnecessary. And even more important, the browser is cross platform. Now we have a tool that gives us uniform look and feel for PCs, Macintoshes and UNIX machines. For those of you who work in or manage heterogeneous client environments, this feature is a lifesaver.

There are some distinct disadvantages to this simple environment. First, the client/server connection is stateless. The server sends a page and maintains no record. This severely limits browser for on-line transaction processing (this issue is being addressed by several vendors). The naive publishing model lacks the dynamic interaction needed for interactive applications

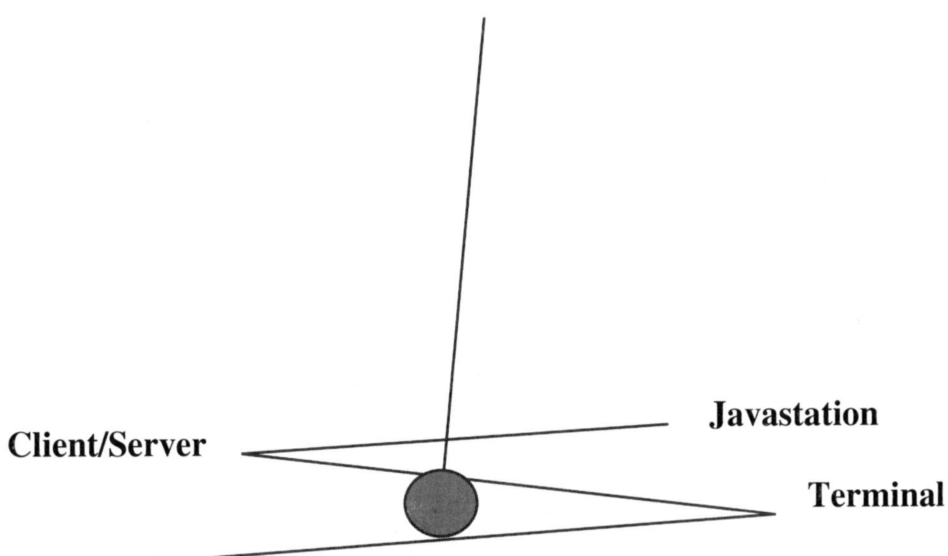

Figure 12-1 Some see Java as the swinging of the client server pendulum back to terminals

Building for the Web – the Java revolution

However, just as the Web has been the enabler of an explosion of information growth, Java has extended the reach of the Web into uncharted waters. Since its introduction in the spring of 1995, the adoption of Java has been explosive. At this writing there were more than 10 million copies of the Java Development Kit (JDK) downloaded from the Web and more than 400,000 developers are writing in Java, almost as many as are writing in Windows.

We are often asked, "what's the big deal about Java?" Isn't a thin client just another terminal? These critics see Java as only a move back to centralized control of client software.

But Java takes us back toward the advantages of the terminal paradigm, but on a totally different level. The network model is no longer host based. We no longer care whether the terminal is a PC or some other device. In short, Java provides flexibility completely unavailable in the terminal model.

Java is a computer language specifically designed to be transported over networks. Security features have been added, some of the insecure attributes of popular languages like C have been removed, and it is designed to be compact and interpreted so that any computer equipped with a Java interpreter, called the Java Virtual Machine (JVM) could download and execute Java code.

Why is this important? The Web demonstrates that the with a directory strategy (URL) a simple transport protocol (HTTP) and a display language (HTML) publishing information in a simple standardized way became easy for everyone.

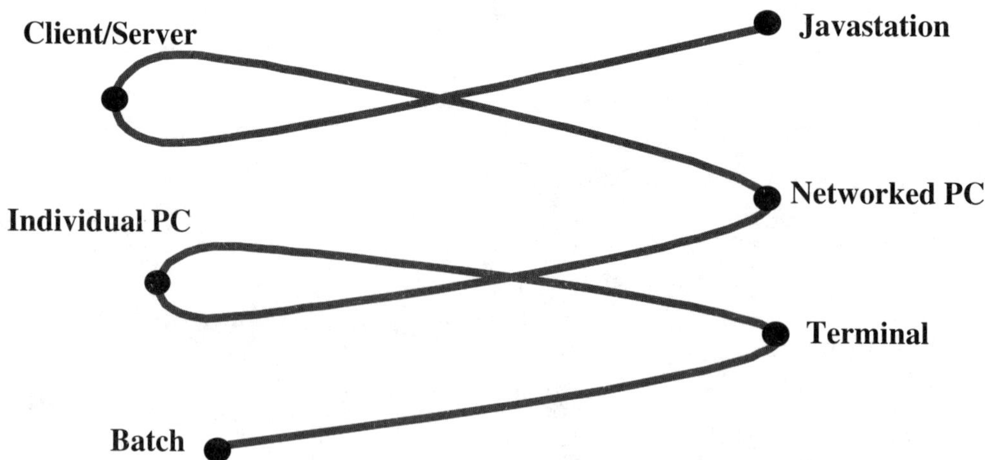

Figure 12-2 Java is a part of the spiral of technical innovation

With the addition of Java, now information content can be provided with a content handler. The network is no longer just a means of data transport, but is also the means of program transport as well. The old days of sharing information in which the sender would bundle a document as an e-mail attachment (or other data stream) and the receiver would have to have the same program as created the data are over. The implications to software development are staggering.

With Java technology a display tool like a browser can become the platform for user interfaces. The Web server can become the means of software distribution throughout organizations. Of most immediate importance, IS departments that faced the continuing challenge of heterogeneity (supporting PCs and Macintoshes, for example) will find their burdens eased, since browsers and JVMs are available for most popular computing platforms.

Enterprise computing vendors have embraced Java because it frees them from the burdens of multi-platform support, and will slim down the large client libraries required for some of the enterprise systems. SAP, PeopleSoft, Oracle, Baan and many other businessware vendors have announced Java strategies and some are beginning to ship Java based products.

Java development tools are proliferating rapidly. Visual J++ and Symantec Café are only two of a rapidly increasing number of Java development tools. These tools extend the visual programming model into the Java environment and greatly speed software development.

Java in the new millennium

As this is written, an intense debate has broken out, with accompanying lawsuits between Sun Microsystems and Microsoft over the ubiquity of Java. Underneath the debate that has broken out in the trade press is a difference of opinion over the value of a universal, centrally administrated thin client, versus a centrally planned network of fatter clients.

Sun and its allies are arguing that commoditizing and slimming the client by interacting through Java enabled browsers is the to reign in excessive IS costs.

On the other hand, Microsoft argues that the individual access to power, performance advantages and the flexibility of fatter client systems, justify the expense, and that the addition of central management tools (under development) will allow IS departments to restrain cost growth.

This debate will continue for years, and we suspect that IS managers will have to pick their own way through the mine field. Early adopters of the Java computing model are likely to be those businesses that are geographically diverse, have only a few core applications, and larger numbers of "heads-down" functional users.

Businesses that are likely to work with fatter clients are those that require a broader range of applications, more individual user power, and have the ability to provide higher levels of user support. However, whether fat or thin, client or server, the Java revolution will continue.

Enterprise-wide services 13

We have written about the importance of building your architecture around standards. Here we show the value of this decision. If we are to achieve the benefits of an inexpensive and easy to manage computing infrastructure, we must automate the management of our infrastructure. We cannot have system administrators going to each server and desktop client for a "laying on of hands" for each problem that arises. That approach is much too expensive today.

Our goal is to build an infrastructure that will allow remote services to be provided to both the desktop and the servers. In this way we can achieve the "glass closet," a lights-out, distributed, low-cost information system.

The goal of enterprise management is to provide basic services in a hands-off fashion. These services are included in the table below:

Table 13-1 Enterprise management provides basic services

Service	Function
Directory and naming services	Enable networking and massaging
Automate software distribution	Save time and provide a standard software suite
Automated diagnostics	Allow remote help services
Security services	Essential for any enterprise
Help desk	Indispensable part of IS department
Management tools	Tools to help the system manager such as system consoles, alarm handlers, reporting tools, load and management analysis tools, etc.

The generic features of an enterprise management software package are straightforward. The typical package contains an agent that is resident on every host The better packages have agents that support all the popular operating systems. The agent monitors services and can create events if a fault is detected, or can respond to a query from the management console. The management server either interrogates the client hosts periodically or responds to alarms generated by the host. All of the popular enterprise management packages are highly flexible and can be customized to handle alarm and out-of-range conditions in a variety of ways. Most packages have the ability to pass information to other centralized services such as event management. One benefit of this technology is that network centers can be given the ability to "follow the Sun" by letting operations centers in geographically diverse locations manage each others' hosts.

The most common protocol to manage the interactions between the local agents and the console is the Simple Network Management Protocol (SNMP). Most popular packages support SNMP. The importance of open protocols is that they allow interoperability across distributed networks and heterogeneous hosts.

Once the enterprise management framework is in place, you can deploy a range of services on top of it. You can automate the management of the servers and clients throughout the enterprise, thus enabling the "glass closet." Servers and networks can be remotely diagnosed, restarted, and frequently repaired by acting on the alarms of the enterprise management software. You can set up autopaging or autofaxing, which frees humans from watching the screens in the data center. Support staff can log-on to systems from home if an alarm sounds after normal working hours.

The basic enterprise management package can be integrated with help desk software to automatically create trouble tickets from alarms or faults. This integration combines the workflow features of help desk software with the diagnostic and reporting features of enterprise management systems. Some additional features are to add Web browser interfaces to enterprise management so that the tools can more easily be used from remote locations, or over the Internet. Enterprise management packages also typically have APIs to allow customization.

Hardware vendors as well as a number of independent software vendors sell systems and tools. Enterprise management software vendors include Sun Microsystems (Solstice Suite) Hewlett-Packard (Open View), IBM (Open Vision), and Microsoft (SMS). Some of the popular independent frameworks are Computer Associates' Unicenter and IBM's Tivoli. See *Networking the New Enterprise* for a more detailed discussion on management systems.

Development

There is an ancient Chinese curse that states "May you live in interesting times." Software developers certainly live in interesting times as pressures to produce more user-friendly and flexible applications is growing. The need to deliver on-time and within budget is higher than ever. The good news is that the art of software engineering has improved with the arrival of new software models and tools. Together, these improve development efficiency by relieving much of the burden from the development team. Rapidly falling hardware prices can often serve as a safety valve, freeing the developer from wringing the last bit of performance from the code.

Although we have come a long way from the Jurassic systems of COBOL on flat file managers, and development the technology is growing ever more robust, we still find most programming projects are not successful. They suffer from significant schedule slippage, cost overruns, or significant functional deficiencies. This disturbing data suggests that some of the fundamental issues in software development are still not solved:

- Aligning with customer needs
- Properly managing customer and managerial expectations
- Architectural failures
- Functional deficiencies

Our objective is not to give you a treatise on programming, (although we provide a number of excellent references) but rather to focus on the issues of how to use the new tools to guide the development process through the thicket of customer demands.

While new tools and development paradigms will increase developer stress, if properly used, they will accelerate the development process and produce systems with sufficient flexibility. This will sustain your business as it transforms itself in response to the rapidly changing economy.

Joint development of standards

The process of unifying the mainframe and client/server groups can be accelerated by agreeing on standards. It sounds easy, right? Wrong!

Critical data for most organizations is housed in mainframes. Standards have lead to safe and secure data centers that protect those data assets. Most client/server systems are in the process of becoming mission-critical, and have yet to embrace mainframe-class standards.

Why have many client/server developers and systems administrators ignored standards? Many believe that the rigid nature of mainframe standards is simply too hideboundor stringent for the fast pace of client/server development. Our experience shows that most client/server systems take the same duration for application development. Applications are now more sophisticated.

It is hard to find IS groups where the staff knows the strategic direction of the organization. Knowing where the strategy for information technology fits the grand scheme of things in the organization goes a long way in supporting the connection between the IS staff and the organization.

For this to occur, the client/server technologists must receive training in the fundamentals of data center management, including:

- Backup and recovery
- Job control
- Scheduling
- Environmental security
- Network security
- Data security

Conversely, mainframers must receive training in the productivity tools that allow client/server technologies to produce modern GUIs and flexible, scalable software that satisfies customers today.

An overview of the network computing technologies coupled with cross-functional teamwork helps both groups understand the issues they face.

Basic standards that must be agreed to are the development methodology, project management techniques, and tools. You must establish naming conventions for data, labels, files, and so on. Development, tests, production source and executable libraries must be created and promotion processes solidified. Customer interfaces for presentation logic must be defined. Quality standards and appropriate walk-through and sign-off processes must be outlined. Network utilization standards must be established to ensure that multiple applications co-exist.

Trends in software engineering

For many managers, the Java explosion is causing confusion, fear, and sometimes loathing. Java is not a fad, and Java will not go away. Java is a poster child of a revolution in software. But before we discuss specific tools and techniques, we want to provide a roadmap of some of the changes we see in software engineering that will be evolving during the next few years. When we strip away the hype several trends emerge.

Components and componentware

The client/server revolution, although far from complete, is fully entrenched. With it have emerged the foundation of new and highly productive software paradigms.

The most significant is the emergence and acceptance of software components. The broad acceptance of tools such as Microsoft's Visual Basic, and Sybase's PowerBuilder have convinced many programmers that the flexibility and productivity of component-based architectures for building applications around functional components. Although these tools (and others such as Delphi) are still popular, the battleground of the late 1990s is between Active X and Java Beans. Regardless of who wins this battle, programmers will emerge with the ability to buy prefabricated code segments that are easily integrated into an application.

We are so confident of Java's success because it is the first of a series of new technologies that have emerged from 40 years of research in computing language and distributed-computing methodologies. Other languages may follow Java, and expand on its desirable properties, but the concept won't die. Java is a breakthrough because it enables safe, highly distributed computing environments. IS managers can now realize the long-sought goal of building highly distributed, manageable systems.

New database technologies

In 1969, IBM's E.F. Codd invented relational database technology. During the 1970s, the technology began to evolve, and as hardware capabilities accelerated in the 1980s, relational engines rapidly increased in speed and capability. Today, relational database technology from Oracle, Informix, Sybase, IBM, and Microsoft forms the basis of most business software applications. They are the underpinnings of most data management code.

This database technology is being extended in several ways that are important to system development today. First, relational database engineers have the ability to handle an increasing variety of data types. Binary Large Objects (BLOBs) such as photographs or sound files, or are streaming media such as video and audio. Some vendors are adding object features into their database technology so that a data set is not just defined by relations between tables, but also by object relationships.

While some small companies are shipping true object databases, most of the major database vendors are letting the technology evolve. As one database vendor told us recently, "Eighty percent of all the data in the free world is still in flat files, so we don't see a particular need to rush to objects." As you develop new applications, the increased capabilities of analytical engines will allow you to build larger and more complex applications.

Another important consideration in working with database technologies is that all vendors are extending their products beyond relational engines with Web-awareness, OLAP tools, and various forms of middleware. We will talk more about multi-tier architectures in the next section, but each of the major database vendors has announced tools and technologies that will allow customers to provide query access across multiple databases and platforms, and will allow access to database applications through the Web.

Database vendors have announced a Java strategy that will allow a customer to connect a Java application to a database through Java Database Connectivity. This means that a customer developing a Web application can create database queries and enable client data access through a Web browser and will not be dependent of client tools such as Visual Basic or PowerBuilder. These developments are powerful extensions of customer capability and productivity.

Multi-tier architectures

Client/server is now established throughout most IS departments, and we read about its limitations in the computer press weekly. Almost every organization has architectures like that shown below. In this approach, the data and business rules are contained in one server. Only the graphical interface and personal productivity tools are contained on the client.

The good news about client/server is that the individual user has access to a broad variety of personal and corporate applications, and customer satisfaction is much higher than the old, dumb, green-screen terminals because of the usability and graphics capability of the Windows interface. But increasingly, IS departments are discovering that the cost of ownership of client server/systems is high and that simple client server architectures do not scale easily or cheaply.

In 1997, Total Cost of Ownership (TCO as it is called) has become a major issue in the trade press, and we agree. We regularly visit IS departments that have thousands of clients (mostly PCs) and hundreds of servers, with no effective way to manage the clients or servers without human intervention. And the high cost is driving IS managers toward more manageable multi-tier architectures. The next extension on client/server is the development of multi-tier architectures. This trend has been popularized in enterprise software by SAP with its three-tier architecture separating application servers from the database server. An illustration of this approach is shown below.

These architectures are proliferating as managers and system architects discover the benefits and as off-the-shelf tools become increasingly available. A multi-tier

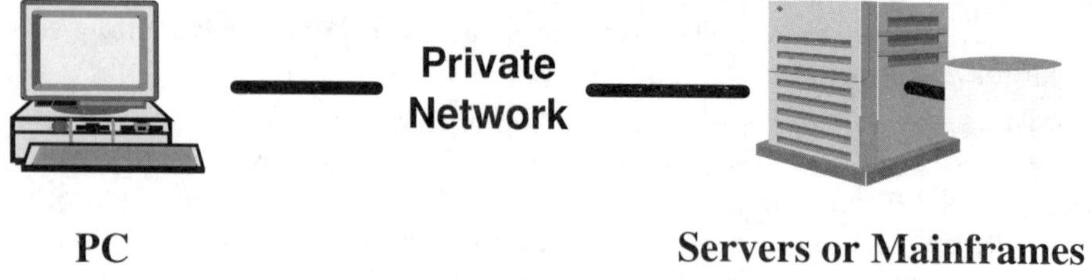

Figure 13-1 A simple client/server architecture

architecture uses a middle layer to manage connections and server access to provide a variety of services to the client. Services such as security and authentication, client software distribution, and connection handling are all enabled on the middle layer of service handlers. In addition the middle layer can manage connections to the back-end servers and can actually manage client applications that rely on multiple heterogeneous server connections.

One trend that emerges in multi-tier architectures is that application business rules are being separated from the data management rules. This development adds tremendous flexibility, since many applications and services can access the same data without the need to replicate it across separate applications. Also, customer satisfaction is greatly increased, since workflow and business process becomes more flexible and easier to change. Gone are the old days when COBOL programs provided both the data access mechanism and imbedded the application business rules — and good riddance. Baking rules in code is a recipe for inflexibility and is the kiss of death to any IS application.

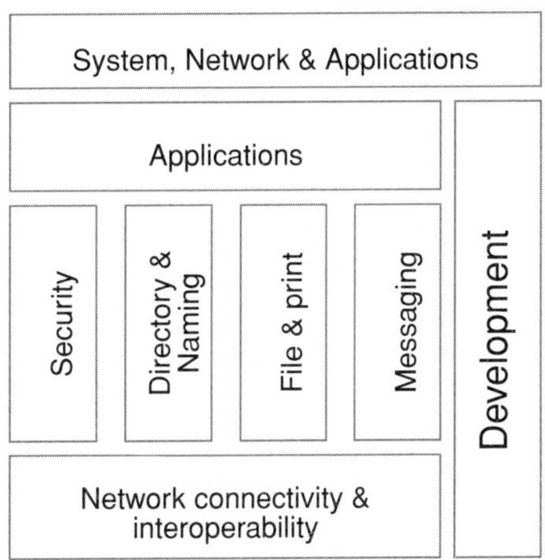

Figure 13-2 An architecture built around specialized services

Customer-centered development

Although new technologies make the developers job easier, the essential challenge remains — how to give the customer what they want, when they don't know what they want (until they see it) and they want it changed more quickly than there is manpower and money to accommodate them. Is it any wonder that IS managers always wish they could be tyrants and impose strict standards on their users? Some can, but don't count on being able to do it in your organization for very long. Your internal customers are reflective of social changes taking place throughout the US — they are more empowered and contentious than ever, and in much more of a hurry.

One way to stay ahead is to surf the wave of change, by using the techniques of Rapid Application Development. These techniques require a significant change in the developmental paradigm, but they can greatly accelerate the development cycle. Increasing customer satisfaction often results from the perception of attentiveness and responsiveness that speed can bring.

Rapid Application Development (RAD)

RAD was once considered a radical concept — fraught with risk and prone to development of unstable applications. But the arrival of new tools and methodologies means that virtually any IS department can do RAD successfully. By RAD we mean that any IS development effort can be completed within a year, major enhancements can be completed within three months, and minor changes can be completed as required. Faster is better, so we encourage you to move more quickly.

RAD processes

We won't discuss specific RAD methodologies because we want you to focus on process changes and paradigmatic shifts that are at the heart of any RAD campaign. The goal of RAD is simple — to break through the waterfall development model, the serial flow of engineering information from requirements through deployment.

In appendix C, we show an example of a waterfall process. This is an example of a management effort to provide a documented and orderly development environment that will function across many different county organizations and will enable the Palm Beach Information Systems organization to begin to have a thoughtful development program. The waterfall is certainly the place to start in any organization that is having difficulty in successfully planning and executing its projects. But it is a long way from being RAD. RAD requires a higher level of organizational sophistication than the waterfall, and it can be nerve wracking to those who like orderly projects. But it provides one important advantage the waterfall lacks — speed.

In breaking through this barrier, we find that the greatest difficulty that many of clients have is that they cannot mentally accommodate the turbulence and confusion that accompanies the change to RAD development. RAD requires a higher level of communication within the development team, between the customers and the developers and between the developers and the operations staff. Elsewhere in this book we discuss the CSPA, a framework for moving systems from development to production, so we won't discuss it further here. But the quality of communication within the development team is key to RAD success just as with the CSPA process.

"Wait," you may say. "We communicate all the time." The problem is that too many IS departments substitute correspondence for communication — a process that cannot possibly work in RAD. It's too slow, and can often hide essential issues rather than bring them to the surface. Managers, who like to communicate through the flow of paper, will often be challenged by RAD. The manager in RAD becomes a facilitator between the development groups, ensuring communication and identifying problems, and also between the customers and the developers to ensure the developers are not drifting away from the project goals.

RAD is parallelism

A RAD project is by definition a highly parallel activity. To breakdown the waterfall, the development team must be prepared to perform all of the development activities at the same time — and here is where the frustrations set in. Those developers who like to do "silver plate" development become quickly frustrated with the confusion induced by RAD.

What is "silver plate" development? It is an infection that exists everywhere — "Until you hand me my assignment on a silver plate I can't do my job." This attitude is death to RAD, because it encourages serial thinking, and encourages silos in the development team. With RAD, no one can toss anything over the wall because nothing is completed until it comes together at the end.

How do we accomplish a project with a lot of parallelism? First, begin with a flexible architecture. Define where the "hard points" are in the architecture and separate that which drives the system and that which can be changed or negotiated. Avoid in architectural decisions, those solutions that have closed APIs or cannot provide the tools to interoperate easily in your systems. Define that boundaries and interfaces that govern the system and again review where negotiation is possible. This sounds like requirement analysis, except that it is intended to be more flexible and focused on possibilities rather than constraints.

Adopt the policy of encouraging trial or pilot solutions and examining their consequences, rather than trying to define the right answer during detailed requirements phases. *Customer satisfaction* means that customer needs are accommodated even if they change during the course of the project. And what traditional managers often fail to understand is that the faster the project proceeds, the less customers will change their minds.

RAD is involvement

Continual involvement from customers and developers is the only way to keep a RAD project on course. This means that the customers of the project need to be continuously involved in reviewing, critiquing, changing, and testing the software. Developers need to stay close to the customers. They need to have familiarity with the operations they are building their systems for, and should have a clear understanding of the project's operational goals, as well as the developmental requirements.

The authors know a development manager who was building a new warehousing system. He had his programmers spend a day working on the receiving dock to gain a better understanding of how their customers actually work. This action had two benefits. First, the developers gained a new appreciation of the challenges their customers faced every day, which gave them new motivation to produce a better solution. Second, by meeting and working with their customers, the developers had a new channel of communication and would often call their new colleagues to discuss issues independent of the management.

RAD is rework

Some managers hate RAD because nothing is ever completed or closed. The ideal RAD project is continually developed, tested, and modified right up to the time it is first delivered to its customers. And after it is delivered, it is further reworked and modified in response to customer's changing needs. This drives some managers crazy, but the rework process is what aligns the system with its customers. And the more radical the system, the more of a departure from previous practice the system is, the more that rework is a valuable alignment tool.

Conference room pilots and disposable prototypes accelerate allignment. Disposable prototypes are snapshots of functionality, populated with small subsets of data. The goal of these prototypes is to draw out requirements and help the customers better understand the system design and the capabilities. Non-RAD programming techniques do not permit the efficient production of disposable code. But using the tools discussed in the next section, anyone can quickly produce a prototype that will often connect with real data.

A variation of disposible prototypes that is often used with larger packaged enterprise systems is the conference room pilot. The pilot requires that the functional users of the new system gather around the prototype in a structured way to critique the system and explore its functionality. The goal of the development team in hosting these pilots is to drive the alignment of the functional users. We often see cases where a conference room pilot reveals

 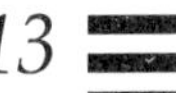

disconnects between the functional groups and a lack of understanding of how the underlying operational process works. If not caught, this leads to the worst kind of IS failure — the inappropriate system.

In keeping with the spirit of rework, RAD projects should be time-phased so that the product is a series of incremental deliveries. With the acceptance of new tools that allow more modular development, it is possible to provide some basic functionality in the first release, and then to rework the first release to add functionality, while fixing bugs and responding to customer requests for changes.

To be effective and to keep momentum up, the timing of these releases should be very short — less than six-month intervals if possible. One of the great benefits of RAD is that it avoids the great pitfalls of waterfall development, namely losing customer interest by taking too long to show results.

RAD is leadership

Because of the turbulent nature of RAD projects, the amount of leadership required to successfully execute RAD is extraordinary. The leader of RAD development needs to focus on assembling a team of people who "get it" — who have a high tolerance for ambiguity, a strong team sense, and a strong commitment to the success of the customer. Developers and managers who do not have (or will not learn) these skills are not likely to be successful (or happy) with RAD.

Remember that RAD is an organized process. The ambiguity caused by breaking down the serial development processes, is not the same as confusion. In RAD development it's OK to get weird. Tradition is the enemy and everything that reminds people of the old paradigm should be reexamined and removed if it is a barrier to communication, customer focus, or results. This includes all institutional behaviors that promote turf, functional silos, or linear thinking. We even suggest that the RAD team redefine the roles traditionally assigned to developers:

Table 13-2 One way to rethink how jobs are labeled

From	To
Team leader	Chief Facilitator
Systems Engineer	Ye Olde Keeper of Tradition
Requirements Engineer	Customer Advocate

We also suggest geographic changes. Developers should be brought together in one space — a war room. The war room serves as the focus of the project and should contain the latest thinking on each aspect of the project. Key decisions and dates should be displayed for all to see. And there should always be a countdown clock on the wall so everyone knows the urgency of each activity.

Tools for development

Until recently, RAD was often a gutsy move — like grabbing a parachute, jumping out of the plane and counting on being able to get it on and open before hitting the ground. However, with the arrival of new tools, RAD is increasingly becoming a way of life in many organizations.

The new tools combine the technologies of objects, components (that may be objects) and new interfaces and protocols required to build systems much more quickly and flexibly. These tools include PowerBuilder, Delphi, and Visual Basic (to name just a few)

The metaphor of visual tools has been extended to C, C++, and Java, so visual tools can accommodate almost any language preference. These tools enable the same approach to reusable code that will easily enable a standard look-and-feel across a variety of applications

Web-centric development

Just as the introduction of the IBM Personal Computer in 1981 was the defining event in computing in the 1980s, the World Wide Web and Java have been the defining events of computing in the 1990s. Navigator and Internet Explorer superseded Mosaic, the killer application that sparked the Web explosion in 1995. However, the growth of the Web from an academic curiosity to a standard means of personal and commercial information exchange, has now surpassed the growth rate of every consumer technology.

One of the Holy Grails of the Web revolution is the ability to communicate with any hardware running almost any operating system. This effort is supported by a number of businessware vendors who are realizing that the cost of supporting multiple platforms is expensive and increasingly unproductive. For example, at a recent meeting, a representative of a large businessware vendor told one of the authors that they support 64 different platforms for their client software. The goal of being able to let a browser provide a common interface across platforms and then to provide interface support through the Web and Java is gaining support. At this writing, SAP, Baan, Oracle, PeopleSoft among others have all announced Web strategies to provide browser-based tools and client software.

Figure 13-3 Replace the private network with the Internet

Another goal of Web-centric development is an effort to replace large and expensive WAN networks with the Internet. Using security technologies such as Secure Key Management for Internet Protocol (SKIP), organizations are developing applications that will work across the supply chain and will also allow individual customer and employee access from anywhere.

There is also a hidden agenda in Web-centric development. The role of the traditional PC is changing, and what we used to think of as the traditional PC desktop is being expanded greatly. Dozens of manufacturers of consumer electronics are adding browsers and Java language capabilities to their products and are enabling their devices to connect to the network to exchange information. Cellular phones, personal digital assistants (PDAs), point-of-sale devices, and appliances are all being equipped to connect to networks. These devices are expected to outnumber PCs on the net by the year 2000. IS managers will soon have the option of connecting bar code scanners, field data terminals, and customer-owned devices directly to their corporate networks.

Customer communication will be enabled through a similarly wide variety of devices, and the traditional PC-centric approach to software development will need to be broadened to include non-PC devices as well. This is already being used to help sales people to use laptops to work in virtual offices and spend more time with their customers. In the future, the traditional PC desktop may be the exception as the standard personal productivity tool, rather than the rule.

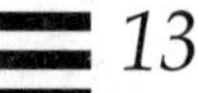 13

Webizing traditional applications

One of the greatest benefits of Web technology is the ability to connect Web-based interfaces to legacy systems. The advantages of moving existing systems to the Web are the ease of maintenance particularly in heterogeneous environments, and the ease of software distribution throughout the enterprise.

The easiest applications to convert are those that use simple forms or queries to enter or extract data. For example, a fixed-asset system may require a simple input of department number or user ID and returns a list of capital property assigned to that number. This type of interface may have to be maintained using client software supplied by the vendor or by using a custom interface written in Visual Basic. To convert this application to the Web, a browser is loaded onto the desktop, and an HTTP server is added to the network to serve information to the browser.

Until recently the standard technique is to prepare a query using CGI (common gateway interface) that is passed from the HTTP server to the legacy system. The results are passed back to the HTTP server that formats the results in HTML and passes the information to the browser. Recently, the Java option has become available. Java Database Connectivity (JDBC) is an open standard that will allow queries developed in Java to be passed directly to those databases supporting Java connections. For those databases that do not yet support direct Java connections, JDBC to ODBC bridges are available.

Transformation of a local government IS department 14 

This is the story of a county government information systems department that set out to change its computers and networks, and the way it managed both. The Palm Beach County, Florida IS department wanted to provide better service and improve customer satisfaction. The County's strategic direction was to interconnect separate operating groups (i.e., Tax Collector, courts, etc.) and to reduce costs by eliminating duplicate data entry and allowing the free flow of information from one department to another. As part of this new strategic direction, the county commissioners combined two existing information systems groups and created a new department to serve all IS needs countywide.

The uniqueness of this case is the technology direction, the organizational structure, and the transition tools selected to provide a smooth transition to a three-tier, client/server environment. It is rare that a medium-sized local government would select a bleeding-edge technology direction (three-tier client/server), but it is even rarer when a local government turns to temporary employees for general staff and management positions to help them during such a big transition.

Background

In 1998, the population of the County was approximately 1 million, making it a medium-size county in Florida. The IS department is responsible for approximately 4,000 peripherals and 125 servers connected to the County's network.

The general governance of the County is the responsibility of an elected board of county commissioners. The county courts as well as property and taxation departments are headed by elected constitutional officers who enjoy considerable power and autonomy in their own right, despite formal budgetary oversight by both state and county governments.

This is a typical Florida county government organizational structure. It poses many issues when dealing with the sharing of data and computing resources.

Information services were provided for many years by a mainframe-based unit under the control of the Property Appraiser. This department was named Automated Information Management. As personal computers began to see wide-scale use, a PC-based Management Information Systems (MIS) department was developed to provided services to County departments other than those using the mainframe.

The existence of two information systems departments created duplication, conflict, confusion, and exacerbated tensions between the County Commission and the constitutional officers. The County Commission, in October 1991, decided to merge the two organizations into one organization called the Information Systems (IS) department. The new department had a combined staff of 181 employees that supported diverse hardware and software combinations running in standalone and network attached environments. In 1991, the two groups merged. Forming a department that consisted of mainframe and personal computer information systems.

The Information Systems Policy Board (ISPB) was formed on February 26, 1992 to set direction and establish policy. The board was made up of three constitutional officers (the Tax Collector, Clerk of the Circuit Court, and Property Appraiser) and two county commissioners. They hired a consultant to oversee the operation and started the merger. In theory, it had ultimate responsibility for all county government information services, including hiring of the director and budgeting. It provided necessary coordination and communication between the various county services.

For the first three years the merger was in name only. Work went on much like before except for considerable increases in conflict over technology selection, ownership of system, training, and other turf issues. New employees were hired in isolated cases only, despite more than 25 vacancies. The same job descriptions used before the merger continued unchanged — a department with approximately 150 people had more than 60 job descriptions.

The ISPB hired a director in May 1992 to oversee the development of the IS department. The new director immediately set out to unify the hardware and software environments. The IS department selected a preferred UNIX vender (Sun Microsystems), a database management systems (Oracle), and an application development environment (Sybase's PowerBuilder). The director and a small group of internal employees also managed to convince the County Commission to fund the development of a new high-speed multi-protocol network.

The director's efforts were focused strictly on the technical infrastructure. By the end of 1993, he had reduced the staff to 151 from 180 employees. As in any merger, duplicate jobs resulted in layoffs and reassignments.

 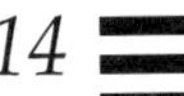

In 1994, the department completed many infrastructure projects and started the development of numerous client/server applications. The county hired a consulting company to help review the county's overall information systems needs.

The consultants conducted numerous interviews, and in January 1995 submitted a transformation plan to the IS department for review and comments. The firm proposed ways to align the county's missions and IS to improve efficiency. In a nutshell, the firm recommended ideas to transform the county's aging information systems to client/server technology, and found better ways to share data.

At the same time, the director hired a deputy director to run day-to-day operations. The deputy director was soon given the responsibility of the transformation project. By the spring of 1995, the transformation plan was approved and the department was directed by IS to commence work.

The transformation

The county's technical transformation was based on the migration from an IBM SNA network to a fiber-optic and level-5, multi-protocol, IP-based network (ATM ready) supporting a heterogeneous mix of clients and servers. The completed network supported universal access from any client (e.g., Windows, Macintosh, Sun SPARCstation, and so on) to any of 125 servers. The server portfolio consisted of Suns, IBMs, DEC Alphas, and Sequents running UNIX; IBM CMOS R51 running MVS and VM; AS400s, System 36s and 38s running IBM's proprietary midrange operating system; and Compaq and Dell servers running Novell NetWare.

The organizational change was aimed to improve customer service. For years, the two ancestors of IS cultivated a negative relationship with other county employees. IS staffers themselves were viewed favorably by IS customers, yet IS management had become an easy target for customer ridicule. Why?

The expense of information technology was exorbitant and investment returns did not materialize as predicted. Many IS customers blamed the change in the IS organization for their own failures. It was easier to point a finger at IS than face the reality that some customer managers were unable to redesign and transform their business processes to fully embrace and use IS.

Based on the consultant's recommendations, IS management decided that the best course of action was to reorganize. The IS department would examine its business processes, evaluate their value, and recommend internally the necessary changes for the transformation. IS management believed this project and the results would be a good use of internal resources. The intent was to refocus the IS department to become an internal information systems consulting organization.

To transform the organization from a product-specific to a service-oriented business; senior management developed new job classifications and changed the organizational structure to better fit what the county departments needed. The IS contracted with a local university to train the staff in team building, matrix management, project management, client/server technologies, telecommunications, graphical languages (e.g., Visual C++ and PowerBuilder), and database theory.

Management knew that they would have peak periods of systems development that would require skills in multiple areas, including networks, applications, server operation, and so on. IS management also knew permanent employees would need help with their regular jobs while they attended class. As a result, the county contracted with an employee-leasing agent to ensure consistent service.

Transformation successes

As we write this in 1998, the transformation is not yet complete, although most of the infrastructure changes are done. Management and operational information is now available from an application software portfolio of one-tier, two-tier, and three-tier client/server information systems developed using PowerBuilder, Visual Basic, COBOL accessing VSAM, and Oracle and DB2 relational databases. A computer output to laser disk (COLD) system, geographic information system, and the initial phases of a paper reduction project are all well underway. The paper reduction project blends specific information technologies such as faxmodems, electronic mail, document imaging, alpha-numeric paging, and GroupWare routing software.The extent of the County's IS transformation, as of the writing of this book, included the following changes:

- The personnel reorganization was complete.
- New job descriptions were completed.
- Management levels were reduced from five to two.
- 75 percent of the training was complete.
- 80 percent of all county buildings had been rewired using level-5 wiring and fiber optics.
- The consulting services group was staffed and operating.
- 15 two-tier and 2 three-tier client/server administrative systems were operating.

- Fiber-optic cable was installed from the downtown office complex the local airport complex, allowing ATM services at 155 megabits per second.
- The network in the new county courthouse was operating fully and supporting 700 clients.
- A research laboratory for testing new technologies was operating.
- Governance and security policies were published.
- An economic cost model was published to guide departments purchasing information technology through the cost justification process.
- A Web page and electronic mail services, via the Internet, were operational.
- Selective outsourcing contracts were signed for one-third of the budgeted services.
- The IS business process was created and published.
- A solution center was started and became a place for the fast turnaround of small problems.
- The IBM mainframe was replaced with new, air-cooled CMOS processors.
- Tape robotics was installed and all backup operations automated.
- An employee manual was created to help new employees adjust to the organization.

IS has been very successful to date. The magnitude of the County's transformation was featured in a July 8, 1996 *Computerworld*[1] article describing the human resource management approach used to train the information systems personnel. The changes were featured in *The Object Technology Casebook — Lessons from Award-Winning Business Applications*, (published by Wiley), included the County's Medical Examiner System, which featured its newest client/server information systems.

Conclusion

The transformation of the County's IS department was multi-year project that still has a long way to go. It required the reclassification of personnel and significant retraining. The significant organizational changes have remained in place. As in any organization, minor modifications have occurred due to changes in the

1. http://www.computerworld.com/

department's leadership. Once the transformation of the organization was complete, the director and deputy director changed the department's leadership to a new senior management team.

The new management team modified the organization structure and business processes as would be expected. Yet, the key transformation components are still intact. Samples of the tools used to build the new enterprise are located in appendixes B and C.

Appendix: IS job descriptions A 

We are often asked, "How should I write the job description for a client/server DBA" or "How will the job descriptions of my Network Administrators change as we implement client/server?" This appendix contains the new job descriptions from a county Information Systems department.

The transition to "open systems" and client/server architecture has a dramatic impact on the role, structure, and staffing of the information systems department. Transitioning to these new technologies is done to gain flexible and the new information systems organization must also be flexible to respond with alacrity.

The basic recommendation for a new operating structure is to move to a customer directed organization with customer satisfaction and solution economics responsibility exacted from a key group of individuals — IS Business Consultants. The IS Business Consultants manages all aspects of the customer relationship and acts as program managers for all projects affecting their clients. Supporting service areas provide the needed expertise to merge the customers' business goals with information technology. Below are some of the job descriptions for the new enterprise:

- CIO
- Deputy CIO
- Manager
- IS Business Consultant
- Senior Software Engineer
- Software Engineer III
- Software Engineer II
- Software Engineer I
- Senior Server Administrator
- Server Administrator
- Server Systems Programmer
- Senior Network Administrator

- Network Administrator
- Network Integration Engineer
- Senior Database Administrator
- Database Administrator
- Senior Technical Architect
- Coordinator
- Shift Supervisor
- Senior Computer Operator
- Computer Operator
- Software Training Specialist
- Customer Representative

Education and work experience scale

A degree in business with a concentration in Management Information Systems, computer science, or related field is recommended for these positions.

Application Development Manager

- Master's degree 5 years experience
- Bachelor's degree 6 years experience
- Associate's degree 8 years experience
- High school diploma 10 years experience

Senior Software Engineer

- Master's degree 3 years experience
- Bachelor's degree 4 years experience
- Associate's degree 6 years experience
- High school diploma 8 years experience

Software Engineer III

- Master's degree 2 years experience
- Bachelor's degree 3 years experience
- Associate's degree 5 years experience
- High school diploma 7 years experience

Software Engineer II

- Master's degree 1 years experience
- Bachelor's degree 2 years experience
- Associate's degree 4 years experience
- High school diploma 6 years experience

Software Engineer I

- Bachelor's degree 1 years experience
- Associate's degree 3 years experience
- High school diploma 5 years experience

Server Administration Services Manager

A degree in business with a concentration in Management Information Systems, computer science, engineering, statistics, or related field is recommended for this position.

- Master's degree 5 years experience
- Bachelor's degree 6 years experience
- Associate's degree 8 years experience
- High school diploma 10 years experience

Senior Server Administrator

A degree in computer science, engineering, statistics, or related field is recommended for this position.

- Master's degree 3 years experience
- Bachelor's degree 4 years experience
- Associate's degree 6 years experience
- High school diploma 8 years experience

Server Administrator

A degree in computer science, engineering, statistics, or related field is recommended for this position.

- Master's degree 1 years experience
- Bachelor's degree 2 years experience
- Associate's degree 4 years experience
- High school diploma 6 years experience

Server Programmer

A degree in computer science, engineering, statistics, or related field is recommended for this position.

- Bachelor's degree 1 years experience
- Associate's degree 3 years experience
- High school diploma 5 years experience

Database Administration Services Manager

A degree in Business with a concentration in Management Information Systems, computer science, engineering, statistics, or related field is recommended for this position.

- Master's degree 5 years experience
- Bachelor's degree 6 years experience
- Associate's degree 8 years experience
- High school diploma 10 years experience

Senior Database Administrator

A degree in computer science, engineering, statistics, or related field is recommended for this position.

- Master's degree 3 years experience
- Bachelor's degree 4 years experience
- Associate's degree 6 years experience
- High school diploma 8 years experience

Database Administrator

A degree in computer science, engineering, statistics, or related field is recommended for this position.

- Master's degree 1 years experience
- Bachelor's degree 2 years experience
- Associate's degree 4 years experience
- High school diploma 6 years experience

Enterprise Center Services Manager

A degree in business with a concentration in Management Information Systems, computer science, engineering, statistics, or related field is recommended for this position.

- Master's degree 6 years experience
- Bachelor's degree 5 years experience
- Associate's degree 7 years experience
- High school diploma 8 years experience

Shift Supervisor

A degree in computer science or related field is recommended for these positions.

- Bachelor's degree 2 years experience
- Associate's degree 3 years experience
- High school diploma 5 years experience

Senior Computer Operator

A degree in computer science or related field is recommended for this position.

- Bachelor's degree 1 years experience
- Associate's degree 2 years experience
- High school diploma 3 years experience

Computer Operator

A degree in computer science or related field is recommended for this position.

- Bachelor's degree 0 years experience
- Associate's degree 1 years experience
- High school diploma 2 years experience

Network Administration Services Manager

A degree in business with a concentration in Management Information Systems, computer science, engineering, statistics, or related field is recommended for this position.

- Master's degree 5 years experience
- Bachelor's degree 6 years experience
- Associate's degree 8 years experience
- High school diploma 10 years experience

Senior Network Administrator

A degree in computer science, engineering, statistics, or related field is recommended for this position.

- Master's degree 2 years experience
- Bachelor's degree 4 years experience
- Associate's degree 6 years experience
- High school diploma 8 years experience

Network Administrator

A degree in computer science, engineering, statistics, or related field is recommended for this position.

- Master's degree 1 years experience
- Bachelor's degree 2 years experience
- Associate's degree 4 years experience
- High school diploma 6 years experience

Network Integration Engineer

A degree in computer science, engineering, statistics, or related field is recommended for this position.

- Bachelor's degree 1 years experience
- Associate's degree 2 years experience
- High school diploma 3 years experience

Customer Services Manager

A degree in business with a concentration in Management Information Systems, computer science, engineering, statistics, or related field is recommended for this position.

- Master's degree 3 years experience
- Bachelor's degree 5 years experience
- Associate's degree 7 years experience
- High school diploma 9 years experience

Customer Services Coordinator

A degree in business with a concentration in Management Information Systems or related field is recommended for this position.

- Master's degree 2 years experience
- Bachelor's degree 3 years experience

- Associate's degree 5 years experience
- High school diploma 7 years experience

Software Training Specialist

A degree in business with a concentration in Management Information Systems or education with a concentration in Management Information Systems or related field is recommended for this position.

- Master's degree 2 years experience
- Bachelor's degree 3 years experience
- Associate's degree 5 years experience
- High school diploma 7 years experience

Customer Representative

A degree in business with a concentration in Management Information Systems, computer science, engineering, statistics, or related field is recommended for this position.

- Master's degree 0 years experience
- Bachelor's degree 1 years experience
- Associate's degree 2 years experience
- High school diploma 4 years experience

Consulting Services: IS Business Consultant

A degree in business with a concentration in Management Information Systems, computer science, or related field is recommended for this position.

- Master's degree 5 years experience
- Bachelor's degree 6 years experience
- Associate's degree 8 years experience
- High school diploma 10 years experience

Planning, Research, & Technology Review Services Manager

A degree in business with a concentration in Management Information Systems, computer science, or related field is recommended for this position.

- Master's degree 5 years experience
- Bachelor's degree 6 years experience
- Associate's degree 8 years experience

- High school diploma 10 years experience

Senior Technical Architect

A degree in business with a concentration in Management Information Systems, computer science, or related field is recommended for this position.

- Master's degree 2 years experience
- Bachelor's degree 4 years experience
- Associate's degree 6 years experience
- High school diploma 8 years experience

Administrative Services Manager

A degree in business with a concentration in Management Information Systems, computer science, or related field is recommended for this position.

- Master's degree 3 years experience
- Bachelor's degree 5 years experience
- Associate's degree 7 years experience
- High school diploma 9 years experience

Administrative Services Coordinator

A degree in business with a concentration in Management Information Systems, computer science, or related field is recommended for this position.

- Master's degree 2 years experience
- Bachelor's degree 4 years experience
- Associate's degree 6 years experience
- High school diploma 8 years experience

Chief Information Officer

Nature of work

This is highly responsible management and administrative work in planning and directing the activities of an Information Systems Services department.

Work involves responsibility for the administration and direction of a large network computer center, development acquisition and maintenance of application systems. Position incumbent is responsible to ensure cost-efficient and -effective information system services to all organizations within the organization and to provide strategic planning to promote operations. Assignments are received in the form of broad policy statements. Work is performed independently. Performance is reviewed periodically through conferences and written reports and results.

Examples of work

- Writes performance evaluations; issues counseling forms/disciplinary actions; handles employee complaints and grievances, recommends the hiring, firing, and promotion of staff.
- Directs and supervises the operation of a large networked computer center through subordinate managers, providing efficient and effective information systems services to the organization.
- Develops policies for the use of information technologies; reviews existing policies and modifies, updates and revises as necessary; attends meetings and conferences with customers to resolve a variety of management problems.
- Authorizes feasibility studies and economic analyses designed to improve effectiveness and efficiency of information systems services; reviews and approves results.
- Develops, presents and supports budget, estimates financial plans concerning acquisition of information technology or developmental costs based on customer direction.
- Plans for and assures the acquisition, installation and operation of information technologies and information systems.
- Performs related work as required.

Required knowledge, skills, and abilities

- Thorough knowledge of the principles of business administration.
- Thorough knowledge of current developments in the field of information technology and information systems.
- Thorough knowledge of applicable County, State and Federal laws, rules and regulations pertaining to departmental operations.
- Ability to plan, organize, and supervise through various levels of management in a manner conducive to full performance and high morale.
- Ability to establish and maintain effective working relationships with the general public, co-workers, senior management and members of diverse cultural and linguistic backgrounds regardless of race, religion, age, sex, handicap, or political affiliation.

Minimum entrance requirements

Bachelor's degree in business administration, computer science, industrial engineering or related field; ten (10) years of experience in a large and complex data processing organization, including five (5) years of experience in an administrative or managerial capacity; or any equivalent combination of training and experience.

Deputy CIO

Nature of work

This is highly responsible administrative and management work assisting the Information Systems Services CIO in the management of activities necessary to ensure the efficient and effective operation of the Information Systems Services department.

An employee in a position allocated to this class is responsible for managing the daily operations of the Information Systems Services Department. Responsibilities include administration of service areas on a day-to-day basis. Additional responsibilities would include monitoring departmental issues being considered by the organization and representing the ISS department in meetings should the CIO be unable to attend.

Work involves providing direction and guidance in formulating and executing administrative policies and practices designed to ensure cost efficient and effective data processing operations.

The primary function for the Deputy CIO, beyond the normal command and control functions, is to act as a team facilitator.

Work also includes acting for the CIO in absence or as delegated. The scope and complexity of duties requires the exercise of considerable independent judgment. Work is reviewed by the CIO through conferences, reports, and observation of results obtained.

Examples of work

- Assists the CIO in the general management of the Information Systems Services department; acts as chief assistant to and may act for CIO.
- Writes performance evaluations; issues counseling forms and disciplinary actions; handles employee complaints and grievances; recommends the hiring, firing, and promotion of staff.
- Manages the daily operation of a large-scale computer center through subordinate executives and supervisors, providing efficient and effective data processing and office automation services.
- Administers policies for the use of automation and telecommunications services. Based on changes to the environment, he assists in reviews of existing policies, and recommends modifications, updates, and revisions as necessary. Attends meetings and conferences with various officials and end users to resolve a variety of management problems.
- Conducts feasibility studies and economic analyses designed to improve effectiveness and efficiency of automation and telecommunications activities.
- Formulates, presents, and supports budget estimates and financial plans concerning acquisition of automation and telecommunication equipment and services along with any necessary software acquisitions or developmental costs based on direction from the CIO.
- Initiates and assures the acquisition, installation and operations of automated data processing equipment
- Performs related work as required.

Required knowledge, skills, and abilities

- Thorough knowledge of the principles of public and business administration.
- Thorough knowledge of the theories and principles of management and administration.

- Thorough knowledge of current developments in the field of automated data processing technology.
- Ability to plan, organize and supervise, through various levels of executives and supervisors, the work of subordinates in a manner conducive to full performance and high morale.
- Ability to communicate effectively, both verbally and in writing.
- Ability to identify, analyze, and solve problems and render advice and assistance in all areas.
- Ability to gather and analyze data and draw logical conclusions.
- Ability to establish and maintain effective working relationships.

Minimum entrance requirements

Graduation from an accredited college or university with major course work in computer science, business administration or related field; five (5) years of experience in a large and complex data processing organization, including three (3) years of experience in an administrative or managerial capacity; or any equivalent combination of training and experience.

IS manager

Nature of work

This is managerial and technical work directing the activities of a technical staff. Work is performed with considerable independent judgment, discretion, and initiative to ensure development coordination, productivity improvement, and quality control.

This position reports to the CIO or Deputy CIO and the work is evaluated based on quality of results obtained, conferences, feedback from customers, and reports.

Examples of work

- Writes performance evaluation, issues counseling forms, and disciplinary actions, handles employee complaints and grievances; recommends the hiring, termination, and promotion of staff.
- Maintains contact with customers and IS service representatives to ensure quality service and provides project monitoring and status information.
- Plans, organizes, and directs a technical staff.

- Coordinates systems maintenance for information technologies/systems under their responsibilities.
- Oversees the planning and design of new and revised information technologies/systems for the business units/divisions.
- Coordinates all development, acquisition, and support activities to ensure the integration of systems and sharing of data.
- Provides recommendations for establishing priorities for the implementation of information technologies/systems.
- Assists in development of RFIs, RFPs and criteria of evaluation of vendor proposals, products, and services.
- Provides recommendations, product support, training, and documentation for information technologies/systems.
- Monitors and ensures the quality and maintainability of all deployed technologies.
- Project management.
- Prepares statistical reports for decision making.
- Ability to express oneself clearly and concisely, both verbally and in writing.
- Budget preparation.
- Performs related work as required.

Addendum — Manager, software engineering services

Required knowledge, skills, and abilities

- Thorough knowledge of current technological trends in the information processing industry.
- Thorough understanding of Information Engineering Methodology and the ability to implement several information plans with differing scopes.
- Thorough knowledge of computer languages (including database management systems and fifth generation languages), applications, operating systems, terminology, communications, networks, and hardware capabilities.
- Knowledge of data modeling and database systems design.
- Thorough knowledge of planning, project management, budgeting, quality assurance, and systems analysis tools and techniques.

- Knowledge of systems integration issues between diverse platforms.
- Ability to plan and supervise the work of others.
- Ability to coordinate and prioritized customer requests with the assistance of other managers and supervisors to ensure an improved level of service to the customer.
- Ability to express oneself clearly and concisely verbally and in writing.

Minimum entrance requirements

Bachelor's degree in business with a concentration in management information systems, computer science, or closely related field; six (6) years experience in the development of information systems; or any equivalent combination of education and experience.

Manager, server administration services

Required knowledge, skills, and abilities

- Thorough knowledge of the design and capabilities of computer operating systems software across all server platforms.
- Thorough knowledge of the operating characteristics, capabilities and limitations of data processing equipment and operating systems.
- Considerable knowledge of research techniques required to gather information relevant to systems programming across all server platforms.
- Considerable knowledge of computer programming and logic.
- Considerable knowledge of file design and programming practices and languages.

Minimum entrance requirements

Bachelor's degree in business with a concentration in management information systems, computer science, or closely related field; six (6) years experience in server administration; or any equivalent combination of education and experience.

Addendum — Manager, database administration services

Examples of work, knowledge, skills, and abilities

- Manages the planning, analysis, and implementation of the security and data integrity controls for computerized data resources.
- Approves all file and data element implementation, ensuring proper integration and file integrity with data resources.
- Provides technical guidance and training in new and modified technology.
- Participates in the analysis and design function for new and existing systems to ensure proper use of data resources.
- Participate in the planning, acquisition, and implementation of software relative to the use, maintenance and support of IS data resources.
- Thorough knowledge of the techniques and methodologies of data management systems including relational, network and hierarchical systems.
- Thorough knowledge of computer capabilities and system development techniques.
- Thorough knowledge of data administration.
- Ability to analyze logical and physical database design for adherence to definition and design standards.

Minimum entrance requirements

Bachelor's degree in business with a concentration in management information systems, computer science, or closely related field; six (6) years experience in data base administration; or any equivalent combination of education and experience.

Addendum — Manager, network administration services

Examples of work, knowledge, skills, and abilities

- Manages the development of communications, networking, and systems standards and policies for connected computing environments.

- Manages the development and implementation of company-wide short- and long-range data communications and networking strategies and implementation plans.
- Manages the staff responsible for monitoring performance of the network environments, tuning performance parameters as necessary.
- Extensive knowledge of LAN, WAN and Data Communications systems analysis and design including knowledge of data communications protocols, access methods and architectures including but not limited to the current market.
- Thorough knowledge of all aspects of the system life cycle (i.e., planning, installation, documentation, training, and management).
- Thorough knowledge of advanced LAN analysis, including protocol/trace analysis, statistic analysis and performance analysis.
- Thorough knowledge of communications standards and limitations.
- Thorough knowledge of security management, access and authorization, data integrity, business recovery, operating environment requirements and physical security.
- Knowledge of licensing, building and fire codes, and legal considerations regarding electronic data communications and cabling.

Minimum entrance requirements

Bachelor's degree in business with a concentration in management information systems, computer science, or closely related field; six (6) years experience in network administration; or any equivalent combination of education and experience.

Addendum — Manager, planning and research services

Examples of work, knowledge, skills, and abilities

- Develops the plans and schedules of technical studies that affect the future direction of information technology.
- Manages the development of specifications, selection criteria, and evaluation parameters for technologies required to enhance the performance of the information systems.

- Manages the development of technical alternatives to compare advantages/disadvantages of different approaches to addressing customer requirements.
- Develops plans and schedules of tasks required for new technology implementation.
- Responsible for long-range planning.
- Manages and develops technical policies, coordinates and publishes technical standards for IS services.
- Coordinates technical and organizational pilot projects.
- Thorough knowledge of systems theory and the systems approach to problem resolution.
- Thorough knowledge of research methods and statistics.
- Thorough knowledge of information engineering and software engineer practices.
- Thorough knowledge of telecommunications.
- Thorough knowledge of database theory.
- Thorough knowledge of strategic and tactical planning.

Minimum entrance requirements

Bachelor's degree in business with a concentration in management information systems, computer science, or closely related field; six (6) years experience in the planning and research of information technologies for large organizations; or any equivalent combination of education and experience.

Addendum — Manager, enterprise center

Required knowledge, skills, and abilities

- Extensive knowledge of operating systems control language (i.e., MVS/XA or MVS/ESA JCL, Unix, etc.) and production automation software.
- Knowledge of the principles of an information systems organization and administration.
- Considerable knowledge of principles and practices of production automation processing.
- Knowledge of production systems analysis.
- Ability to plan, manage, and evaluate the work of others.

- Ability to communicate effectively both verbally and in writing.
- Ability to coordinate, plan, and schedule production software production and technical staff.
- Ability to establish and maintain effective working relationships at all levels.

Minimum entrance requirements

Bachelor's degree in business with concentration in management information systems, or closely related field; and five (5) years experience in enterprise center services; or any equivalent combination of education and experience.

Addendum — Manager, customer services

Required knowledge, skills, and abilities

- Thorough knowledge of planning, project management, budgeting, and business planning.
- Thorough knowledge of product presentation and salesmanship.
- Thorough knowledge of customer support management.
- Thorough knowledge of telephone support management.
- Knowledge of information server organizations.
- Knowledge of business administration.
- Knowledge of quality improvement processes.
- Ability to develop customer feedback processes to provide the organization with information for management decisions.

Minimum entrance requirements

Bachelor's degree in business with concentration in management information systems or closely related field; and five (5) years experience in customer services; or any equivalent combination of education and experience.

Addendum — Manager, administration services

Required knowledge, skills, and abilities

- Thorough knowledge of all the functions, components, and activities of a large-scale information processing operation.

- Thorough knowledge of the purpose and functions of each of the divisions in IS.
- Thorough knowledge and understanding of current and evolving trends in information processing.
- Considerable knowledge and understanding of data processing accounting procedures and cost recovery systems.
- Knowledge of research techniques, methods, and practices.
- Knowledge of and ability to use project management tools.
- Knowledge of cost accounting.
- Knowledge of fund accounting.
- Knowledge of human resource practices.

Minimum entrance requirements

Bachelor's degree in business with concentration in management information systems or closely related field; and five (5) years experience in customer services; or any equivalent combination of education and experience.

IS business consultant

Nature of work

This is advanced technical and administrative work assisting customers with the use of information technology as it relates to their business plans. An employee in this position is accountable for maintaining contact with assigned customers, assuring quality service, and providing overall project monitoring and status information.

An individual in this position is responsible for the collection of application requirements and the creation of conceptual designs. To perform these functions, the IS Business Consultant often leads facilitated sessions and drives a heterogeneous audience to a consensus solution. The IS Business Consultant is required to develop knowledge specific to the business needs of the customer. As project manager for implementing projects for information technology customers, the IS Business Consultant must supervise multiple projects simultaneously while bringing each of them in within budget and on time.

This position reports to the CIO and the work is evaluated based on quality of results obtained, conferences, feedback from customers, and reports.

Examples of work

- Maintains contact with customers and IS service representatives to ensure quality service and provides project monitoring and status information.
- Coordinates systems maintenance for information technologies/systems under their responsibilities.
- Oversees the planning and design of new and revised information technologies/systems.
- Coordinates all development, acquisition, and support activities to ensure the integration of systems and sharing of data.
- Provides recommendations for establishing priorities for the implementation of information technologies/systems.
- Assists in development of requests for proposal, requests for information, and criteria of evaluation of vendor proposals, products, and services.
- Provides recommendations, product support, training, and documentation for information technologies/systems.
- Monitors and ensures the quality and maintainability of all deployed technologies.
- Project management.
- Prepares statistical reports for decision making.
- SLA preparation and coordination as required.
- Performs related work as required.

Required knowledge, skills, and abilities

- Thorough knowledge of Information Strategic Planning and Business Area analysis and the related tools and techniques required to assess business needs and direction.
- Thorough knowledge of planning, project management, budgeting, business planning and systems analysis.
- Thorough knowledge of computer applications, operating system, terminology, communications networks, and hardware capabilities.
- Knowledge of the IS procedures for billing and budgeting for services.
- Knowledge of enterprise and system modeling.
- Knowledge of object-oriented analysis (OOA).
- Knowledge of project management tools and personal productivity PC tools (word processing, spreadsheets, graphics).

- Knowledge of benchmark techniques.
- Knowledge of planning for client/server, database server engines, front-end packages, middleware, and distributed DBMS.
- Knowledge of operating systems.
- Knowledge of GUI design.
- Knowledge of network design issues.
- Knowledge of process innovation and process improvement techniques.
- Ability to analyze requests and assembles functional and technical feasibility information.
- Ability to establish and maintain effective working relationships both in and outside of the organization.
- Ability to communicate effectively both verbally and in writing.
- Ability to successfully mange multiple projects concurrently.
- Ability to express oneself clearly and concisely, both verbally and in writing.

Minimum entrance requirements

Bachelor's degree in business with a concentration in management information systems and six (6) years experience in the development of information systems; or any equivalent combination of education and experience.

Senior software engineer

Nature of work

This is professional analysis and technical work involving the deployment or procurement of software systems. An employee in this position is responsible for the analysis, design, and implementation of application software information systems.

This position reports to a Manager of Software Engineering Services and the work is evaluated based on quality of results obtained, conferences, feedback from customers, and reports.

Examples of work

- Coordinate tasks and participates in the completion of designated projects to ensure that objectives are met in accordance with prescribed priorities, time limitations and funding conditions.

- Coordinates the implementation of packaged software applications for IS customers.
- Develops criteria for building or buying new information systems solutions.
- Provide technical guidance to team members, so their abilities and project quality is both enhanced.
- Keeps IS Business Consultants and management informed of project problems and progress.
- Conduct, facilitate and document Joint Application Development and Joint Requirements Planning sessions with our customers.
- Coordinates with vendors and consultants when necessary to achieve desired results.
- Train existing staff in leading edge technologies.
- Communicates clearly and concisely both verbally and in writing.
- Write technical reports and manuals.
- Establishes and maintains effective working relationships at all levels.
- Performs related work as required.
- Responsible for quality reviews and standards.

Required knowledge, skills, and abilities

- Thorough knowledge of full application development life cycles.
- Thorough knowledge of current development methodologies including 3-tier, 2-tier, and *n*-tier client server development.
- Thorough knowledge of relational database technology.
- Thorough knowledge of systems integration issues between heterogeneous platforms.
- Thorough knowledge in project planning including use of leading project management software.
- Ability to led JAD and RAD sessions.
- Knowledge of data and process modeling techniques.
- Ability to express oneself clearly and concisely both verbally and in writing.
- Ability to train others in various aspects of information technology.
- Thorough knowledge of data processing standards and procedures.
- Extensive knowledge of state-of-the-art information systems methodologies, techniques, and tools.

- Ability to review, analyze, and evaluate the work of project team members.
- Ability to establish and maintain effective working relationships with IS customers and staff.
- Knowledge of object-oriented analysis (OOA).
- Ability in personal productivity PC tools (word processing, spreadsheets, and graphics).
- Knowledge of benchmark techniques.
- Knowledge of planning for client/server.
- Knowledge of database server engines.
- Knowledge of middleware products.
- Knowledge of distributed DBMS.
- Knowledge of GUI design.
- Ability to perform process analysis.
- Ability to perform process redesign.
- Thorough knowledge of SQL.

Minimum entrance requirements

Bachelor's degree in business with a concentration in management information systems, or computer science; and four (4) years experience in the development of software information systems; or any equivalent combination of education and experience.

Software engineer III

Nature of work

This is highly skilled technical and analysis work involving the applications development function of IS. This position is responsible for participating through the planning, analysis, design, and implementation phases of system development and/or software procurement.

This position reports to a Manager of Software Engineering Services and work is evaluated based on quality of results obtained, conferences, feedback from customers, and reports.

Examples of work

- Lead analyst in developing business models to support decisions on building or buying new information systems solutions.
- Provide internal consulting services for individual projects.
- Conduct, facilitate, and document joint application development sessions to identify business processes and information needs.
- Perform system integration for various computer systems that reside on heterogeneous platforms.
- Develop systems using current IS methods and tools.
- Train customers on the use of new application software.
- Communicates clearly and concisely both verbally and in writing.
- Write technical reports and manuals.
- Establishes and maintains effective working relationships at all levels.
- Performs related work as required.

Required knowledge, skills, and abilities

- Thorough knowledge of information systems standards and procedures.
- Thorough knowledge of all phases of the systems development life cycle.
- Thorough knowledge of modern information systems methodologies, techniques and tools.
- Ability to express oneself clearly and concisely both verbally and in writing.
- Knowledge of current development methodologies including 3-tier, 2-tier, and n-tier client server development.
- Thorough knowledge of relational database technology.
- Knowledge of systems integration issues between heterogeneous platforms.
- Ability to participate in JAD and RAD sessions.
- Thorough knowledge of data and process modeling techniques.
- Thorough knowledge in application development tools for client/ server, open systems development.
- Ability to train others in various aspects of Information Services.
- Knowledge of object oriented analysis (OOA).
- Ability in personal productivity PC tools (word processing, spreadsheets, and graphics).

- Knowledge of database server engines.
- Knowledge of middleware products.
- Knowledge of distributed DBMS.
- Knowledge of GUI design.
- Ability to perform process analysis.
- Ability to perform process redesign.
- Knowledge of data modeling and logical database design.
- Thorough knowledge of SQL.

Minimum entrance requirements

Bachelor's degree in business with a concentration in management information systems, computer science, or closely related field; and three (3) years experience in the development of software information systems; or any equivalent combination of education and experience.

Software engineer II

Nature of work

This is technical and analysis work involving the applications development. This position is responsible for Participating as a team member through the planning, analysis, design, and implementation phases of system development and/or software procurement.

This position reports to a Manager of Software Engineering Services and the work is evaluated based on quality of results obtained, conferences, feedback from customers, and reports.

Examples of work

- Develop business models to support decisions on building or buying new information systems solutions.
- Supports the building and/or implementation of new information systems.
- Perform Business Systems Analysis, Business System Design, and/or Business System Implementation.
- Develop systems using current programming languages and database system.

- Documents joint application development and joint requirements planning sessions with our customers.
- Communicates clearly and concisely both verbally and in writing.
- Writes technical reports and manuals.
- Establishes and maintains effective working relationships at all levels.
- Performs related work as required.

Required knowledge, skills, and abilities

- Thorough knowledge of information systems standards and procedures.
- Knowledge of current 2-tier, 3-tier, and *n*-tier development methodologies and tools.
- Knowledge of data and process modeling techniques.
- Ability to review, analyze, and critique the work of others.
- Ability to train others in various aspects of Information Services.
- Knowledge of data processing standards and procedures.
- Knowledge of all phases of the systems development life cycle.
- Thorough knowledge of modern information systems methodologies, techniques and tools.
- Ability to express oneself clearly and concisely both verbally and in writing.
- Thorough knowledge of SQL.

Minimum entrance requirements

Bachelor's degree in business with a concentration in management information systems, computer science, or related field and three years experience or any relevant combination of education and experience.

Software engineer I

Nature of work

This is technical work involving the applications development function of IS. This position is responsible for Participating as a team member developing applications and/or supporting software packages.

This position reports to a Manager of Software Engineering Services and the work is evaluated based on quality of results obtained, conferences, feedback from customers, and reports.

Examples of work

- Design program logic to meet business specifications. Program using IS standard programming languages.
- Maintain existing programs; modify programs to enhance functionality.
- Document programs in accordance with department standards.
- Serve as scribe for joint application development sessions.
- Communicates clearly and concisely both verbally and in writing.
- Establishes and maintains effective working relationships at all levels.
- Performs related work as required.

Required knowledge, skills, and abilities

- Knowledge of information systems standards and procedures.
- Knowledge of current programming techniques.
- Knowledge of current information systems methodologies, techniques, and tools.
- Ability to express oneself clearly and concisely both verbally and in writing.
- Knowledge of current 2-tier, 3-tier development methodologies and tools.
- Knowledge of data and process modeling techniques.
- Ability to establish and maintain effective working relationships.
- Knowledge of application languages.
- Knowledge of SQL.
- Ability to develop software information systems using an RDBMS.
- Knowledge of current operating systems.

Minimum entrance requirements

Bachelor's degree in business with a concentration in management information systems, computer science, or closely related field; and one (1) year experience in the development of software information systems; or any equivalent combination of special education and experience.

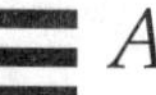

Senior server administrator

Nature of work

This is an advanced technical and analytical work with responsibilities for technical consulting, server design, planning, implementation, management, and operational support of servers.

An employee in this position has full access to the server operating system, program products, recovery, and system utilities. The employee is responsible for analyzing and recommending server system software configurations for any/all existing server platforms. Independent judgment is necessary to accomplish tasks and a high degree of coordination is maintained with other administrators, analysts, operations personnel, vendors, and customers.

This position reports to the Manager of Server Administration Services and is evaluated based on quality of results obtained, conferences, feedback from customers, and reports.

Examples of work

- Performs project coordination function for the evaluation, installation, monitoring, debugging, audits, and maintenance of server software on variety of hardware platforms.
- Plans, documents and communicates all changes to server software minimizing customer disruption.
- Assists IS Business Consultants in assessing the needs of the customer to determine the suitability of specific server hardware and software solutions.
- Confers with vendors, other IS personnel, and customers to determine suitability of server software.
- Writes user documentation as appropriate.
- Install, tests, and implements server operating system upgrades and enhancements.
- Prepares specification for server software and hardware systems that adherence to technical standards and ensures interoperability with other servers.
- Responds to emergency calls relating to server performance, diagnosis of problems, repairing problems or calling upon appropriate technicians.
- Diagnoses server and operational problems and develops effective solutions.
- Maintains data integrity and security of server software.

- Monitors server software products and tracks server performance.
- Evaluates placement of data or devices for the purpose of optimum server performance.
- Monitors server DASD and CPU utilization for effective capacity management.
- Performs related duties as required.
- Responsible for quality reviews and standards.

Required knowledge, skills, and abilities

- Thorough knowledge of the server operating characteristics, capabilities, and limitations of the appropriate system, including hardware and server operating systems.
- Thorough knowledge of the design and capabilities of server operating system software.
- Knowledge of the use of on-line systems used in central computer systems and system utilities.
- Knowledge of open systems network concepts.
- Ability to plan, document, install and effectively implement complex server software across all various computing platforms.
- Ability to diagnose server system/operational problems and develop effective solutions.
- Ability to monitor server performance in an existing environment as well as new environments.
- Ability to express oneself clearly and concisely both verbally and in writing.
- Ability to establish and maintain effective working relationships at all levels.

Minimum entrance requirements

Bachelor's degree in computer science, engineering, statistics, or closely related field; four (4) years experience in server administration or any equivalent combination of education and experience.

 A

Server administrator

Nature of work

This is technical and analytical work responsible for server systems support involving planning, installing, maintaining and troubleshooting multiple vendor operating systems software.

An employee in this class has work assignments on the server operating systems, program products, recovery, and system utilities. The employee is responsible for analyzing and recommending server operating system software configurations. Independent judgment is necessary to accomplish tasks and a high degree of coordination is maintained with other administrators, analysts, operations personnel, vendors, and customers.

This position reports to the Manager of Server Administration Services and work is evaluated based on quality of results obtained, conferences, feedback from customers, and reports.

Examples of work

- Evaluates, installs, monitors, debugging, audits, and maintains server operating software on a variety of hardware.
- Plans, documents, and communicates all changes to server software minimizing customer disruption.
- Confers with vendors, other IS personnel and customers to determine suitability of server products.
- Installs, tests, and implements operating system upgrades and enhancements.
- Prepares specifications for new software and hardware systems that adheres to technical standards and ensures interoperability with other servers.
- Responds to emergency calls relating to systems performance, diagnosis of problems, repairing problems or calling upon appropriate technicians.
- Diagnoses server and operational problems quickly and develops effective solutions.
- Maintain data integrity and security of server software.
- Monitors server software products and tracks server performance.
- Performs related duties as required.

Required knowledge, skills, and abilities

- Thorough knowledge of server operating characteristics, capabilities, and limitations of the appropriate system. Including hardware, server operating system, and application software across.
- Thorough knowledge of the server operating system software.
- Thorough knowledge of server programming and logic.
- Knowledge of the use of on-line systems used in the central computer system, system utilities.
- Knowledge of telecommunication network concepts.
- Ability to plan, document, install, and effectively implement complex server software.
- Ability to diagnose server system/operational problems quickly and develop effective solutions.
- Ability to monitor server performance in an existing environment as well as new environments.
- Ability to express oneself clearly and concisely both verbally and in writing.
- Ability to establish and maintain effective working relationships at all levels.

Minimum entrance requirements

Bachelor's degree in computer science, engineering, statistics, or closely related field; and two (2) years experience in server administration; or any equivalent combination of education and experience.

Server systems programmer

Nature of work

This is professional and technical work responsible for server systems programming involving installing, maintaining and troubleshooting multiple vendor operating systems software.

An employee in this class works on the server operating systems, program products, recovery, and system utilities. The employee is responsible for recommending server operating system software configurations. A high degree of coordination is maintained with operations personnel, vendors, and customers.

This position reports to the Manager of Server Administration Services and work is evaluated based on quality of results obtained, conferences, feedback from customers, and reports.

Examples of work

- Installs, monitors, debugs, audits, and maintains server operating software.
- Documents and communicates all changes to server software minimizing customer disruption.
- Writes user and operations documentation as needed.
- Installs, tests, and implements operating system upgrades and enhancements.
- Responds to emergency calls relating to systems performance, diagnosis of problems, repairing problems or calling upon appropriate technicians.
- Diagnoses server and operational problems quickly and develops effective solutions.
- Maintain data integrity and security of server software.
- Monitors server software products and tracks server performance.
- Performs related duties as required.

Required knowledge, skills, and abilities

- Thorough knowledge of the server operating characteristics, capabilities, and limitations of the appropriate system, including hardware, server operating system, and application software.
- Thorough knowledge of the server operating system software.
- Knowledge of the use of on-line systems used in the central computer system, system utilities.
- Knowledge of telecommunication network concepts.
- Ability to diagnose server system/operational problems quickly and develop effective solutions.
- Ability to monitor server performance in an existing environment as well as new environments.
- Ability to express oneself clearly and concisely both verbally and in writing.
- Ability to establish and maintain effective working relationships at all levels.

Minimum entrance requirements

Bachelor's degree in computer science, engineering, statistics, or closely related field; and one (1) year experience in server software support; or any equivalent combination of education and experience.

Senior database administrator

Nature of work

This is professional and technical work related to the administration of all computerized database management systems, data resources residing in those systems and the facilitation of data sharing among users. Work in this area involves the use of database software packages to ensure data integrity, consistency, and security, recovery, database space management, and database schema management.

Reports to the Manager of Database Administration Services. Work is evaluated on quality of results obtained, conferences, feedback from customers, and reports.

Examples of work

- Evaluates enterprise wide database infrastructure, develops detailed analysis reports and recommendations for database systems.
- Plans, designs and implements databases on a variety of platforms.
- Plans and implements database backup and recovery procedures.
- Analyzes and participates in the security and data integrity controls for all computerized database resources.
- Performs the analysis, definition, creation, and implementation of database technical standards.
- Participates in the analysis and design function for new and existing systems to ensure adherence to technical standards, data standards, and integration with other data resources.
- Participates in the planning, acquisition, and implementation of systems and application software.
- Participates in development and implementation of company-wide short- and long-range database strategies.
- Coordinates and provides technical direction, advanced technical support, and training to appropriate external and internal technical staff.
- Coordinates quality audits of database systems to ensure consistency throughout the enterprise.
- Provides budget preparation assistance regarding database systems.
- Establishes and maintains effective working relationships at all levels.
- Responsible for quality reviews and standards.
- Performs related work as required.

Required knowledge, skills, and abilities

- Thorough knowledge of the techniques and methodologies of data management systems, including relational, network and hierarchical systems.
- Extensive knowledge of computer capabilities, limitations, and system development techniques.
- Write efficient SQL statements through the correct use of the SQL language.
- Experience in distributed database concepts and implementation.
- Experience in data modeling, logical and physical database design and implementation.
- A working knowledge of middleware standards (i.e., DCE & DTP) and GUI application development tools (i.e., Java).
- Experience with database monitoring, tuning, and capacity management.
- Experience in the operation and use of database administration tools.
- Experience in database software installation and maintenance, database creation, startup and shutdown, backup and recovery procedures.
- A thorough understanding of database I/O and memory allocation and in implementing tuning methods.
- An understanding of locking, transaction, and concurrency controls within databases.
- An understanding of database security and auditing functions.
- A working knowledge of programmatic interfaces.
- A working knowledge of the operating systems that are used by the organization.
- A working knowledge of computer networking, such as the TCP/IP protocol.
- An understanding of client/server architectures and standards.
- Keeps professional skills updated and consistent with current database and information systems technology.
- Communicates clearly and concisely both verbally and in writing.

Minimum entrance requirements

Bachelor's degree in computer science, engineering, statistics, or closely related field; and four (4) years of experience in database administration; or any equivalent combination of education and experience.

Database administrator

Nature of work

This is technical work related to the analysis, design, and implementation of database information including logical and physical database modeling, definition, and maintenance. Work in this area involves the use of database software packages, CASE tools, and other data modeling software tools.

This position reports to the Manager of Database Administration Services and is evaluated based on quality of results, conferences, and customer feedback.

Examples of work

- Ensures sound physical data models supporting application requirements.
- Maintains efficiency, integrity, consistency, and security of database objects.
- Monitors database schema performance and storage management.
- Performs planning, design and implementation of data structures use by database applications.
- Plans and conduct interviews with Systems Analysts and other functional experts.
- Analyzes and Participates in the security and data integrity controls for all of the computerized database resources.
- Assists with technical training of application developers and other users of database management systems.
- Participates in the analysis and definition of technical standards relating to database resources.
- Participates in the analysis and design function for new and existing systems to ensure adherence to technical standards, data standards, and integration with other data resources.
- Participates in quality audits of database systems to ensure consistency throughout the enterprise.
- Keeps professional skills updated and consistent with current database and information systems technology.
- Communicates clearly and concisely both verbally and in writing.
- Writes technical reports and manuals.
- Establishes and maintains effective working relationships at all levels.
- Performs related work as required.

Required knowledge, skills, and abilities

- A thorough knowledge of data modeling techniques.
- Experience with monitoring and auditing procedures of databases.
- Extensive knowledge of computer capabilities, limitations, and system development techniques.
- Enforcement referential integrity using foreign keys and primary keys.
- Uses entity-relationship diagrams to design the physical database model.
- Experience in optimizing single- and multi-table queries through the correct use of indexes.
- Experience in the use of middleware standards (i.e., DCE, DTP, etc.)
- An ability to use database monitoring tools to tune performance of database schema's data.
- A through understanding of storage efficiency for database objects.
- Experience in performing quality assurance and tuning of database manipulation language (DML).
- Ability to use Systems Design Methodology tools, such as LBMS, to create an efficient physical database design from a logical design.
- Ability to write efficient SQL statements through the correct use of the SQL language.
- Experience in creating and maintaining a database data dictionary by creating and maintaining tables, views, indexes and sequences through the use of database definition language (DDL).
- Experience in using performance tools, such as EXPLAIN PLAN and the SQL trace facility.
- A working knowledge of the operating systems that the organization uses.
- An understanding of client/server architecture and standards.

Minimum entrance requirements

Bachelor's degree in computer science, engineering, statistics, or closely related field; and two (2) years of experience in database administration; or any equivalent combination of education and experience.

Senior network administrator

Nature of work

This is an advanced technical and analytical position responsible for technical consulting and systems design for implementation, management, and operational support of information network communication systems.

An employee in a position acts as a designer and analyst of simple and advanced complex information network systems.

Reports to the Manager of Network Administration Services. Work is evaluated on quality of results obtained, conferences, feedback from customers, and reports.

Examples of work

- Performs communication and networking systems analysis and design planning for integration of computer systems into a Local/Wide Area network based upon business analysis research.
- Evaluates customer requests or projects; analyzes requirements and pertinent technical information; then develops and implements quality, cost effective solutions.
- Installs, customizes and tests network communications and Desktop workstation systems.
- Evaluates enterprise networking components and infrastructure, develops detailed analysis reports and recommendations for network and data communications systems.
- Performs communication and networking systems quality analysis of integrated computer systems into a Local/Wide Area network(s).
- Analyzes and Participates in the development of security standardization and implementation of security controls for Local and Wide Area Networks.
- Participates in the development and enforcement of communications and networking systems, and desktop workstation standards and policies for connected computing environments.
- Participates in the development and implementation of company-wide short- and long-range data communications and enterprise networking strategies.
- Provides budget preparation assistance regarding data communications systems and desktop workstations.
- Keeps professional skills updated and consistent with current information systems networking technology.

- Coordinates and provides technical direction, advanced technical support, and training to appropriate external and internal technical staff.
- Coordinate system changes with appropriate support staff, to ensure uninterrupted computer services to Company Departments and elected officials.
- Performs related duties as required.
- Responsible for quality reviews and standards.

Required knowledge, skills, and abilities

- Extensive knowledge of LAN, WAN, and data communication systems operation, analysis and design.
- Extensive knowledge of data communication protocols, access methods, and architectures.
- Thorough knowledge of advanced protocol/trace analysis, statistical analysis and performance analysis.
- Thorough knowledge of communication standards and limitations.
- Working knowledge of the operating systems that the organization uses.
- Considerable knowledge of the various types of computer hardware and peripheral equipment.
- Considerable knowledge of network data communications and computer system diagnostic aids and tools and the ability to isolate and resolve hardware and software problems.
- Knowledge of licensing, building and fire codes and legal considerations regarding electronic data communications and cabling.
- Knowledge of network security management, access and authentication, data integrity, business recovery, operating environment requirements and physical security.
- Ability to express oneself clearly and concisely both verbally and in writing.
- Ability to establish and maintain effective working relationships at all levels of the organization.
- Working knowledge of problem analysis, troubleshooting, and repair skills.

Minimum entrance requirements

Bachelor's degree in computer science, engineering, statistics, or closely related field; and four-years experience in the support of networks and network connected device; or any equivalent combination of education and experience.

Network administrator

Nature of work

This is advanced technical work involving the design, implementation, management, and operational support of information network communication systems.

An employee in a position in this class is responsible for planning, implementing and coordinating the installation, enhancement or operational support of simple and advanced complex information network systems and desktop workstations.

This position reports to the Manager of Network Administration Services and the work is evaluated based on quality of results obtained, conferences, feedback from customers, and reports.

Examples of work

- Evaluates customer requests or projects tasks; analyzes requirements and pertinent technical information; then develops and implements quality, cost effective solutions.
- Installs, customizes and tests network communications and desktop workstation systems.
- Monitors current network and computer system configurations and performance; creates technical reports, recommendations and solutions to meet short and long range goals.
- Provides operational and technical support of advanced information network hardware and software.
- Maintains inventory control system and network connection inventory to ensure proper asset management.
- Coordinate system changes with appropriate support staff, to ensure uninterrupted computer services to Company Departments and elected officials.
- Analyzes and Participates in the development of security standardization and implementation of security controls for Local and Wide Area Networks.
- Participates in the development and enforcement of networking systems and desktop workstation standards and policies for connected computing environments.
- Reviews problem reporting and customer request systems and updates status or resolution text with current information.

- Keeps professional skills updated and consistent with current information systems networking technology and desktop workstations.
- Provides problem determination, repairs or upgrades to desktop workstations and peripherals at customer sites or in the IS lab facility.
- Performs related duties as required.

Required knowledge, skills, and abilities

Extensive knowledge of LAN, WAN, and data communication operations, analysis, and design.

Thorough knowledge of data communication protocols, accesses methods and architectures.

- Thorough knowledge of advanced protocol/trace analysis, statistical analysis and performance analysis.
- Considerable knowledge of the various types of computer hardware and peripheral equipment.
- Considerable knowledge of network data communications and computer system diagnostic aids and tools and the ability to isolate and resolve hardware and software problems.
- Working knowledge of the operating systems that the organization uses.
- Knowledge of communication standards and limitations.
- Knowledge of network security management, access and authentication, data integrity, business recovery, operating environment requirements and physical security.
- Ability to express oneself clearly and concisely both verbally and in writing.
- Ability to establish and maintain effective working relationships at all levels of the organizational structure.
- Working knowledge of problem analysis, troubleshooting, and repair skills.

Minimum entrance requirements

Bachelor's degree in computer science, engineering, statistics, or a closely related field; and two-years experience in the support of networks and network-connected devices; or any equivalent combination of education and experience.

Special requirement

Ability to lift 40 lbs. and must possess a valid driver's license.

Network integration specialist

Nature of work

This is a technical position that provides field servicing of network data communications and desktop workstation systems.

An employee in this position is responsible for installation, operational (troubleshooting and repair) support of simple and complex information communications and cabling equipment.

Reports to the Manager of Network Administration Services. Work is evaluated on quality of results obtained, conferences, feedback from customers, and reports.

Examples of work

- Evaluates customer requests or projects tasks; analyzes requirements and pertinent technical information; then develops and implements quality, cost effective solutions.
- Installs, customizes and tests network communications and Desktop workstation systems.
- Monitors current network and computer system configurations and performance; creates technical reports, recommendations and solutions to meet short and long range goals.
- Provides operational and technical support of information network hardware and software.
- Maintains inventory control system and network connection inventory to ensure proper asset management.
- Coordinate system changes with appropriate support staff, to ensure uninterrupted computer services to Departments and elected officials.
- Participates in the development and enforcement of communications and networking systems, and desktop workstation standards and policies for connected computing environments.
- Keeps professional skills updated and consistent with current information systems networking technology and desktop workstations.
- Provides problem determination, repairs or upgrades to Desktop workstations and peripherals at customer sites or in the IS lab facility.
- Uses hardware and software tools to isolate, troubleshoot, and repair data communications and computer system problems.
- Performs related work as required.

Required knowledge, skills, and abilities

- Considerable knowledge of network data communications hardware and cabling topologies.
- Considerable knowledge of computer hardware and peripheral devices.
- Knowledge of network data communications and personal computer diagnostic aids and tools.
- Knowledge of personal computer based operating systems and applications software.
- Ability to gather information from technical reference manuals, hardware specifications and troubleshooting guides to formulate computer solutions.
- Ability to understand and carry out complicated written and oral instructions.
- Ability to express oneself clearly and concisely both verbally and in writing.
- Ability to work independently.
- Ability to establish and maintain effective working relationships at all levels.

Minimum entrance requirements

Bachelor's degree in computer science, engineering, statistics, or closely related field; and one (1) year experience in the support of networks and network connected devices; or any equivalent combination of education and experience.

Special requirement

Ability to lift 40 lbs. and must possess a valid driver's license.

Senior technical architect

Nature of work

This is responsible administrative work coordinating special projects and research of new technologies. An employee in this position is responsible for assisting management in a variety of matters necessary for effective and efficient operations of the Information Systems Services department. The wide scope of assignments requires independent judgment and the exercise of a high degree of responsibility. The employee in this class must be able to supervise the work of several concurrent projects.

This position reports to the Manager of Planning, Research, and Technology Review and work is evaluated based on the quality of results obtained, conferences, feedback from customers, and reports.

Examples of work

- Coordinates the completion of designated projects to ensure that objectives are met in accordance with prescribed priorities, time limitations, and funding conditions.
- Monitors projects in order to inform the management team of the status of projects.
- Analyzes and develops financial alternatives to assist the management team in major financial decisions.
- Initiates and carries through to completion programs and projects.
- Contributes to strategic and tactical plans.
- Coordinates and develops plans and schedules for new technology implementation, including acquisition and training issues.
- Researches technologies that can be used to enhance Company and Constitutional Offices' business activities.
- Performs related work as required.
- Coordinates quality standards and organizational policies and procedures.

Required knowledge, skills, and abilities

- Thorough knowledge of the theories, principles, and practices of information technology.
- Thorough knowledge of the systems approach to problem resolution.
- Thorough knowledge of research methodologies.
- Thorough knowledge of the theories and principles of management and administration.
- Thorough knowledge of the organizational structures, functions, operations, objectives, and goals of information technology.
- Knowledge of quantitative and qualitative evaluation techniques.
- Knowledge of descriptive and inference statistics.
- Ability to identify, analyze, and solve administrative problems and render advice and assistance in these areas.
- Ability to gather and analyze data and draw logical conclusions.

- Ability to express oneself clearly and concisely both in writing and verbally.
- Ability to establish and maintain effective working relationships at all levels.

Minimum entrance requirements

Bachelor's degree in business with concentration in management information systems, computer science, or closely related field; and four (4) years experience in information technology infrastructure development; or any equivalent combination of education and experience.

Coordinator

Nature of work

Professional administrative work involving the coordination of activities that support the internal workings of the Information Systems Services department.

An employee in this position is responsible for coordinating activities that may relate to assets, system access, help desk, business recovery, facilities management, training, account registration, etc. These are supporting activities that enable the IS department to function on a daily basis.

This position reports to a member of the management team and work is evaluated based on quality of results obtained, conferences, feedback from customers, and reports.

Examples of work

- Coordinates activities that may relate to training, assets, facilities management, purchasing of software and professional services (including but not limited to requests for proposal, requests for information, and the competitive bid process), and other internal information technology support functions.
- Coordinates with information technology staff to ensure necessary technical information is provided to avoid delays.
- Negotiates the terms and conditions, reviews and monitors all contracts for information technology.
- May analyze expenditures to determine appropriate accounts for posting and ensures adherence to budget, making appropriate adjustments as required.
- Assists with the preparation, maintenance, and reporting of the departmental records related to audits and budgets.

- Researches and advises staff of cost-effective alternatives for the acquisitions of equipment, software and services.
- Performs related duties as required.

Required knowledge, skills, and abilities

- Considerable knowledge of applicable contracts, laws and ordinances as they pertain to information processing equipment, software, and services.
- Considerable knowledge of accounting, purchasing, and financial practices, including laws pertaining to contracts and contract compliance.
- Knowledge of the business of running a large complex information systems services department.
- Knowledge of the functions, organization and administration of governmental organizations.
- Knowledge and experience with automated accounting systems.
- Ability to formulate and analyze financial information, prepares detailed reports, and present material to the management team with appropriate recommendations.
- Ability to analyze and apply contract requirements as they relate to acquisition of data processing goods and services.
- Ability to communicate effectively both verbally and in writing.
- Ability to establish and maintain effective working relationships with company officials, department/division heads, outside agencies and public.

Minimum entrance requirements

Bachelor's degree in business with a concentration in management information systems or closely related field; and three (3) years experience in infrastructure support; or any equivalent combination of experience and education.

Addendum — Coordinator, Physical Assets

Nature of work

This is professional administrative work involving the coordination of activities that support the internal workings of the Information Systems Services department.

Responsible for coordinating activities that relate to physical assets.

Reports to the manager of Customer Services. Work is evaluated on quality of results obtained, conferences, feedback from customers, and reports.

Examples of work

- Coordinates activities that relate to physical assets.
- Coordinates with IS staff to ensure necessary technical information is provided to avoid delays.
- Assists with the preparation, maintenance, and reporting of the departmental records related to audits and budgets.
- Researches and advises staff of cost-effective alternatives for the acquisitions of equipment, software and services.
- Performs related duties as required.

Required knowledge, skills, and abilities

- Considerable knowledge of applicable contracts, laws and ordinances as they pertain to information processing equipment, software, and services.
- Considerable knowledge of accounting, purchasing, and financial practices, including laws pertaining to contracts and contract compliance.
- Knowledge of the business of running a large complex information systems services department.
- Knowledge of the functions, organization and administration of governmental organizations.
- Knowledge and experience with automated accounting systems.
- Ability to formulate and analyze financial information, prepares detailed reports, and present material to the management team with appropriate recommendations.
- Ability to analyze and apply contract requirements as they relate to acquisition of data processing goods and services.
- Ability to communicate effectively both verbally and in writing.
- Ability to establish and maintain effective working relationships with department/division heads, outside agencies and general public.

Minimum entrance requirements

Bachelor's degree in business with a concentration in management information systems or closely related field; and three (3) years experience in infrastructure support; or any equivalent combination of experience and education.

Shift supervisor

Nature of work

This is technical supervisory work involving the direct supervision of the operations of computer equipment.

An employee in this class is responsible for coordinating all the activities of the assigned team on a specific shift. Work in this area involves analysis of production systems that result in efficient cost effective improvement.

This position reports to the Manager of Enterprise Center Services and the work is evaluated based on quality of results obtained, conferences, feedback from customers, and reports.

Examples of work

- Monitors production schedules and plans an optimum and accurate course of action for team processing.
- Monitors system applications and malfunctions and initiates corrective action to maintain schedules and to ensure the integrity of production files and output.
- Coordinates work related activities of subordinates.
- Trains new personnel.
- Plans and coordinates with customers, programmer analysts, and server administrator to ensure that all production schedules are met.
- Oversees and maintains a high level of quality service and participates in the monitoring and status reporting.
- Participates in data and physical integrity controls for the Data Center.
- Participates in the planning, acquisition, and implementation of applications, monitoring tools and physical equipment.
- Oversees system availability verification procedures to ensure service level requirements.
- Participates in performance evaluation for employees on their shift.
- Participates in budget preparation.
- Meets with other team supervisors to assure proper continuation and completion of work in progress.
- Assists in the evaluation and implementation of new software productivity tools.

- Analyses all assigned problem reports and makes modifications to the environment to improve productivity.
- Plans physical environment for all information systems hardware and supporting equipment.
- Monitors and executes changes to the production system though Change Management when appropriate.
- Performs related duties as required.
- Responsible for quality reviews and standards.

Required knowledge, skills, and abilities

- Ability to plan and supervisor the work of others.
- Ability to understand and carry out complex oral and written instruction.
- Considerable knowledge of operating systems.
- Knowledge of principles and practices of automated data processing concepts.
- Considerable knowledge of teleprocessing networks such as SNA and TCP/IP.
- Knowledge of editing tools such as ISPF or Visual Editor. Considerable knowledge of principles and practices of production automation processing.
- Ability to diagnose a networking failure that results in unavailable service to the customer and ability to take appropriate steps to correct them.

Minimum entrance requirements

Bachelor's degree in computer science or closely related field; and two-years experience in enterprise center services, or any equivalent combination of education or experience.

Senior computer operator

Nature of work

This is skilled and advanced technical work which involves maintaining and monitoring production schedules, networks, applications and systems.

An employee in this class identifies system malfunctions and ensures the integrity of all production files and output. Work in this area involves analysis of production systems, problem determination, and resolution. Duties include administration and use of system monitoring software tools.

This position reports to the Manager of Enterprise Center Services and the work is evaluated based on quality of results obtained, conferences, feedback from customers, and reports.

Examples of work

- Interprets system software, hardware of application malfunctions that relate to customer's performance, actively diagnoses the problem, and takes the necessary effective action.
- Monitors and follows production schedules and plans an optimum and accurate course of action to ensure that all deadlines are met.
- Monitors batch streams or procedures for possible problems and makes corrective recommendations.
- Performs and oversees systems shutdown and startup which executes a complex set of instructions that starts up the system, network and customer data files.
- Assists in keeping problem reports up to date.
- Operates a variety of information processing tools and equipment.
- Performs system availability verification procedures to ensure service level requirements.
- Keeps professional skills updated and consistent with information systems technology.
- Communicates clearly and concisely both verbally and in writing.
- Writes operating procedures.
- Participates in the implementation of new applications and sub-systems for the production environment.
- Administrates production automation tools.
- Performs related duties as required.

Required knowledge, skills, and abilities

- Considerable knowledge of operating systems.
- Knowledge of principles and practices of automated data processing concepts.
- Considerable knowledge of teleprocessing networks.
- Knowledge of editing tools.

- Considerable knowledge of principles and practices of production automation processing.
- Considerable knowledge of production systems analysis.
- Knowledge of operating software to guide and direct computer operators in the event of abnormalities not covered in the computer operations standard operating procedures.
- Ability to perform complex system shutdown and startup as per procedure.
- Ability to diagnose a networking failure that results in unavailable service to the customer and ability to take appropriate steps to correct them.
- Ability to understand and convey complex oral and written instructions.
- Ability to communicate effectively both verbally and in writing.
- Ability to coordinate, plan, and schedule production software products and technical staff.

Minimum entrance requirements

Bachelor's degree in computer science or closely related field; and one (1) year experience in computer operations; or any equivalent combination of education and experience.

Computer operator

Nature of work

This is technical work involving monitoring of production network, applications, and systems. An employee in this class maintains the highest level of system efficiency by ensuring that all production requirements are met. Performs administrative support for vendor software. Monitors quality and accuracy of all output material that has been generate by the IS/Data Center Services department. Maintains tape library, enforces tape security regulations and control of tapes stored in vaults and remote locations. Maintains all system documentation of current production systems and prepares and maintains production schedules

This position reports to the Manager of Enterprise Center Services and the work is evaluated based on quality of results obtained, conferences, feedback from customers, and reports.

Examples of work

- Responsible for preparing, scheduling and monitoring production program jobs to be processed on system.
- Day-to-day systems management, administration, and monitoring.
- Ensures that the quality and accuracy of all data leaving the department meets the highest standards. Reviews jobs/procedures for successful completion.
- Provides special production assistance to all IS staff and customers.
- Maintains control of the tape data set cartridges stored in local and remote off-site vaults.
- Maintains the production load library and emergency load libraries on the computer system.
- Updates and maintain the production libraries.
- Coordinate and monitor production workflow of programs.
- Performs various tasks associated with migrating test applications to the production environment.
- Generates all the necessary production documentation for every production procedure.
- Operates a variety of information processing tools and equipment.
- Performs system availability verification procedures to ensure service level requirements.
- Performs related task as required.

Required knowledge, skills, and abilities

- Knowledge of operating systems.
- Knowledge of principles and practices of automated data processing concepts.
- Knowledge of teleprocessing networks.
- Knowledge of operating system commands.
- Knowledge of editing tools such as ISPF or Visual Editor.
- Knowledge of file utilities, directories, and catalogs.
- Ability to understand and carry out complex oral and written instructions.
- Ability to deal courteously with all IS customers.

- Ability to clearly document status reports, problem reports, change management reports and other technical reports.
- Knowledge of system monitoring and administration tools used in an open/systems client/server environment.

Minimum entrance requirements

Associate's degree in computer science or closely related field; and one (1) year experience in computer operations; or any equivalent combination of education and experience.

Software training specialist

Nature of work

This is professional work planning and delivering software-training programs. An individual in a position in this class is responsible for meeting training needs through individual and group instruction for standard Office Automation software, as well as programs and/or systems developed by internal staff. Preparation of course outline, training schedules, training aids and course handouts development are required to support the function.

Work is performed under the direction of the Manager of Customer Services and is reviewed through conferences, reports, and customer feedback.

Examples of work

- Develops course outlines, visual aids, and end user handouts for training classes offered.
- Participates in the evaluation and determination of standard Office Automation software products.
- Receives and processes training requests.
- Schedules training classes to ensure adequate levels of response to customer requests.
- Evaluates effectiveness of courses and makes changes as needed.
- Learns new and/or revised software applications to provide training as required.
- Develops useful documentation to support instruction given.
- Researches new products to assess and recommend adequate support levels.

- Receives training in developed applications to allow support in the customer environment.
- Maintains student history of classes attended.
- Performs related duties as required.

Required knowledge, skills, and abilities

- Thorough knowledge of adult education theory and effective methods and techniques of skills training.
- Considerable knowledge of computer systems technology, including networking and interfacing capabilities.
- Considerable knowledge of standard Office Automation software packages.
- Ability to use audio/visual equipment and interactive training aids.
- Ability to create and use job aids to supplement training.
- Ability to critique the effectiveness of training methods, and materials and to monitor progress of training participants.
- Ability to tailor and present individualized and group instruction to non-technical staff.
- Ability to learn unfamiliar and updated versions of applications software uses manufacturer or developer documentation.
- Ability to communicate effectively both verbally and in writing.
- Ability to establish and maintain effective working relationships at all levels.
- Bachelor's degree in Computer Science, Human Resources Development, Adult Education or closely related field and three years of experience conducting training classes in standard Office Automation software products and providing end user documentation; or any equivalent combination of related training and experience.

Customer representative

Nature of work

This is technical work providing a central point of contact for customer help, problem status, and feedback to customers. An employee in this position is the focal point for reporting and minor system problem resolutions including monitoring of data communications, on-line applications, and large complex network systems on a variety of hardware platforms.

This position reports to the Manager of Customer Services and the work is evaluated based on quality of results obtained, conferences, feedback from customers, and reports.

Examples of work

- Answers Solution Center telephones and uses first-level problem determination techniques to analyze and solve problems
- Operates a variety of data processing equipment including computer consoles, personal computers, modems, controllers, and office equipment.
- Interfaces with internal staff, external service providers, and customers to facilitate timely resolution of all reported problems.
- Performs system availability verification procedures to ensure service level requirements.
- Initiates recovery procedures for terminals, printers, modems, controllers, and all telecommunications devices.
- Maintains contact with all customers until a problem has been resolved informing them of current status.
- Provides recommendations to Problem and Change regarding any configuration, problem, or change concern.
- Provides electronic mail support.
- Performs related duties as required.

Required knowledge, skills, and abilities

- Knowledge of customer relationships.
- Knowledge of help desk software.
- Knowledge of client/server technologies.
- Knowledge of LAN technologies.
- Knowledge of WAN technologies.
- Knowledge of desktop operating systems.
- Knowledge of network management systems.
- Knowledge of large mainframe systems using production operating systems.
- Knowledge of data communications software.
- Knowledge of information management problems, change and configuration management software.
- Knowledge of word processing software.

- Ability to administer electronic mail system.
- Ability to maintain effective working relationships at all levels.
- Ability to apply technical knowledge in a logical progression to diagnose customer problems.
- Ability to communicate effectively with strong emphasis on telephone skills.
- Ability to troubleshoot problems through the use of computer diagnostic tools.

Minimum entrance requirements

Bachelor's degree computer science or closely related field; and one (1) year experience in an information systems services environment; or any equivalent combination of education and experience.

Appendix: IS business processes

B 

The Information Systems (IS) department described in the case example developed the following business process. The merger of the mainframe and personal computer departments required a new way of addressing customer needs and of processing work internally. Senior management sponsored the project and selected an external consultant to record and draft the business process. Once the document was in a draft form, a review team composed of staff from all segments of the department reviewed and modified the document until there was a consensus.

The next step was to distribute the document to the staff for review and comment. Many suggestions were received and the review team evaluated each suggestion and submitted a final document to management.

Each manager gave a formal presentation to the members of their service area (e.g., Server Administration Services). Once this step was complete, the document was officially adopted.

The focus of the document is to provide the IS staff with a navigational tool to aid them during the transformation process. Information systems used to capture data for the internal running of the IS department were than developed around this business process.

Aligning the IS business process with the supporting information systems allowed the right information to reach the right employee while the employee was addressing customer service requests.

Customer satisfaction and productivity increased as a result of the business process. Employees worked together to provide the highest level of service because they understood how the work product of their fellow workers became the final product or service.

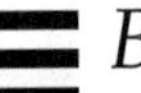 *B*

County government information systems services department business process

Introduction and overview

The following is an excerpt from the organization's transformation planning document.

> **IS Business Consultant** — These individuals will be responsible for the collection of application requirements and creation of conceptual designs. To perform these functions, the IS Business Consultant should be able to lead facilitated sessions and drive a heterogeneous audience to a consensus solution. The IS Business Consultant should have domain knowledge of the agency in which the application resides. His/her level of expertise should be such that the business leaders in their customer agencies look to them for practical assistance in the area of business process design and other forms of planning. As the team leader for implementation projects involving his/her customers, the IS Business Consultant must be fully proficient in supervising multiple projects simultaneously while bringing each of them in under budget and on time. As ultimate quality assurance officer for his/her customers, the IS Business Consultant must know how to verify system requirements and integration upon project turnover.

ISS Business Process

Customer Information Officer

Solution Center

Consulting Services

ISS Service Areas

Trust

Respect

This document supports the spirit and intent of the IS Transformation Plan. It is produced to provide a benchmark in the development of an ongoing IS Business Process that will mature over the next twelve months. Material included within this document is subject to varied interpretation and modifications are anticipated.

Information systems services — leadership

Responsibility, Accountability, and Management are essential factors in the in the daily routine of Information Systems (IS) Department. Consulting Services (IS Business Consultants) and the associated Service Area Managers are primarily responsible for leading the IS organization through the established business process.

Duties and responsibilities are defined in the Transition Plan. The official Job descriptions for IS Business Consultants and Service Area Managers detail the variety of management and technical qualities inherent to the positions. This document presents a perspective of the IS Business Consultant and Service Area Managers as documented and implied in these source materials.

Trust and respect

Although not specifically addressed in the Transformation Plan, the greatest challenge to Information Systems is to establish a feeling of *Trust* and *Respect* for the client. These are the important items to the success of IS.

Without trust and respect, Information Systems will never achieve the level of partnership required to be effective. That feeling, or the lack of it, may be the product of numerous unfortunate experiences with segments of the former IS environment. Those qualities must be earned over time.

IS image

IS must do whatever is required to promote a positive image within the client population. Indeed, the smallest detail to the largest project must be performed on time, within budget, and without error. This includes a simple PC installation or handling a Solution Center call.

Project methodology concepts

As information technology organizations mature and become successful, a major contribution to that success is the development of specific project concepts. These concepts are woven into a project methodology. The components of a *project methodology* are:

- Business Principles

- Business Policies
- Proven Methods
- Documented Procedures
- Approved Practices
- Process Definitions

Traditional IS situations

The development of formal IS methodology is eventually required by most organizations when migrating to a mixed client/server, mainframe environment. Practices that were appropriate in the mainframe only network all of a sudden do not adequately manage the new development and management requirements. Problems leading to a re-engineering of the business practices and processes include:

- The development cycle is too long
- Projects are completed late, if ever
- Cost overruns are common
- Quality is poor
- Immediate system or application modifications are required to adequately use the product
- Maintenance is a problem because of poor documentation and/or unstructured code

Project methodology concepts address these issues and promote a positive and professional relationship between the information technology organization and the customer.

Project methodology considerations

The function of information technology is to convert requirements into deliverables within given constraints on budget, time, resources, and quality. A project methodology helps to explain how the deliverables are obtained. Therefore, a project methodology considers and involves such items as:

- How projects are initiated
- Input constants and variables
- Output constants and variables
- Work required to convert input to output
- How that work is to be performed
- How the work will be planned

- How the work will be managed
- Customer expectations
- Quality measurements
- Customer satisfaction
- Resource requirements

Required project characteristics

Before defining the components, a brief definition of a project should be considered. Every project, large or small, system or application should consider the basic characteristics of an information technology project.
They are:

- Established beginning or start date
- Well-defined purpose and scope
- Formal, documented cost-value analysis
- Well defined product, including performance
- Defined completion or closure criteria
- Established end date or completion date

Aspects of a project methodology

Addressing the required characteristics of a project, a project methodology is presented that addresses each of these important project aspects. Specifically, the project methodology then must contain aspects addressing:

- Work items, divided into events, and tasks
- Procedure for producing the product
- Policies and procedures for:
    - Contracting
    - Project Planning
    - Data collection procedures
- Standard terminology
- Client expectation measurements
- Quality definitions
- Defined deliverables
- Acceptance criteria
- Completion criteria

- Definition of associated risk
- Change management procedures
- Standards for documentation
- Standards for project organization
- Clearly defined responsibilities

Consultants and Project Leaders may use this checklist to appraise the completeness and viability of project plans.

Problem resolution process

Throughout the development and implementation stages of any project, numerous unanticipated events or problems may occur. The basic technique for problem resolution is provided below. When applied, this technique will reduce the overall time required to identify and solve these problems.

1. Identify and document the problem
2. Select best solution through brainstorming
3. Implement solution — document results
4. Review problem; return to Step 1, if required

Problems associated with an IS project must be documented and available in the project file.

Organization — function responsibilities

IS, as an organization, has the responsibility of providing a clear and precise set of operational and environmental management and operational guidelines.

In turn, the functional areas are responsible for using the guidelines and resources available to provide quality products to the IS customer community.

Table 14-1 IS responsibilities

Organization	Functional Areas
Mission	Quality
Practices	Management
Procedures	Accountability
Standards	Auditability

High-level work plan

The diagram presented above is theoretical. It is important because it provides the framework for building a complete and manageable business driven environment. That environment is supported by a simple work process logic.

IS work process

- Planning performance
- Observing performance
- Measure plan to actual
- Adjust as required

Process improvements

IS has the obligation to continually improve the working business process model. Each employee should look for efficiencies in areas such as:

- Product quality
- Effective resource allocation
- Cost-effective development
- Process standards development
- Positive customer relationship

Project methodology standards

Each information technology project is unique. No methodology can consider all possible aspects of any significant project. An attempt, then, is made to develop standards that will accommodate the majority of conditions under controlled situations. A minimum listing of information technology standards is provided below. Using this listing as a guide, IS must develop and use these standards in the performance of every project.

- Project Management
- Change Management
- Planning Standards
- Estimating Standards/Models
- Form Design Standards/Models
- Acceptance Standards
- Documentation Standards
- Security Standards

- Project Work Standards:
  - Analysis
  - Tracking
  - Reporting
  - Design
  - Coding
  - Testing
- Quality Assurance
- Business Assessment
- Cost Value Analysis (CVA)
- Service Quality Assessment (SQA)
- Technical Risk Analysis

Project management team

Table C-2 illustrates the responsibility distribution for standard IS projects.

Modifications to this model are anticipated as no two projects are exactly alike. Additional influences such as personnel availability, experience of the team members, and technology considerations may require modification to the presented model. However, under normal business conditions the model should be followed and will provide the appropriate organization, planning, management, and performance guidelines.

Table 14-2 IS responsibilities in more detail

Customer	
Select Projects	Contract Services
Appropriate Funding	Monitor Progress
Define Requirements	Evaluate Results
Consulting services	
Define Requirements	Monitor Progress
Generate Proposal	Report Status
Generate Project Plan	Manage Change
Service Area Managers	
Contribute to Proposal	Control Quality
Service Area Work Plan	Team Performance

Table 14-2 IS responsibilities in more detail

Customer	
Allocate Resources	Monitor Progress
Project Leaders	
Report Status	Assign Tasks
Monitor Progress	Team Meetings
Manage Change	Daily Contact

Note: The IS Business Consultant is responsible all project management activities. As such, the items listed for the Project Leader may indeed be performed by the IS Business Consultant.

Building an IS business process

In the previous sections of this chapter, six topics were presented. Alone, the sections simply introduce a variety of thoughts pertaining to the topic subject. Together, they form the foundation for the development of an ongoing business process.

These are the elements that will define and establish the business rules and practices that will guide IS to become a premier provider of information technology services.

- Components of a Project Methodology
  The basic building blocks of a methodology
- Project Methodology Considerations
  Turning requirements into products
- Aspects of a Project Methodology
  Areas that define project management and control
- Organizational and Functional Responsibilities
  High-level perspective of business management
- Project Methodology Standards
  Documented criteria for process management
- Project Management Team
  High-level responsibility distribution

Combining the elements from each component yields the IS business process.

IS business process

- Components of Project Methodology

- Project Methodology Considerations
- Aspects of Project Methodology
- Organization/Function Responsibilities
- Project Methodology Standards
- Project Management Team

Responsibilities — project management

This listing provides a summary of standard responsibilities associated with project management. These duties should be defined and assigned during the project concept stage. Items within the list should be distributed between the three major participants: IS business consultant, service area manager, and project leader.

Table 14-3 Summary of standard IS project management responsibilities

	Business consultant	Service manager	Project leader
Responsible and accountable for project development			
Accountable for project support activity			
Instruct team leaders in overall Project Plan execution			
Identify project activities			
Negotiate project activities with service area managers			
Set the direction for project and team leaders			
Identify software and hardware requirements			
Communication to client management of Project Plan			
Facilitate with client, activities involving client personnel			
Facilitate resolution of issues and problems			
Schedule with client, equipment & facilities requirements			
Consult with IS and client on procedures and methods			

Table 14-3 Summary of standard IS project management responsibilities

Responsible and accountable for project development	Business consultant	Service manager	Project leader
Establish standards for delivery of products and services			
Direct, track, and control project execution			
Recommend/develop training programs for client			
Collect actual performance data for analysis			
Analyze project execution trends			
Recommend process improvements			
Recommend future directions to optimize benefits			
Resolve customer complaints			
Lead meetings (progress reporting, team, client)			
Define Project Quality Plan			
Establish acceptance procedure with client			
Define test planning process			
Analyze trends in account and cross account metrics			
Conduct project quality evaluation			
Development of Master Plan			
Participation in development of Service Area Work Plans			
Development of Project Plan			
Performance of Risk Analysis			
Assign and review activities with team members			
Provide guidance to technical staff			
Conduct team meetings			
Recognize and resolve issues			
Communicate issues and problems			
Identify and report change activity			
Prepare project activity reports			

Table 14-3 Summary of standard IS project management responsibilities

	Business consultant	Service manager	Project leader
Responsible and accountable for project development			
Monitor applications programming/analysis procedures			
Coordinate activities following Work Plan			
Assist in user training procedures			
Coordinate client concerns and questions			
Respond to daily routine problems and issues			

IS environment

In IS, Service Area Managers and IS Business Consultants potentially influence large numbers of internal and external personnel and projects. Any given consultant or manager may be responsible for projects that cost $500,000 or more.

IS Business Consultants are responsible for the overall management of the client/IS relationship. That includes all projects, current and projected, and the successful completion of those projects.

Project leaders

Project management is the responsibility of the IS Business Consultant. As such, they are responsible for all project activity. It is possible that, under the appropriate conditions, an IS Business Consultant may require a Project Leader to assist in the project. The IS Business Consultant may even request various contributing Service Areas to supply an additional Project Leader for a specific project.

To assist in the daily management and control of these projects the IS Business Consultant may be assisted by a Project Leader, assigned by a Service Area Manager, to facilitate the development and "hands-on" support supervision of the account.

The Span of Control of the Project Leader is limited to the responsibilities determined appropriate for the account by the IS Business Consultant and the appropriate Service Area Manager. Therefore, the Project Leader may perform task related project items and other responsibilities as directed by the IS Business Consultant and the Service Area Manager.

The overall responsibility for the account remains with the IS Business Consultant. The overall management of the Project Leader remains with the Service Area Manager. All three work in concert to provide the highest level of service to the account.

Managing the business process

The business-driven, quality processes will allow IS to provide products and services that are *repeatable, predicable,* and *measurable.* This is only possible by forming a cohesive bond with the customer community. Together, by following established business rules and with full participation in the project management process this relationship will mature and thrive. Without that spirit of cooperation and joint venture, it will be difficult to address the numerous business opportunities in the future.

Table 14-4 Processes allow IS to provide services that are repeatable, predicable, and measurable

Process management	
Business rules	**Project management**

- Application Development
- Internet/Intranet
- Network Services
- Enterprise Center Services
- Customer Services
- Solution Center
- Data Base Administration
- End User Training
- Desktop Support
- Client/Server Development
- Server Administration

IS2000 perspective

Client Information Officer *ISS Consulting Services*

ACCOUNT MANAGEMENT

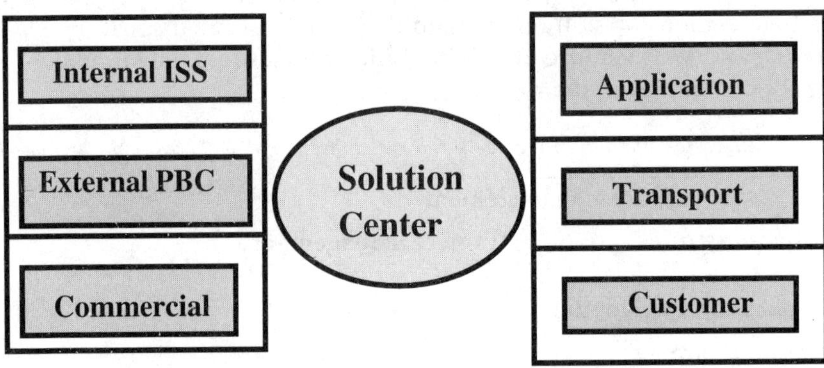

Communication Services
Training and Education Services
Bidirectional Point of Contact
User Access Management

The emphasis on account management will evolve along with the development of a 'Managed Services' deployment. Managed Services implies that IS will manage the performance of routine tasks and but not necessarily perform the task.

A reserve of skilled technical personnel may be called to perform routine services with IS responsible for marketing, contracting, and managing the opportunity. Ideal candidates for this policy are: Training, Solution Center, Desktop, and Transport.

Elements of process management

Considering the vast number of responsibilities and the variety of associated management and leadership qualities inherent with the IS Business Consultant, it would appear that this position is impossible to perform. In reality, the total spectrum of the IS Business Consultant's role is encompassed within three very distinct and specific categories. They are:

1. Concept
2. Execute
3. Closure

These categories span the entire IS business process. They directly align with the project management process and fully support the role of IS Business Consultant as a member of the IS Management Team. Other IS Business Consultant duties, (CSR Processing, Purchasing Processing, SLA Development, Monthly Reporting, and Customer Information Exchange Meetings, are performed in the interest of or on behalf of the client. That is managing the customer relationship, and client relationship is a major influence or factor in conceiving or establishing the business concepts.

On the following pages, a direct relationship between the IS Business Consultant and the IS business process and the IS Project Management process is established.

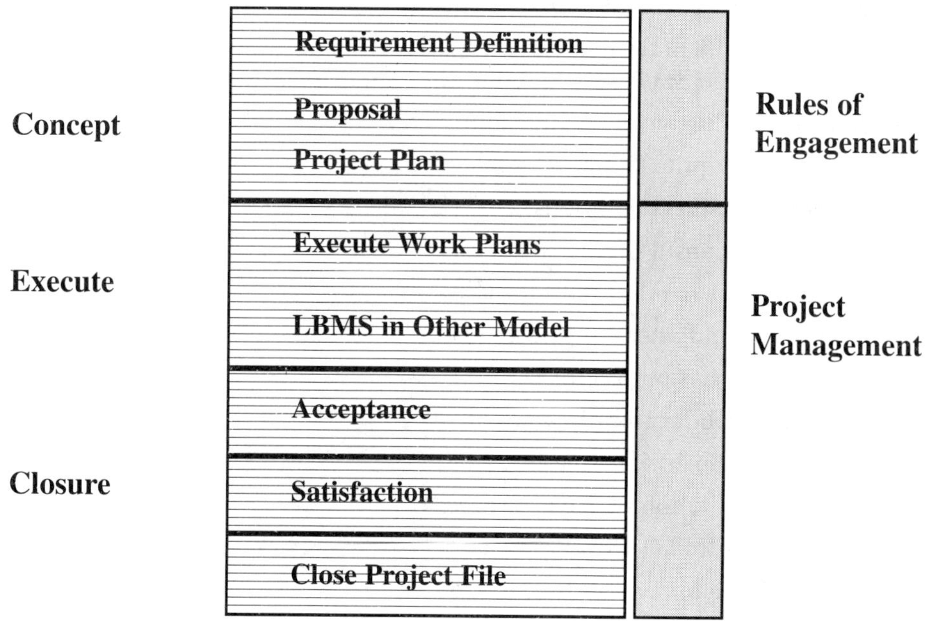

Process management perspective

Process Management provides the framework to develop a cohesive but flexible environment to produce quality products and services. Within that framework, the development of individualized work plans is anticipated and encouraged. Sources for these plans may be many. LBMS and other sources may require modification to conform to the Process Management model.

During the Execute Stage, Process Management requires a distinct phase review process. The IS Business Process model provides a standard work plan configuration for consideration. Terms and conditions agreed upon in the Project Plan are the Rules of Engagement. This document includes the models for:

- Technical Risk Analysis
- Service Quality Assessment
- Evaluation/Assessment Process
- Change Management
- Status Reports
- Information Economics Model

Each item is essential in establishing the IS Business Process.

Concept layer — process management

The concept layer includes the following areas of concentration and dedication. These areas are specifically addressed within the IS Transformation Plan.

- Consultant/Customer Relationship
- Understanding the Business Problems
- Providing Business Solutions
- Technology Consulting
- Forming a Partnership With the Customer
- Oversee Development of Master Plan
- Overall Supervision of Projects
- Training and Education Development
- Interface to IS Service Areas
- Oversee Generation of Project Proposal
- Assist in Work Plan Development
- Oversee Development of Project Plan
- Budget and Financial Consulting

 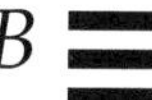

In general, the concept layer includes those activities and functions that relate to the ongoing IS/customer relationship. The development of a vibrant cohesive bond between the consultant and the customer requires trust and respect from both parties and must be nurtured and earned.

Analysis of customer business processes and work products is essential. Opportunities for process enhancement and/or methodologies that are more efficient may surface.

IS Business Consultant — Information Officer

The IS Business Consultant will work with the Client Information Services Officer to develop strategies that will enhance performance and reduce long term expenditures through business solution practices. Although an Information Officer has not been assigned for every agency, the current client contact should be considered the Information Services Officer.

Business solutions, mutually developed and agreed upon by the consultant and the Information Services Officer are expressed in the form of a Master Plan.

Master plan development (requirements)

The Master Plan contains a high level or *conceptual* description of the specific business problem areas or conditions or desired production scenarios. This may be referenced as a requirements specification, wish list, or an expectation document. In any event, it represents the high level perspective of the client's requirements.

The business solution is presented to include known or possible development alternatives and the anticipated requirement for an IS service area or cross-service area participation. The Information Economics Model should be used on projects costing $10,000 or more. Anticipated schedules and known contingencies are documented. Budget considerations and other constraints are included within the Master Plan. Upon approval, both the Information Services Officer and the IS Business Consultant sign and date the official Master Plan document.

The master plan is a mutually developed solution that addresses the client's business requirements. The client or Consulting Services may enter an IS Customer Service Request (CSR) as the Master Plan. The response from IS is the generation of an official proposal document. The proposal addresses the client's requirements and provides a high level evaluation of procedures suggested to address the client's expectation. The Master Plan is not a contract, the IS Proposal Document is a contract.

Proposal generation process

The Master Plan, in the form of a Customer Service Request (CSR) is presented to IS for analysis and consideration. IS may also receive CSRs directly from any given County Agency. The IS Business Consultant will work with the associated Service Area Managers to develop a response to the client. That response may be in the form of an immediate scheduling of activity or the development of a formal proposal to the client. Utilizing input from the associated IS service areas, the IS Business Consultant will generate the formal proposal. The proposal will include all the information required by the client to make an informed business decision relevant to the project. The client will be instructed in the IS proposal process and will have verified the contents and technical nature of the document.

Proposal approval process

Upon approval of the proposal document by all associated Service Area Managers, the document is signed by the IS Business Consultant and delivered to the customer. A specific meeting is scheduled to review the proposal and to work out any last minute alterations or problems. Time frames and budget considerations are discussed and agreed upon.

At that point, the client may ask for alterations and the document is returned to the consultant for amendment. The final product of this process is a signed proposal that will be utilized by IS for further development of the product or service.

Work plan development

With the signed proposal, the IS Business Consultant may assist each Service Area Manager or Project Leader to develop a **Work Plan** representing that areas participation. Service area Work Plans are combined into the formal Project Plan by the IS Business Consultant. Although the responsibility of the Service Area Manager, the Project Leader may develop the actual Work Plan. *The IS Business Consultant is responsible to combine the produced Work Plans into the Project Plan.*

Project plan

The **Project Plan** is very specific in nature and details the development process and the IS commitment to that process. A detailed review of the requirements for IS Project Plan development is included in the document. Planned status meetings are required through the life of the project. During actual product development, each Phase must be completed through a formal Phase Review meeting. Upon completion, the Project Plan is reviewed by the client and the IS Business Consultant. Modifications and alterations are worked out by the Service Area Managers, the client, and the IS Business Consultant. The product of this process is a signed agreement between the two organizations.

At that time, specific resources are identified by the service area managers or as assigned by the manager, the Project Leader. It is expected that these resources will be available and will remain on the project. Appropriate entry is made into the Project Management tool to reflect the Project Plan. Additional entries for *Risk Assessment* and Phase Reviews are scheduled. The IS Business Consultant will conduct a Project Team meeting and review the entire spectrum of the commitment.

Table 14-5 The proposal generation process

Master plan	Proposal	Project plan
	Client — Information Officer	
	Consulting services	
	IS management team	

A ***Project Leader*** (as required) may be identified by the Service Area Manager(s) and the specific responsibilities of this resource will be agreed upon. Provided the concurrence of the responsible Service Area Managers, the project is placed in a pending status and the Concept level is completed. Over time, standard project responsibility levels will be established for the Project Leaders.

Execute layer — process management

In accordance with the Project Plan, the project is executed. Prior to execution (start date), the IS Business Consultant will assemble the respective partners and verify the start date and review the overall Project

Plan. As the project develops, the Project Team will inform the IS Business Consultant of all issues, problems, and changes.

A formal ***change control*** process is identified within the *Proposal* and specified in the *Project Plan*. A standard for project management Change requests is established. All projects must include an approved Change Control process.

The IS Business Consultant will oversee or conduct formal Phase Reviews (milestones within the project) and gain the client's concurrence to the review. *Daily activity and project management at the event and task level are the responsibility of the assigned Project Leader.*

The Project Leader will be responsible for timely status reports and the communication of all issues and changes through the approved process. *Daily customer contact will be directed to the IS Business Consultant or the Project Leader, if applicable.* This process is also contained and agreed upon within the formal proposal document.

The execute layer continues through system test, installation, training, documentation, and post install reviews as directed by the Project Plan. Upon formal agreement to the contracted deliverables, the project is complete and the CSR must be updated to reflect that status. This marks the end of the execute layer. *The project is not closed, it is complete as contracted.*

Closure layer — process management

It is important that a project management tool be utilized to record and track project activities. Upon completion, project activities must be updated to reflect the appropriate status. Upon completion of the contracted project, the IS Business Consultant will assemble the appropriate client representatives and the IS Project Team and conduct a Project Review meeting. The product of this meeting is to turn over the project to the client and gain signature closure to the contract.

Prior to this meeting, an agreement for ongoing maintenance, support, and other considerations will have been negotiated. These provisions may also be included with the Project Plan and within the formal Proposal document.

Upon a signed mutual agreement, the project is closed. The CSR should be updated to reflect the Closed Status of the project. This is only done with the consent of the client. The Project Team will assemble all pertinent documentation, including contracts, change requests, problem reports, status reports, Phase Reviews, and signed agreements and place the collection in a permanent Project File. *This completes the Closure level. Appropriate entries into the project management and time tracking tools complete the documentation process.*

SS business-driven quality

It is the policy of the Information Systems Department to achieve Business-Driven Quality in meeting the requirements of external and internal IS customers. Business-Driven Quality means understanding who the customer is, what the requirements are, and meeting those requirements within budget, without error, on time, every time.

Proposal generation model — MPR

The process presented below is specifically tuned for information systems projects. It contains the basic essentials required for proper project management and IS/Customer management review. As a rule of thumb, all items contained within the template should be included in the final proposal document. If an item is not applicable for this project, so state that fact.

Minimum Project Requirement — MPR

Within this document, several items are identified as *MPR*. This identifier stipulates that information and/or content of the identified item is mandatory to comply with the IS Business Process. Additional material may be included as directed or required by the Customer Information Services Officer and/or IS Consulting Services

Proposal generation definitions

1. Project Scope

Describes the business and technical areas included within this proposal, and where possible, list those areas to be excluded. The Scope should be written to serve as an Executive Overview for client and/or functional IS management. Include: business objectives, boundaries of investigation, and outline of solution.

2. Assumptions

Details all assumptions that must be considered, including availability and participation of client or functional management personnel, availability of facilities, tools, and other resources.

3. Deliverables

Identifies the specific services, materials, reports, which will constitute the tangible end product of the project.

4. Responsibilities

States the specific work responsibilities of each participant, organization, team, and/or project. Provides project management assignments and project control assignments.

5. Training and education

Describes any training and education that will be developed, provided, performed, or required of addressing management, users, and technical personnel during or at the conclusion of the project.

6. Estimated costs

Outline Project phases and provides estimated or projected Cost Value Analysis (CVA). Projects of $10,000 or more require the IS Information Economics Model results.

7. Completion criteria

States the specific deliverables, products, and conditions that constitute the successful completion of the project.

8. Payment schedule

Includes the charge back process and how IS will expect payment. The client should verify that appropriate funds are available.

9. Change control

Describes the process to be followed for any modifications or alterations to the contract of record. Includes a statement which provides notice that any changes may result in an adjustment to the terms and conditions of the contract, including price, dates, and completion criteria.

10. Project management

Identifies the parties responsible for: overall project, specific areas or deliverables or segments of the project. Includes approval and project communication methods.

11. Facilities required

Lists all requirements for offices, conference rooms, supplies, terminals, printers, access hours, and security.

12. Risk assessment

Defines any specific or potential situations or conditions that may put the successful completion of the project at any degree of risk. Identifies the risk in terms of high, medium, or low risk.

13. Estimated start/stop dates

States the specific date upon which activities will commence and the estimated date of completion or conclusion. The IS Business Consultant, Service Area Managers, and the customer Information Services Officer must establish a doable and acceptable date parameters.

14. Customer acceptance criteria

Documents the specific conditions and requirements established to mutually complete the project.

15. Proposal expiration date

State the actual date upon which the terms and conditions of this proposal will expire unless expressly extended in writing.

Service quality assessment (SQA)

The IS Business Consultant continually strives for improvements in customer satisfaction. In order to achieve true customer satisfaction, the IS Business Consultant must obtain a precise and comprehensive understanding of the customer's perspective and expectations.

The **Service Quality Assessment** (SQA) is the vehicle utilized to accomplish that perspective. A SQA should be performed on every major contract and all contracts that cross IS Service Area boundaries. This vehicle is designed for face-to-face contact with the customer Information Services Officer and/or executive and management personnel. The results of this process will generate a baseline for the current and future projects with the agency.

The objective is to gather the client's perspective on the selected processes, skills, and work products. When reviewing the assessment with the customer assign a value between 1 to 10 to the component being discussed. Low evaluations indicate items of relative low value to the client. High evaluations indicate items important to the client. Tabulate each section and note areas that might influence (positive or negative) the project. These observations or conclusions should be included in the IS Proposal and/or IS Project Plan.

Service Quality Assessment (SQA)

- Requirements & specifications
- Quality management requirements
- IS staff performance expectations
- IS staff conduct & actions
- IS business consultant/management

The SQA process is performed at the beginning and at the end of each major project. This produces a clear interpretation of the customer's expectations and forms the baseline for evaluating customer satisfaction.

Technical risk analysis — MPR

Within the IS business and Project Management process, Risk Analysis is an important component. The IS Business Consultant is responsible for performing risk analysis as part of the project management process. The items below summarize five areas associated with risk analysis.

A Technical Risk Analysis should be incorporated into every project requiring multiple phase approach and/or the commitment of IS personnel over extended periods of time and/or projects that cross service area boundaries.

The purpose of a Technical Risk Analysis is to ensure that those responsible for planning, authoring, or managing project activities are aware of the risk factors that may influence the successful completion of the project.

This model is based on Harvard University's Security By Analysis (SBA) method, adjusted to comply with the IS environment. When performing the analysis assign a value between 1 to 10 to the component being reviewed. Low evaluations indicate items of relative low risk to the client and to the project. High evaluations indicate items that could influence the project in a negative manner. Tabulate each section and note areas that might influence (positive or negative) the project. These observations or conclusions should be included in the IS Proposal and/or IS Project Plan.

Technical risk analysis

- Quality & definition of scope
- Experience of the project team
- Technology factors
- Project organization
- Environmental factors

Evaluation/assessment process — MPR

In the role of consultant, the IS Business Consultant may be required to evaluate or assess a particular project or process. A standard three-stage review process is presented below for consideration.

Although not all-inclusive, this process does cover the majority of items that one should consider in a project, product, process, or documentation review.

When evaluating a process or product, assign a value between 1to 10 to (1=Low 10=High) the component being reviewed. Tabulate each section and then tabulate the average score for the entire study.

While performing the evaluation look for areas that might influence (positive or negative) the project. These observations or conclusions should be included in the IS Proposal and/or IS Project Plan.

Note: Templates from a variety of process and management tools are available for specific tasks. This process provides a general overall evaluation of the selected application, system, or process. It may be used with a more specific technical template.

Summary of process

- Performance criteria

- Qualified & quantified
- Process management

Change control procedure

The incorporation of a vigorous and uniformly enforced Change Control process is an essential element in the management of all projects. Within the Proposal and Project Plan documents, a standard format for Change Control should be utilized. The intent is to present a common element between every IS project.

Project scope (proposal and project plan)

Changes to this statement of work will be processed in accordance with the procedure described in the 'change control procedure' section of this document. investigation and the implementation of changes may result in modifications to the schedule, charges, or other terms and conditions of this contract.

Assumptions (proposal and project plan)

Deviations from the Project Plan and schedule, mutually agreed to by the IS Business Consultant and the Information Services Officer may necessitate the application of Change Control procedures identified in the 'Change Control Procedure' section of this document.

Responsibilities (proposal and project plan)

The IS Business Consultant assumes full project management responsibility for this project. The objective of this task is to provide direction and control of the project and to provide a framework for project communications, reporting, and procedural and contractual activity, including but not limited to:

- IS Business Consultant will maintain project communications through the customer Information Services Officer.
- Coordinate and conduct review sessions, as appropriate, for project Phase completion.
- Coordinate and conduct, as required, project status meetings.
- Manage the Change Control Procedure through signature authority.
- Manage and provide bi-directional issue and problem resolution.

Change control — process (project plan)

Changes to this Statement of Work may be requested at any time by either party (IS Business Consultant) or (customer Information Services Officer). Since a change could affect the cost, schedule or other terms of this agreement (contract), both the IS Business Consultant and the customer Information Services Officer must approve each change before amending this Statement of Work and implementing the change.

This procedure will be used by IS and the customer to control any and all changes to the Statement of Work, as described within this document, that add, influence, modify, generate, or remove: Terms and Conditions, schedules, deliverables, cost, and quality.

- All project change requests will be submitted in writing utilizing the approved Change Request form provided by IS. They will describe the change and include any justification, conditions, rationale and/or estimated effect the change will have on the Statement of Work.
- The IS Business Consultant and/or the customer Information Services Officer, as appropriate, will review the proposed change. It is then accepted or rejected for submission to the other party. If rejected, the Change Request form is returned to the originator, along with the reason for the rejection.
- The IS Business Consultant and/or the customer Information Services Officer, as appropriate, will then sign the completed Change Request form and submit the form to the other party. Approval of the Change Request form for investigation by both parties constitutes authorization by the customer for charges incurred by IS to investigate the change request. Appropriate staff work will take place at that time and the effect on the cost, estimated schedule or other terms and conditions of the Statement of Work will be documented.
- The completed investigation, including all conditions and contingencies, will be presented to the other party for consideration and the change will be approved/disapproved for implementation. Approved changes will be incorporated into the Statement of Work through a written change authorization that will be appended to the original contractual document or materials.
- The IS Business Consultant will maintain a history log of all approved changes to the original Statement of Work. This history file will be available for review at all project, phase, and/or status reviews and included in the IS project File.

Note this procedure, in total, may be included in an Appendix to the contractual material and referenced within the document as Appendix *n*.

Process time estimates

Task or process	Ref. pgs	Responsible party: A/C	SAM	Client	Staff	Est. time	Support tool	Project layer
Evaluation Assessment	32-33	X			X	4 hours	form p33 (model)	Concept
Technical Risk Analysis	29-31	X	X		X	4 hours	p30-31 (model)	Concept
Service Quality Asmt.	26-28	X		X		2 hours	p27-28 (model)	Concept Closure
Proposal Generation	23-25	X	X		X	7 hours	page 23 (model)	Concept
Cost/Info Model	58-63	X	X			3 hours	page 62 (model)	Concept
Project Plan Generation	38-42	X	X		X	8 hours	page 40 (model)	Concept Clist p43
Project Mgmt Model/detail	44-48	X	X			30 min	sample page 46	C/E/C Clist p49
Status Reports	45-47	X			X	1 1/2 hours	page 56 (model)	Execute page 56
Issue Resolution	41-57	X			X	1 1/2 hours	page 57 (model)	Execute page 57
Change Control	34-35	X	X	X	X	2 hours	page 54 (model)	C/E/C
Project Closure	44-45	X	X	X	X	8 hours	page 48 (detail)	Closure

Material presented in this model represents the approximate time and personnel required to perform various process and documentation tasks. These numbers consider that personnel are familiar with the various techniques. A major consideration is that significant portions of the Proposal and Project Plan are 'standard' or 'modeled' and do not change from contract to contract.

Project plan overview

To conduct a successful project, a complete and effective project plan is essential. *The IS Business Consultant is responsible to oversee the development and processing of the Project Plan.*

The Project Plan validates and expands on the written description of the customer's goals, objectives, and expectations of the project as documented in the IS Proposal.

The IS Business Consultant evaluates the Project Team responsibilities and work commitments and documents, in detail, exactly how the work will be performed, resources that are required, and deliverable content and conditions for closure.

The IS Project Plan should contain five (5)-required sections or segments. Each segment should be complete and present both the IS and customer perspectives.

Modifications to the development process for the Project Plan are anticipated as experience and technology influence our business.

1. Project description

This segment expands the content and detail provided in the IS Proposal. The term 'Statement of Work' is often associated with this segment.

2. Project management plan

This segment details the management practices that will govern the development process. This segment is often associated with 'Rules of Engagement.'

3. Deliverable description

This segment provides the development and approval process required to generate the final deliverable product. This should include reports, documentation, diagrams, and other forms of a deliverable.

4. Development environment

Describes the physical development requirements and processing procedures.

5. Project work plan

The Project Work Plan(s) detail assumptions and responsibilities required for a successful completion of the project. This includes Phases, Events, Tasks, and the associated responsibilities and date parameters.

Project plan summary — MPR

The diagram below presents the five sections of the Project Plan and the associated events that constitute the levels within the section.

Material contained within this section was drawn from documentation provided or detailed within publications from IBM Corporation, CTG Corporation, LBMS, and comments and suggestions from the IS staff.

1. **Project description**
   a. **Description**
   b. **Goals and Expectations**
   c. **Objectives**
   d. **Scope**
   e. **Limitations**
   f. **Risk Analysis Results**
      - Quality and Definition of Scope
      - Experience of Project Team
      - Technical Factors
      - Project Organization
      - Environmental Factors
2. **Project management plan**
   a. **Communication Procedures**
      - Status Meetings
      - Status Reports
      - Team Meetings
   b. **Staffing Procedures**
      - Staff Selection Procedure
      - Orientation Procedure
      - Training Procedure
   c. **Project Control Procedures**
      - Issue Resolution Procedure
      - Change Control Process
      - Configuration Management
      - Acceptance Procedure
      - Budget Management Procedure
      - Project Scheduling and Tracking

- Activity Status — Schedule Variance
- Quality Assurance Procedure
- Project Completion Procedure

3. Deliverable description

a. Description of Deliverables

b. Acceptance and Performance Criteria

c. Standards: Format and Content

d. Quality Control Procedures

i. Verification Procedures

ii. Verification Activities

iii. Testing Approach

- Unit Testing
- Integration Testing
- System Acceptance Testing
- User Acceptance Testing

4. Development environment

a. Facilities Description

- Furnishing/Supply Requirements
- Hardware Requirements
- Software Requirements

b. Environment Procedures

- Facility Management
- System/Computer
- Security Procedures

5. Project work plan(s)

a. Project Breakdown by Function

b. Estimating Assumptions

c. Resource Distribution

- Responsibilities
- Project Roles

- User Responsibility
- Management Responsibility
- Support Roles Required

Note: Each Project Plan developed by the IS Teams should follow the framework presented above. If items are not applicable, so state that fact.

Process and project methodology

The illustration below presents a diagrammatic perspective of the Process and Project Management methodology that will be utilized to manage and control this project.

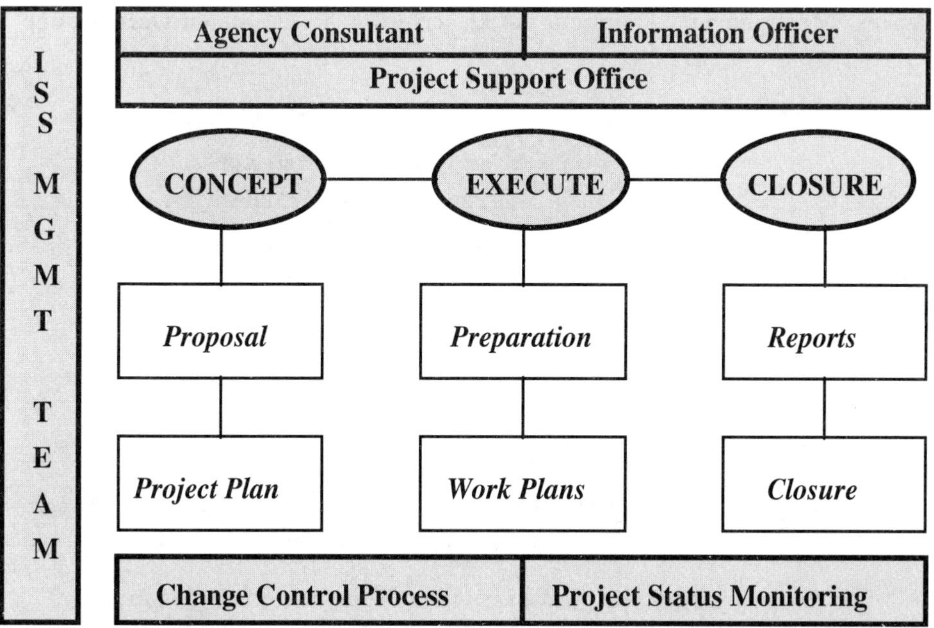

Phase development

The work plans illustrated in the diagram below are constructed using a four-phase development scenario. The four phases (Requirements, Development, Implementation, and Review) include the combined work plans for each participating IS Service Area.

Phases	Requirements	Development	Implementation	Review
APS				
DBA				
NAS				

Process management — project overview

Process Management	Functional Description	Estimated Date Model
Concept Layer 1.1	Generate Proposal	Initiation ___________ Completion ___________
Concept Layer 1.2	Generate Project Plan	Initiation ___________ Completion ___________
Execute Layer 2.1	Project Preparation	Initiation ___________ Completion ___________
Execute Layer 2.2	Project Execution	Initiation ___________ Completion ___________
Closure Layer 3.1	Report Generation	Initiation ___________ Completion ___________
Closure Layer 3.2	Project Closure	Initiation ___________ Completion ___________

The Project Overview diagram above provides the estimated date parameters for major project milestones, as established through the IS methodology. It is anticipated that the provided date parameters may fluctuate due to the influence of the dependencies and assumptions associated with this project. Provided dates may change as the result of approved project changes and/or modifications to the Terms and Conditions of this project plan.

The diagram above should be used as a model within the Work Plan of the Project Plan. It should be completed by the IS Business Consultant from information provided by the participating Service Area Managers. The model includes the specific areas required for within the IS Business Process. The diagram of the Process and Project Methodology illustrate that concept.

Further development of the Work Plans requires that this important milestone project overview be completed with as much accurately as possible. This information will also be very useful to the customer in planning associated business tasks and assignments.

Project work plan control model

Work Plan Phase Mgmt.	Initiate Phase	Complete Phase	Phase Review	Estimated Hours	
Requirements					
Development					
Implementation					
Review					

The table above provides estimated date parameters for initiation and completion of the four phases within the Execute layer of this project. Detailed definitions for associated project events and tasks are managed by IS utilizing an automated project management facility that provides time and personnel management along with budget and project tracking. Items marked '?' contain additional documented material. That material is presented following this section of the Project Plan.

The diagram above should be used as a model within the Work Plan of the Project Plan. It should be completed by the IS Business Consultant from information provided by the participating Service Area Managers. The model includes the specific areas required for within the IS Business Process. The diagram of the Process and Project Methodology illustrate that concept.

Combined with the Project Overview diagram (on the previous page) they provide a complete view of the project and associated activities. The four sections of the Work Plan are illustrated in the diagram. These calculations will be utilized in establishing the final 'Work Plan' parameters within Plan view.

IS functional area responsibility

IS Service Area	Project Function	IS Manager

This project will require personnel resources and active participation on the part of the above IS Service Areas. Input into the development of this project plan was provided and approved by the above management team. Additional information pertaining to the management and control of this project will be provided by the responsible IS Business Consultant through scheduled Status Meetings and scheduled Phase Reviews.

Within this project plan, Change Control and Issue Resolution processes are detailed. Modifications to the Terms and Conditions detailed within this document must follow the approved Change Control and Issue Resolution processes.

The diagram above should be used as a model within the Work Plan of the Project Plan. It should be completed by the IS Business Consultant from information provided by the participating Service Area Managers. Thus, the 'Work Plan' section of the IS Project Plan should contain:

- Project Overview Diagram
- Work Plan Model Diagram
- Functional Area Responsibility

Additional and/or more detailed project information and schedules will be available within the Planview tool. Reports on project Status, Changes, Issues, and Event and Task assignments will also be available to the IS Business Consultant, IS Management, and potentially the Customer.

The next chapter (4.8) details the proposed entry that will be required into Planview to effectively and efficiently manage and monitor the project. The previous material will be used as a foundation in the building of the actual detailed 'Work Plan'.

Building the development model

Within the Execute Layer of the project life cycle detail, work plans must be generated. A plan for each participating Service Area is required. The developed plans are then consolidated into one comprehensive work plan. The final plan is represented in Planview. Development of the consolidated Work Plan is expedited by following an established routine. This chapter illustrates and details a routine that provides the appropriate management and control while allowing freedom and creativity to the associated Service Areas.

It is assumed that the appropriate date parameters have been established for the project. The required parameters were discussed in the previous chapter.

Defining the established phases

The appropriate phases (Requirements, Development, Implementation, and Review) are placed in a master timeline. A sample is provided below. To initiate the timeline, display the four phases.

Table 14-6 Defining established phases

	Description	**Start** mm/dd/yy	**Complete** mm/dd/yy
Phase 1	Requirements		
Phase 2	Development		
Phase 3	Implementation		
Phase 4	Review		

Table 14-7 Add the associated service areas events

Phase	Description	**Start** mm/dd/yy	**Complete** mm/dd/yy

Table 14-8 Major 'milestones' as tasks and phase reviews

Phase	Description	**Start** mm/dd/yy	**Complete** mm/dd/yy
Phase 1	**Requirements**		
Event	APS		
Task	Detail analysis		
Task	Document analysis		
Event	DBA		
Task	Detail analysis		
Task	Document analysis		
Task	Phase Review		
Phase 2	**Development**		
Event	APS		
Task	Define screens		
Task	Build screens		

Table 14-8 Major 'milestones' as tasks and phase reviews

Phase	Description	Start mm/dd/yy	Complete mm/dd/yy
Task	Test screens		
Event	DBA		
Task	Define DB		
Task	Build DB		
Task	Test DB		
Task	Phase review		
Phase 3	**Implementation**		
Event	APS		
Task	Install software		
Task	Integration test		
Task	Train users		
Event	DBA		
Task	Install DB		
Task	Integration test		
Task	Train users		
Task	Phase review		
Phase 4	**Review**		
Event	APS		
Task	Dual systems		
Task	Production test		
Event	DBA		
Task	Tune DB		
Task	Production test		
Task	Phase review		

Project distribution—classification

A variety of request generation channels are funneled to the responsible IS Business Consultant. All product and service requests must follow this path. Delegation for specific Type C services is appropriate.

In addition, the analysis of a given project may generate the requirement for up-front or preliminary analysis and/or data collection through an additional Customer Service Request.

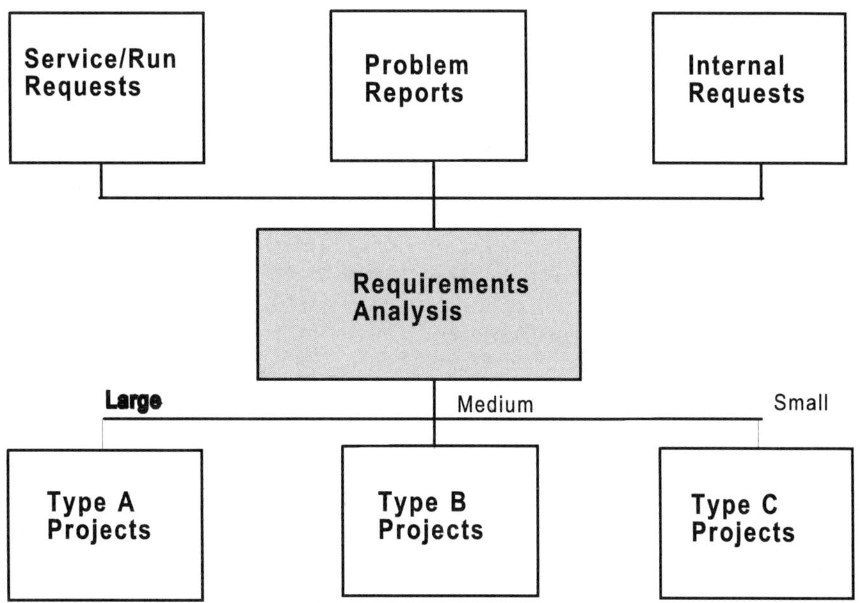

Figure 14-1 ***Type A** $10K or more, 80 hours or more, cross-function **Type B** Less than $10K, 40-80 hours, cross function **Type C** Less than 40 hours, one or two service areas*

Project classification

It is the mission of Information Systems (IS) to provide products and services that are predictable, repeatable, and measurable. To address that lofty ambition, business processes and procedures must be established that facilitate the management, accountability, and utilization of **resources** and **projects**. These processes and procedures must address both the resource and project perspectives of the IS environment. With this goal in mind, a three-channel distribution process has been established for managing and performing IS product and services requirements.

Type A — (Large Size/Effort Project)

As presented in the IS Business Process document, Type A services must follow a full process and project management routine. These projects require large amounts of personnel time and the participation of multiple IS Service Areas. Coordination and communication are the essential elements in managing these involved and important product development efforts. To accommodate this challenge, the entire Concept, Execute, and Closure layers of the IS Business Process must be followed.

Type B — (Medium Size/Effort Project)

Type B projects require 40 or less billable hours and may performed by two or more IS Service Areas. The Type B process follows the Concept, Execute, and Closure model in an abbreviated fashion. Typically, the contractual document includes elements from the Proposal generation and Project Plan generation models. Signature authorization to the document completes the Concept Layer. Execution of the 'Statement of Work' contained within the Description section of the document begins the Execute Layer. Signature approval by the client verifies the 'Completion Criteria' and project Closure.

Type C — (Small Size/Effort Project)

Type C is established to efficiently address client opportunities that require 40 or less billable hours. The contractual instrument is the signed Service Level Agreement. An abbreviated, template driven document confirms the service request and provides basic management and tracking of the service request. Type C follows the Concept, Execute, and Closure IS model. An important element of Type C projects is the Change Control procedure. This procedure must be followed and monitored for time and dollar escalation.

A review of Types A, B, and C projects follow this page.

Type A — Large projects

As detailed within this document, Type A projects are subject to the entire project and process management practices as approved by the IS Management Team. Full development of the Proposal and Project Plan models is required. Appropriate customer and IS signature approval is required. Full Change Control and Status Reporting processes must be implemented and enforced. Appropriate business process tools (Technical Risk Analysis, Service Quality Assessment) must be performed and documented in the Proposal and Project Plan. Work Plans from the associated project Service Areas must be complete and available in the Project Plan.

A completed Information Economics Model should be available in the Proposal and Project Plan documents.

High-level process overview

Proposal Generation	Concept 1.1
Project Plan Document	Concept 1.2
Execute Preparation	Execute 2.1
Work Plans	Execute 2.2
Report Generation	Closure 3.1
Project Closure	Closure 3.2

Project plan construction

Section 1.	Project Description
Section 2.	Project Mgmt Plan
Section3.	Deliverable Description
Section 4.	Development Environment
Section 5.	Project Work Plans

The diagrams above illustrate the high-level business process and the components of the IS Project Plan. These perspectives are detailed in the IS Business Process documentation. Full development of these components is required for all Type C projects. Indeed, elements of the entire process are contained within the Type B and Type C project models. This provides uniformity and continuity in the development and delivery of IS products and services.

Type B — Medium projects

Within the IS Business Process three levels of product and services support are provided. These levels are distinguished by work effort time, total expense, and IS Service Area participation. The analysis and classification is managed by the assigned IS Business Consultant. This document provides an overview of the contractual instrument required for **Type B** opportunities.

Type B Documentation Model

A	Description of Project
B	Scope of Project
C	Assumptions/Dependencies
D	Training and Education
E	Time Estimates (in hours)
F	Completion Criteria
G	Payment Schedule/Process
H	Change Control Procedure
I	Estimated Start/Stop Dates
J	Client Contact — Manager
K	Work Plan Overview
L	Signature/Authorization

Type B characteristics are: Less than $10K, 40-80 development (billable) hours, and two or more IS Service Areas involved. Type B incorporates items and functions associated with the 'Proposal' and 'Project Plan' utilized in Type A projects.

Signature authorization from the client completes the 'Concept' layer of the IS Business Process. Generic 'template' text is available to expedite the completion of this contractual instrument. The Change Control Procedure associated with this service must be followed in a timely and complete manner.

Type C—Small projects

Type C provides the vehicle for expeditiously responding to service requests. This would include Training, report generation, panel modifications, network installs, and many more contract services. Provided as a fast path, Type C service requests follow a simple and logical contracting and performance model that allows flexibility, management, and control in the execution of the selected service. This page provides an overview of the contractual instrument required for Type C service opportunities.

Type C documentation model

A	Description of Project
B	Scope of Project
C	Time Estimate (in hours)
D	Estimated Start/Stop Dates
E	Payment Schedule/Process
F	Change Control Procedure
G	Completion Criteria

Type C characteristics are: Less that $10K, 1-40 development (billable) hours, and one or more IS Service Areas are involved. Type C incorporates items and functions associated with the 'Proposal' and 'Project Plan' utilized in Type A projects.

Although abbreviated, Type C provides elements of the Concept, Execute, and Closure model supported by the IS Business Process. The Description, Payment, and Change Control elements are representative of the Concept Layer. The Description combined with the Start/Stop dates are representative of the Execute Layer. Closure is represented by the Completion Criteria. Thus, Type C follows the three-layered Business Process model. This provides a defined, manageable, and trackable service platform for IS and its client population.

In addition to accommodating the IS Business Process, Type C also follows the project management model required by the Planview implementation. A generic 'template' is available to expedite the completion and processing of this document.

The completed document, signed by the IS Business Consultant, should be forwarded via GroupWise, Facsimile, or paper copy to the appropriate client representative. Type C documentation provides the parameters and management guidelines of the services.

Business/process environment

For any business process to mature, an understanding and appreciation of the operation and related elements must be developed. A business process is not a collection of rules and regulations. Documentation and project management requirements are not developed to create work, nor are they obstacles that hinder true progress and development. The integrated collaboration between each element within the business environment contributes to the efficient and efficient growth and maturity of the business process. A number of major process environment factors are presented below. Each contributes a specific value or contribution to the overall IS Business Process.

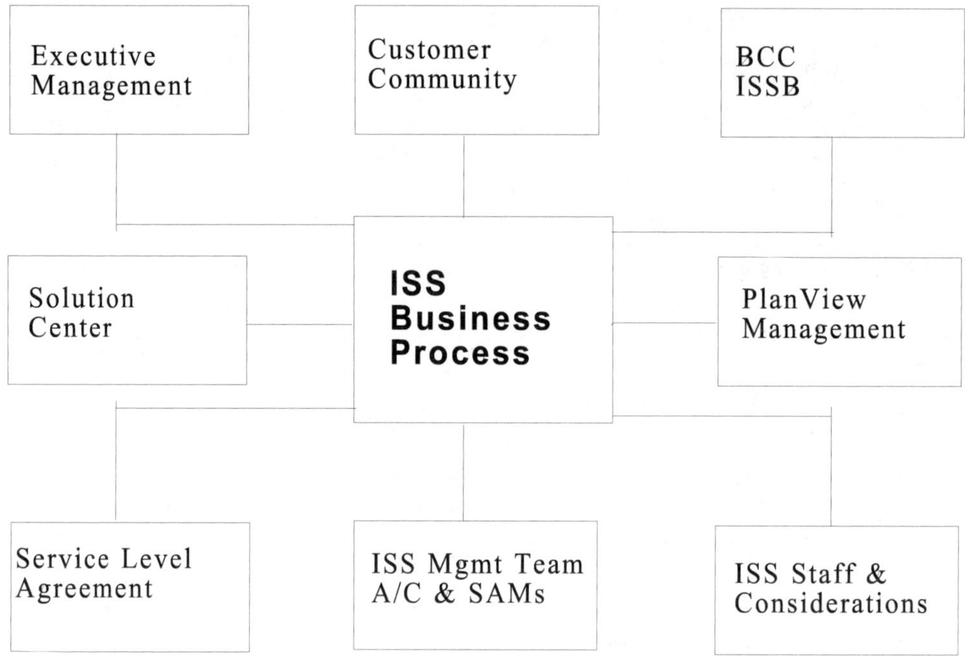

When addressing process development, modifications, implementation, or problems — each of these factors must be considered and evaluated. No one factor works without the combined cooperation of the associated factors. In brief, the IS Business Process is the glue that combines all of these contributing factors. Without the glue, all that you have left is a group of disassociated entities that are inefficient and non-functioning.

A business process brings these factors together to mutually address the challenges and rewards of the IS business environment.

Project management model — MPR

The IS business process is conducted by following an established set of business rules. Project Management is an integral portion of that rule set. This section provides a review of a three-stage project management model that conforms to the IS Business Process as detailed or implied within the IS Transformation Plan.

Prior to the implementation of the Project Management Model, a Master Plan should have been developed and approved by the customer Information Services Officer and the responsible IS Business Consultant. Acceptance of the plan by the IS Management Team indicates the beginning of the Concept Layer of the project management process.

Layer One — Concept model

The Concept Model includes activities that are performed generating, analyzing, contracting, and planning IS solutions for client business driven requirements.

Layer Two — Execute model

The Execute Model provides for project preparation and project execution. This considers the fact that a period of time may elapse between the Concept and Execute stages of the project.

Layer Three — Closure model

The Closure Model provides project review and client signature acceptance of the deliverables, and the completion of the service contract.

Project management summary — MPR

1. **Layer One — Concept**
   a. Generate Proposal (Phase I) (Proposal Generation Model)
      i. Compile and Document Proposal (Event 1.1.1)
      ii. SS Signature Approval of Proposal (Event 1.1.2)
      iii. Proposal Presentation to Client (Event 1.1.3)
      iv. Client Signature Acceptance of Proposal (Event 1.1.4)
   b. Generate Project Plan (Phase II) (Project Plan Model)
      i. Compile and Document Project Plan) (Event 1.2.1)
      ii. IS Signature Approval of Project Plan (Event 1.2.2)
      iii. Presentation to Client (Event 1.2.3)
      iv. Client Signature Acceptance of Plan (Event 1. 2.4)
2. **Layer Two — Execute**
   a. Execution Preparation (Phase I)
      i. Prepare Environment (Event 2.1.1)
      ii. Assign Human Resources (Event 2.1.2)

iii. Adjust Project Plan (Event 2.1.3)

b. Execute Project Plan (Phase II)

i. Manage Budget (Event 2.2.1)

ii. Manage Contingencies (Event 2.2.2)

iii. Manage Environment (Event (2.2.3)

iv. Manage Human Resources (Event 2.2.4)

v. Report Status (Event 2.2.5)

vi. Present Deliverables (Event 2.2.6)

vii. Compile Project File (Event 2.2.7)

3. Layer Three — Closure

a. Project Reports (Phase I)

i. Project Summary Report (Event 3.1.1)

ii. Quality Assurance Report (Event 3.1.2)

b. Project Closure (Phase II)

i. Confirm Customer Satisfaction (Event 3.2.1)

ii. IS Project Close Meeting (Event 3.2.2)

Project management — execute detail stage two

1. Execution Preparation

a. Prepare Environment

- Request/Receive Supplies
- Establish Physical Environment
- Install Hardware
- Install Software
- Develop Environment Report

b. Assign Human Resources

- Request Resources
- Select Project Team
- Project Team Meeting
- Prepare/Conduct Training
- Prepare/Conduct Orientation
- Develop Staffing Report

c. Adjust Project Plan
   - Update Project Plan
   - Obtain Client Approval

2. Execute Project Plan (example)
   - Phase I Requirements
   - Phase II Development
   - Phase III Implementation
   - Phase IV Review

a. Manage Budget
   - Establish Budget Spreadsheet
   - Establish Process for Financials
   - Generate Budget Report

b. Manage Contingencies
   - Identify: Events, Issues, Changes
   - Log Events, Issues, Changes
   - Analyze Impact to Project
   - Report Impact to Client
   - Obtain Client Signature Approval
   - File all related material

c. Manage Environment
   - Request/Receive Supplies
   - Adjust Physical Environment
   - Adjust Hardware Requirements
   - Adjust Software Requirements

d. Manage Human Resources
   - Conduct Project Staff Meetings
   - Direct Project Staff
   - Document Performance
   - Provide Training / Education

e. Report Status

- Internal Staff Reports
- Report Status to Client
- Report Status to Consulting Services
- Report Status to IS Managers
- File all Status Reports

f. Present Deliverables

- Package Deliverable Components
- Inspect Deliverable Package
- Review Deliverables with Client
- Conduct Acceptance Test
- Client Sign-off or Exceptions

g. Compile Project File

- Gather and maintain Project Data
- Present Project File to Consulting Services

This completes *Layer Two: Execute*

Project management — closure detail

This section details the activities associated with the Closure layer of project management.

1. Produce Project Reports

a. Compile Summary Report

- Project Execution Summary
- Description of results
- Description of Acceptance
- Factors That Influenced Project
- Financial Overview
- Changes From Original Plan
- Recommendations to Client
- Review Report With Client

b. Quality Assurance Report

- Major Activities
- Project Plan Completed

- Deliverables Were Accepted
- Changes Have Been Completed
- SQA Objectives Have Been Met
- Problems and Issues Resolved
- All Sign-offs Are Provided
- Conformity to Client/IS Standards

2. **Project Closure**
   a. Confirm Customer Satisfaction
      - Conduct Service Quality Assessment
      - Review Findings With Client
      - Obtain Signature Approval
   b. IS Project Close Meeting
      - Return Hardware
      - Restore Project Site
      - Review Project Summary
      - Review Service Quality Assessment
      - Total/Close Financials
      - Close Project File

This completes *Layer Three: Closure*

Project plan review/evaluation

Upon completing the Project Plan, the IS Business Consultant, Service Area Manager(s), and the Project Leader should review the completed document. Utilized during that meeting, the checklist provided below will assist in detecting omissions and/or errors in the proposed plan. Upon the completion of the review, the review document should be included in the IS Business Consultant's project file.

1. Are all the required service area work plans included?
2. Are the work plans consistent with the anticipated project time line?
3. Do time estimates appear to be realistic?
4. Does the Cost Value Analysis support project development?
5. Has a time and personnel allowance for possible rework been included?
6. Have holidays, vacations, and illness been factored into project time line?

7. Have provisions for project security been established?
8. Do time plans include adequate time for Reviews and Approvals?
9. Is there a mandated completion date?

If yes, what provisions were established to accommodate the date?

____

10. Are responsibilities defined and assigned for each project task?
11. Are the proposed resources available at the appropriate time?
12. Are the physical facilities adequate?
13. Is administrative and/or clerical staff available, if required?
14. Are testing facilities adequate and assigned?
15. Is their in-house experience in similar projects?
16. Will additional resources (virtual staff) be required?
17. Have training procedures for the project team been provided?
18. Have training procedures for the end user been provided?
19. Has the client been appropriately involved in project development?
20. Has client approved completion and closure criteria?

If any of the above questions are answered with a NO, detail the situation on this form, and include this, and any other associated documentation in the project file.

____

____

____

____

____

Project leader (IS business consultant)

The appropriate service area manager assigns project Leaders to specific projects. As directed by the manager, a specific resource may be assigned to a specific customer for an extended period of time. The customer may also request the resource, as availability and business conditions permit. The IS Business Consultant may select to have event or task related items communicated directly from the client to the Project Leader. New requirements or project changes should always be communicated back to the IS Business Consultant.

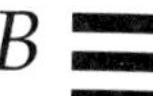

Business relationship with IS business consultant

The business relationship between the IS Business Consultant and the Project Leader is an important one. The IS Business Consultant, with full responsibility for the account, may delegate, as appropriate, a range of latitude to the Project Leader or Project Team. It is also possible that more than one Project Leader will be active in a given account, but only one per project. Establishing Standards for Project Leaders would increase the effectiveness of this valuable resource.

The IS Business Consultant assigned to the account is always the primary interface to the customer. Also, the IS Business Consultant is responsible for coordinating resources from the various service areas. Upon request or prior understanding, the Project Leader may perform this function. Project members should not be substituted without the IS Business Consultant and the clients knowledge and approval.

Projects may involve a number of service areas to provide services to complete the project. Each service areas may select a Primary Contact representing that resource group. In this case, it would be appropriate that the assigned Primary Contacts select a Project Team Leader to coordinate and communicate various aspects of the project. *Once again, the IS Business Consultant is always responsible for the satisfactory completion of the project.*

Project management perspective

The formal Proposal and Project Plan have been signed and accepted, and the project is scheduled for execution. This diagram illustrates the continued participation by the IS Management Team, the IS Business Consultant, assigned Project Leader(s), and the technical support staff.

The 'PSO' Project Support Office, will monitor activity at the Phase and Event levels. A 'Status Report' process must be implemented to relay timely information to the PSO.

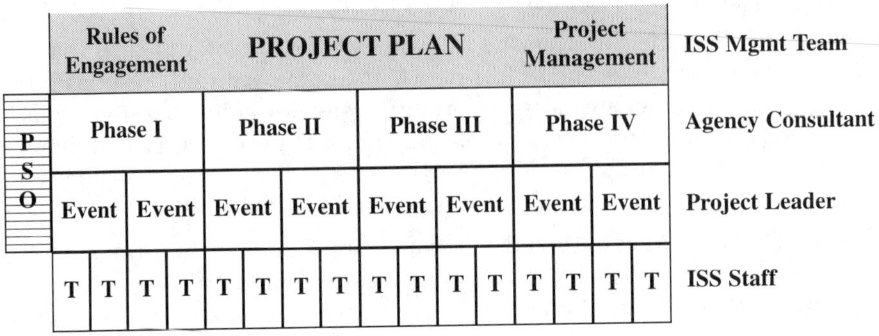

	Rules of Engagement	PROJECT PLAN		Project Management	ISS Mgmt Team
PSO	Phase I	Phase II	Phase III	Phase IV	Agency Consultant
	Event | Event	Event | Event	Event | Event	Event | Event	Project Leader
	T | T | T | T	T | T | T | T	T | T | T | T	T | T | T | T	ISS Staff

Modifications to the **'Terms and Conditions'** of the contract (signed Project Plan) must be administered according to the Change Control procedure stipulated in the contract. Terms and conditions mutually agreed upon in the Project Plan are the **'Rules of Engagement'.**

Process/Project Management

The diagram below illustrates the interaction and responsibility alignment associated with the IS Process Management and IS Project Management practices. Notice the customer involvement throughout the process. This is essential for continuity and communication between the IS staff and the client.

Process/Project Management

CUSTOMER	*CONCEPT*	ISS MGMT TEAM	
	PHASE	AGENCY CONSULTANT	EXECUTE
	EVENT	PROJECT LEADER	
	TASK	ISS STAFF	
	CLOSURE	PROJECT TEAM	

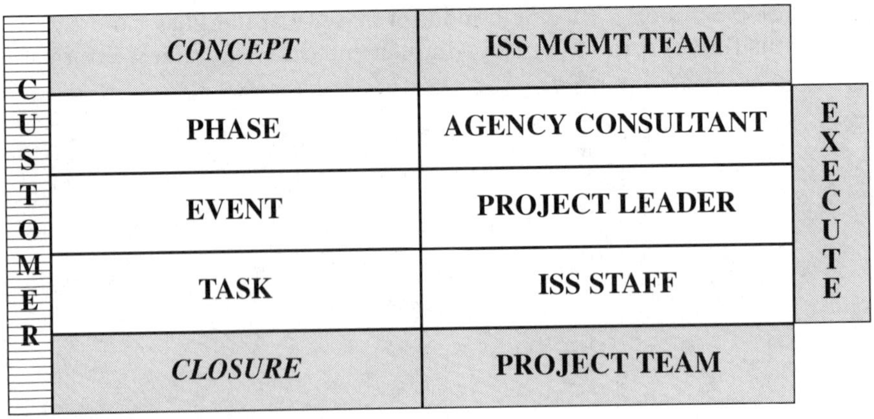

Working with the customer, IS will follow this comprehensive methodology designed to produce quality products and services that are *predictable, repeatable,* and *measurable.*

The heart of this methodology is effective Project Management and Process Management, and effective Change Control.

Project management forms processing

This section reviews four processing forms that will facilitate process and project management. Each form was developed with the cooperation and participation of the IS Management Team. The approved process forms follow the suggested approach supported through the Planview (process and project management) implementation. Thus, the automated control facility will contain like online documents that will support the IS Business Process.

Change request form

Communicate and approve/disapprove all modifications to the 'Terms and Conditions' of the IS/Customer contract. Changes are categorized as Major or Minor. Both IS and the customer must approve major changes. As appropriate, the change becomes an addendum to the contract — detailing the adjustment in the 'Terms and Conditions'. Minor changes (those that do not impact the customer or the 'Terms and Conditions' require IS Service Area Management and IS Business Consultant approval.

Change request summary

Maintained by the IS Business Consultant, this summary includes all approved change requests processed for a given project. The form reflects the current status of each request. Through Planview, this form is automatically generated.

Project status report

Completed, as required, by the Project Leader and/or IS Business Consultant to track and communicate current status of a given project. Reviewed at status and phase review meetings with the customer. Project status reports are generated through Planview from the captured phase and event levels.

Issue description form

Vehicle for communicating conditions and concerns and other situations that may influence project performance or may influence the 'Terms and Conditions' is not addressed. Planview provides the capture and reporting of project issues.

Appendix: Sample governance policies

C 

Information systems goals

County agencies and constitutional organizations (the county) shall become fully responsible for the cost/benefit justifications presented for information technology they deploy in their operations. *Conversion costs and training costs must also be included.* Agencies/Organizations will assume full accountability for delivering the productivity gains derived from information technologies, as committed in their business plans.

County operations shall be supported with information technology solutions that offer the most effective information-handling capabilities available.

The county shall make information productivity one of the essential indicators of performance and include it in all periodic performance evaluations.

The county shall make it possible for employees to satisfy the majority of their communication needs using electronic means.

County employees and the public shall be able to contact the county anytime, by computerized means, to obtain needed information.

County employees shall work more effectively as well as communicate and cooperate electronically better.

The county's information systems shall integrate communications, computing, and systems support functions automatically by means that do not require personal intervention, except in cases involving information security.

The county's voice, data, video, and image information systems shall be interoperable and secure so that employees will be able to retrieve, on an authorized computing device, a display of information from any authorized information source.

The county's information systems shall enhance the information productivity and work quality of employees, suppliers, and contractors.

The county's enterprise-wide information systems shall share resources effectively and efficiently through adoption of common standards, common data, and common software capabilities.

 C

To manage the county as an integrated, inter-operable and low cost organization, compatible management processes and shared resources are needed. The following sections define how it may be feasible to achieve that objective.

Statement of principles

The county shall manage information through centralized control over standards, efficiency, security, and the sharing of assets.

The county shall manage information through central policy direction and decentralized execution to assure responsiveness, quality, learning, and innovation.

The county shall require eliminating redundant tasks and then simplifying all information processes prior to building new applications.

The county shall enhance existing information systems whenever the need arises for additional automation instead of opting for new systems development as the preferred choice.

The county shall, in selecting any new data processing hardware/software, give primary consideration in the decision-making process, to the legitimate business needs of current system user(s), particularly where the replacement of an existing system is involved.

The county shall subject existing and proposed business methods to risk-adjusted cost-benefit analyses using for comparison the best public and private sector results.

The county shall prove and validate new business methods in pilot installations prior to full-scale implementation.

The county shall use common applications software for all information systems that perform the same function, unless verifiable proof exists that some functions should remain unique.

The county shall hold Information Services Officers at all levels accountable for all benefits and costs of developing and operating their information systems.

The county shall develop and enhance information systems according to standard enterprise-wide methods in order to enhance the speed of such development and realize benefits swiftly.

The county shall pursue a policy of small, incremental system development before considering any investments in large and comprehensive programs.

The county shall develop and enhance information systems using standard process models that document business methods.

The county shall make computing and communication networks transparent to the information systems that rely upon them.

The county shall adopt countywide data definitions and standards for all data.

The county shall acquire information services through competitive bidding that considers internal as well as external offerings.

County information services shall meet the criteria of being proven, interoperable, scalable, low cost, and well supported, and, have clearly defined migration strategies toward further technological evolution.

The county shall enter data into the information system only once, at the point of origin.

The county shall assign safeguards to data elements that assure close to zero errors at points of origin.

The county shall facilitate, control, and limit access to information according to universally applicable security principles.

The county shall protect information assets against deliberate attack by technically experienced adversaries.

The county shall safeguard information against unintentional or unauthorized alteration, destruction, or disclosure.

The county shall standardize graphic presentation formats for ease of communication between users and to enhance learning the use of applications.

Responsibilities at the enterprise and business levels

The IS Board shall consent to and issue all county information management goals, principles, policies, and objectives.

The Director of IS shall be a senior executive who reports to the IS Board. The Director of IS will be responsible for independently assessing whether the information management plans are aligned with the approved county business plans.

The Director of IS shall be responsible for long range human resource planning for county personnel involved in information management, including the skill and career advancement of information technology personnel.

The Director of IS shall report monthly, to the IS Board on the state of information management. This report must document whether current information assets are enhancing or detracting from the economic value-added to the citizens of Palm Beach County.

Each county agency and constitutional organization (business unit) shall appoint a business unit information officer with responsibility for that unit's information management. This responsibility includes assuring the accuracy, consistency, and timeliness of the data for which their organization is accountable.

Additionally, the business unit information officer shall be responsible for assessing the alignment of the business unit's information management plans and resources with the approved goals, principles, policies, and objectives of the business unit as well as the county.

Responsibilities of IS management team

Regardless of the organizational level, all information systems managers - defined here as all managers who control information systems - shall adhere to the following principles:

Information managers shall be responsible for providing superior responsiveness to customer needs, enhancing the value of information products and services, and supporting employees to increase their productivity and the quality of their work.

Comparisons of actual results against those proposed in the business plans and budgets shall be used to evaluate information managers' contributions.

Information managers shall be responsible for authorizing access to information bearing in mind security requirements. They will be also accountable for any lapses in information security.

Information managers shall be responsible for providing training and assistance to all users of information services, even when such support originates from vendors.

Information managers shall comply with county policies regarding security, safety, survivability, technology sharing, technology investment planning, data integrity, data access, applications inter-operability, and cross-functional integration.

Responsibilities of the information technology officer

Information Services Officers shall be responsible for ensuring that information systems deliver results as planned or better. They shall be accountable for both the costs and benefits of their information resources. They will measure their information productivity and report on their progress in achieving committed objectives.

Information Services Officers shall be accountable for the planning, design, implementation, quality, and operational performance of all information systems necessary to support their missions.

Information Services Officers shall be responsible for granting security access to information.

Information Services Officers shall be accountable for surpassing their organization's peers/counterparts in the effectiveness of their information systems.

Information Services Officers shall use information management to realize organizational gains and enhance economic value-added.

Information Services Officers shall be responsible for assuring that employees understand how to apply information systems effectively while meeting or exceeding quality standards.

Planning and finance

County business plans must show how information systems contribute to achieving planned operating results.

Business plans shall include information systems implementation plans that are consistent with the stated financial and operating targets.

Support services, whether provided from shared facilities or managed locally, shall adhere to standard cost accounting practices. Service providers shall benchmark their costs and performance against the best organizations, regardless of industry.

Activity-based standard costing shall be used in billing for information services. Services shall be priced and billed by activity that consumes information services, as recognized by the IS Board Cost Recovery Sub-Committee.

The established practice of billing by computer resource units, central processor time, number of tape mounts, and kilo packets shall not be used. Invoices shall indicate only those elements agreed upon by the IS Board Cost-Recovery Sub-Committee.

Information services shall be competitively priced and reflect the rapidly declining unit costs of information technologies.

Favorable comparisons with the most efficient among similar commercial services shall be demonstrated after discounting competitive prices for profit and marketing expenses.

Contracting

Information processing and software development shall be contracted out only if quality, cost, security and service standards are equivalent to or better than those found within the organization. All bids shall be evaluated against fully allocated internal costs instead of directly budgeted expenses.

Resources for information services shall not be expended by business units on systems that in any way duplicate services available from another business unit or from commercial source.

Analytic methods based on economic value-added shall be used to justify discretionary expenditures for information management projects in excess of limits set by the IS Board.

Care for customers of internal information services

County personnel at points-of-use shall determine the acceptability of the human-machine communication and the quality of the performance features of all information systems. They shall evaluate the quality, utility, responsiveness, and effectiveness of the information systems on which they depend.

Information management shall operate on the principle of assigning single point accountability for the successful completion of every information management services task. The organization that has the single point of accountability shall have the capacity to perform every diagnostic test and draw on all required expert assistance to correct any defects and answer any customer queries.

Approaching zero defects shall be established as the achievable quality standard for information services.

Customer satisfaction shall be measured only as seen from the customer's point of view, and not as defined by the providers of services.

Every customer complaint shall be accounted for. Every corrective action shall be recorded and reported to the organization that has been assigned the responsibility for auditing compliance with policies, principles, and standards.

Process improvements that result from error corrections shall be routinely reviewed jointly by information systems and operating management in order to avoid frequently repeated mistakes that originate from error-prone business procedures, inadequacies in training or mistakes in applications design.

All customers of information services shall be provided with facilities, tools, and training to evaluate the quality, price, and utility of the organization's providers of information services.

Data management

All information acquired or created by county employees while conducting business, except that which is specifically exempted as personal or private, is a county resource. The intellectual or property rights to all county information produced while on the county payroll belongs to the county.

Business units or local management may receive a temporary authority to become custodians of enterprise-level data. In such cases, the methods, rules, and conditions of custody cited in county information management policies and standards will apply.

All data elements shall be entered into the information system only at authorized points of origin. All subsequent uses of such data elements shall rely on copies of the original entries. Methods for positively identifying the originating source of all county data elements will be included in all systems designs.

Calculated summaries and aggregations of data, such as totals and subtotals, shall be derived only from original data entries to maintain information integrity at all times. Summary data obtained by other means shall not be entered into the information system, except as authorized.

The points of origin, authorization, security, context and definition of all data be documented using standard data model description methods.

Information configuration policies

Information management shall follow levels of accountability, which describe the information management master plan. Definitions of a seven-level structure are:

Level 1: Global

All functions, services and standards that assure the inter-operability of the enterprise with suppliers, customers and vendors of information technologies.

Level 2: Enterprise

All services and standards that set the rules of governance to assure the cost effectiveness and inter-operability of information systems.

Level 3: Functional Processes

All functions that support common business processes and assure horizontal integration of activities, across the entire enterprise, that have interrelated work flows regardless of location or business.

Level 4: Business

All systems that are unique to the products or service delivered by an autonomous organizational unit.

Level 5: Application

All systems features that uniquely satisfy the operating needs of personnel who perform similar tasks.

Level 6: Local

All systems features and practices that are unique to individuals or groups who require modifications of the standard processes not provided by higher organizational levels.

Level 7: Personal

All data that individuals wish to keep private. The purpose of the assignment of levels to the master systems configuration framework is to define the applicability of policies and standards. Configuration management calls for close adherence to standards at higher levels while providing maximum flexibility at the local and personal levels.

A formal management process, administered by the IS Board, shall define the application services performed at each level of the master design framework.

Information management functions that are not expressly reserved for a higher level shall be delegated to the next level. The IS Board shall not delegate what has been already reserved for enterprise level accountability.

The Director of IS shall be responsible for keeping track of unresolved interpretations of the principles of information management governance and bring them to the attention of the IS Board without delay. The Director of IS shall also be responsible for resolving any incidents that interfere with the capacity of the organization to react to competitive actions or expose the enterprise to jeopardy, especially when they involve matters of information security.

Decentralization policies

Information processing capabilities shall be available at the local and personal levels, except for those services expressly reserved for operations at the business, process, or enterprise levels.

Operating decisions about communications capabilities, document management, computing resources, applications support and training shall be made wherever local management has discretionary powers over budgets and performance.

Point-of-use personnel, provided they use only standard software tools provided for this purpose shall do designing screens, creating local applications and making ad-hoc inquiries.

Adequate resources shall be made available to Information Services Officers for local training, integration and innovation needs.

Personnel development policies

The IS Board shall review at least annually an independent assessment, and preferably from a consulting firm, of the quality of the personnel who support information management services.

The Director of IS shall monitor the progress of all personnel development programs that concern information management.

A professional corps of information managers and technical experts shall focus on innovation and business value creation irrespective of any outsourcing of computer services to commercial providers. The Director of IS shall be accountable for this activity.

Collegial and peer group electronic communications shall be established for all information systems personnel, regardless of geographic location or organizational level.

Every information management professional shall share knowledge, cooperate in finding solutions to problems, identify opportunities for improvement, promote innovation and assist personnel who have less developed skills. This shall be accomplished by establishing and maintaining a secure information communications network.

Standard computer-aided systems engineering tools and standard project management methods shall be applied in planning, management, and implementation of systems projects.

Distance learning and on-line services shall be used to improve the affordability and timeliness of information systems training. Remote diagnostics for just-in-time tutoring shall be available for all applications. Distance learning, tutoring, and distance applications support shall be a feature of all applications.

Systems design policies

Systems integration shall be established as the core competency of the systems development organization. Systems integration is the capacity to build low cost, secure and technically inter-operable systems according to rules that follow the prescribed systems standards for each level of the enterprise.

Full systems integration capabilities for the enterprise will be demonstrable when any authorized individual can easily share information without regard to application, operating system, or computer hardware.

Integration services shall be available within each organizational level, which will promote the reuse of standard software and data models. The IS systems integration staff will assist in adopting integrated systems engineering methods and help in distributing for general use successful adaptations of local applications.

Design principles

Standard software tools shall be supplied to local personnel to increase the range of choices available to them, within the constraints imposed by architectural standards. These tools will enable experimental prototyping of local variants or additions to existing standard applications.

Software tools shall become available at all levels of the architecture for constructing unique local applications and databases. Data originating from one level shall not enter a higher level without first complying with standards prescribed for the higher level.

Locally developed applications shall be encouraged, provided that they comply with the master systems design framework and security standards. These duplications must not introduce nonstandard data definitions for further distribution outside their local scope.

The best of locally developed applications shall be considered for migration to higher levels to become enterprise, business, or functional level systems. Criteria for their selection shall include: low operating and maintenance costs; features that satisfy a list of required new functions; a systems design possessing the best prospect of being upgraded; and a design that complies with open systems standards.

The design of any major new application shall be authorized only after the completion of business process improvement studies that trace the workflow of the existing business processes and compare it with what is proposed.

All new application developments or major software enhancements shall follow an evolutionary path towards open systems that conform to the approved enterprise standards.

The cost of information systems operations shall be reduced by avoiding periodically printed reports, eliminating all printing except for local exception reporting, and using tools so that customers may specify their own output formats.

Design costs and making widely accessible a repository that stores customer-conceived templates of useful system solutions shall reduce implementation schedules.

Contractors, consultants and suppliers engaged in the development of new county applications must comply with the approved county design standards and procedures so that their work is reusable elsewhere and does not keep up a dependency on maintenance services from the original designers.

Technology advancement

Designing while prototyping shall accelerate the systems specification process.

Applications shall be rapidly enhanced by means of add-on modular features in preference to redesigning or modifying the application itself.

Using leading-edge users to conduct experimental testing of pilot applications shall shorten the design cycle. The systems staff shall be frequently rotated from technical design tasks to the operating environment through short term and diversified assignments.

Experimental installations of leading-edge technologies shall surpass the most advanced competitors. The rapid pace of innovation makes the most advanced technologies also the most economical to operate. Early pilot demonstrations of the commercial feasibility in new technologies shall be funded to assemble a portfolio of opportunities that offer potential competitive advantages.

Reuse

Accumulated process knowledge from legacy systems shall be salvaged through reverse engineering and redesign.

Data element, software component, software object, and business process reuse shall be maintained using distributed but centrally coordinated configuration catalogs of all systems designs.

A standard graphic systems workflow description notation shall be used throughout the county. This symbolic notation shall be at a sufficiently comprehensible level so that any Information Services Officer, without extensive technical training, will be able to understand systems proposals using these methods to comprehend the contemplated changes in business procedures.

Developers, contractors, consultants, and suppliers shall segregate the software development environment from the software execution environment to increase software portability from an existing operation to a totally new computing system.

Telecommunications

A shared telecommuting network shall be capable of securely delivering voice, data, image, and video information on demand, anywhere and anytime in a high quality, timely and cost-effective manner which also assures privacy and the protection of the information that is conveyed.

Dependence on local support personnel shall be reduced through central online diagnostics, remote help desk support, and network control services.

A communications redundancy classification shall be assigned to every personal computer, workstation, gateway, server or communications switch on the network. This classification shall determine how many alternate communication channels must be available for traffic to move without disruption if a network failure occurs. This classification will also guide the decision how and when to replicate local databases to backup sites.

Risk management

System designs shall use multiple identical databases to assure survivability under conditions of failure.

Application designs shall use local databases to improve transaction response times and minimize the dependence on communications links.

Applications shall be location and data source independent. In the event of a local disaster, it shall be possible to reconstitute operations from an alternate site without deterioration of customer service. Formal actuarial methods shall be used to determine the economic affordability of risk protection.

Technology acquisition

Commercially available technologies, services, and software shall be used. Modification of vendor-maintained commercial software will not be allowed except where the ability to make modifications is a standard option of the software.

The adoption of open systems shall be enforced by procurement guidelines that specify which standards must be met.

Consultants or contractors shall use only prescribed standard software development and maintenance tools. Acceptance tests will assure that purchased or contracted for software remains portable, and will assure independence from having to continue the consultants' or contractors' engagements after contract completion.

Applications shall not be dependent on hardware, operating systems, systems engineering tools, management methods or computer languages that are available only from a single source of supply.

Security

Computing power shall continue to be available anywhere within the organization, on short notice, regardless of any disruptions of services. A continually tested and independently certified contingency plan shall be documented based on criteria set by the IS Board.

Information services support for customer-support operations shall be restored, within a specified time period, subsequent to any incident of physical destruction caused by natural disaster or professionally executed sabotage.

Only essential services shall be maintained when a specified fraction of facilities, defined by the IS Board, become inoperable.

All workloads shall be shifted geographically within the enterprise or to commercial providers as the need arises to meet emergencies. The IS Board shall specify how rapidly this must occur.

Software revisions for critical applications shall be subjected to an independent change management and control process that tracks all software change actions and monitors test results.

At least two independent levels of authorization shall be used for granting network access privileges to any software repository or for making software modifications in critical county applications.

Dual security access authorizations to confidential databases shall be required in all cases where the alteration of such databases would have severe consequences.

Multilevel security software and hardware shall permit the acquisition, display and manipulation of secure as well as open information in a single display, without compromising security.

Redundant network control centers and archival data repositories at fully protected sites shall be established and continually tested.

Data network services, including online data network diagnostic capabilities for local area networks, shall have the capacity to achieve rapid service restoration of local computing facilities from a remote site.

1.0 Information technology survey

The purpose of this document is to identify and qualify the elements required to develop a comprehensive infrastructure statement of direction for the selected Information Systems (IS) client.

Inherent to the completed statement of direction, a detailed and specific implementation plan, including alternatives and cost estimates will be included.

The Statement of Direction is a comprehensive report detailing the consensus design and support structure required to meet or exceed requirements. Detailed within the report are process and application dependencies and contingencies.

Detailed performance criteria for application, hardware, process, and support are also presented.

The Statement of Direction provides the framework to develop and implement a unified efficient and effective infrastructure support management business process.

1.1 Project management

IS will utilize a comprehensive project management methodology to manage and monitor the performance of this valuable service offering. This process will assure that both the client and IS are in concert and concur to all activities, milestones, problems, and progress associated with the successful completion of this project.

IS will assign a Project Leader to actively manage the performance and client communication associated with this service. The selected Project Leader will provide oral and documented progress reports to the responsible IS Agency Consultant overseeing the performance of this service.

In turn, as appropriate, the IS Agency Consultant will conduct a series of Phase Reviews with the client to communicate project status.

1.2 Scope of project

The scope of this project includes the acceptance of this proposal, an IS team to conduct the survey and gather the results, and a documented deliverable as to the results and recommendations of the survey.

This survey will be conducted through the following areas:

- Review (general client information)
- Transport an
- Client Information/Presentation
- Application Software Survey
- Staff Review

Note: Some of the information for the Data Facility Review and Application Software Survey may have already been collected or may be immediately available. This information should be given to the IS staff performing the survey before the survey begins.

Survey summary schedule

Survey Areas	Schedule Date
Client Information	
Transport/Presentation	
Application Survey	
Staff Review	

1.3 Project projections

During the project Implementation or initiation meeting the follow outlines should be completed. They will become part of the permanent record of the service. They will also allow IS and the client to plan personnel and other project events.

 C

Project time projections

	Start Phase	Complete Phase	Status Review
Client Information			
Transport & Pres.			
Application			
Staff Review			

Complete this projection outline and include in project status review meetings with the project team and the client. This information will become part of the final project report.

1.4 Project timetable

	Week 1	Week 2	Week 3	Week 4	Week 5	Week 6	Week 7	Week 8
Phase 4							Final	Report
Phase 3								
Phase 2								
Phase 1								

Project Management Process

Record of commitment (document schedule and all time commitments)

1.5 Project deliverables

The IS team performing this survey will gather observations and information for compilation and evaluation. Using the combined talent and experience of the customer and IS team, a set of recommendations will be prepared. The developed recommendations will be specific. The recommendations will include a list of activities, which may be followed by the client to accomplish the recommended actions.

For acceptance, all documents will be delivered to:

____

(name)

____

(Title)

1.6 Project utilities

Throughout the performance of the Technology Survey, a series of forms associated with the project will be employed. These forms provide the official communication between the IS Project Leader, the IS Agency Consultant, and the client Information Officer.

- Survey Initiation Meeting
- Enterprise Representative
- Current Operation Analysis
- Potential Benefit Analysis
- Change Request Form
- Status Report

1.6.1. Survey initiation meeting

General Information

Account Name ____________________Agency Consultant _______________

Date of Meeting ___________________Time ________________________

Location of Meeting ________________Project Leader __________________

IS Representatives

Name ___________________________Title __________________________

Name ___________________________Title __________________________

Name ___________________________Title __________________________

Name ___________________________Title __________________________

Name ___________________________Title __________________________

Account Representatives

Name ___________________________Title __________________________

Name ___________________________Title __________________________

Name ___________________________Title __________________________

Name ___________________________Title __________________________

Name ___________________________Title __________________________

Comments:

____

____

____

____

____

____

1.6.2. Enterprise Representatives

General Information

Account Name ____________________ Agency Consultant ________________

Information Officer __________________ Project Manager __________________

Start Date __________________________

Client Representatives

Name ____________________ Title ________________ Phone ___________

Name ____________________ Title ________________ Phone ___________

Name ____________________ Title ________________ Phone ___________

Name ____________________ Title ________________ Phone ___________

Name ____________________ Title ________________ Phone ___________

Name ____________________ Title ________________ Phone ___________

Name ____________________ Title ________________ Phone ___________

Name ____________________ Title ________________ Phone ___________

Name ____________________ Title ________________ Phone ___________

Name ____________________ Title ________________ Phone ___________

Name ____________________ Title ________________ Phone ___________

Name ____________________ Title ________________ Phone ___________

Name ____________________ Title ________________ Phone ___________

Name ____________________ Title ________________ Phone ___________

Name ____________________ Title ________________ Phone ___________

Name ____________________ Title ________________ Phone ___________

Name ____________________ Title ________________ Phone ___________

Name ____________________ Title ________________ Phone ___________

Name ____________________ Title ________________ Phone ___________

Name ____________________ Title ________________ Phone ___________

Comments:

____

____

____

____

Use additional copies of this form, as required

1.6.3. Current Operation

General Information

Account Name ____________________Agency Consultant ________________

Information Officer __________________Project Manager __________________

Start Date _________________________

Key Strengths and Weaknesses

____

____

____

____

____

Areas For Improvement

____

____

____

____

____

Documentation of Process

____

____

____

____

____

Management Costs and Control

____

____

____

____

____

Comments

____

____

____

____

Use additional copies of this form, as required

1.6.4. Potential benefits analysis

General information

Account Name ____________________ Location ____________________

Information Officer ________________ Start Date ____________________

Evaluation Completed ______________ Function ____________________

Agency Consultant ________________ Project Manager ______________

Cost Reduction Analysis

____

____

____

____

____

Productivity Enhancements

____

____

____

____

____

Control Improvements

____

____

____

____

____

Business Process Improvements

____

____

____

____

____

Comments

____

____

____

Use additional copies of this form, as required

1.6.5. Change request form

General Information

Account Name ____________________ Location ____________________

Agency Consultant ________________ Project Leader ________________

Request Initiated By: ______________ Change ID # ________________

Summary of Change ______________ Priority ____________________

Reason For Change

____

____

____

Scope of Proposed Change

____

____

____

Additional Information

____

____

____

Impact on Schedule and Fees

____

____

____

____

Agency Approval for ____________ By ________________________

IS Approved ________________ Date of Approval ______________

Comments

____

____

____

____

Use additional copies of this form, as required

1.6.6. Survey status report

Account Name ____________________Location ______________________

IS Agency Consultant _____________Project Leader __________________

Reporting Period: From ________To ________

Milestones Completed

____

____

____

Work in Progress

____

____

____

Change Orders

____

____

____

Problem Areas/Issues

____

____

____

Planned Activity/Milestones

____

____

____

Comments

____

____

Completed By: ___________________________ Date _____________________

Use additional copies of this form, as required

 C

2.0 Client information review

The following sections will be completed by IS with help from the customer. If the customer chooses to actively participate in this, and enter his or her own responses, please be sure that you read each Explanation section before proceeding to the Question section. Each Explanation section was written to help in providing specific responses to the questions listed.

The following sections contain important information that will assist you in accurately completing this questionnaire. Please read it prior to answering the questions.

In order to make accurate and meaningful comparisons across multiple agencies, it is necessary that we use a common format for collecting information. This may mean that the terminology or categories used by the questionnaire may be different from that which you normally use. Often times, the most time-consuming part of data collection is this "re-fitting" of your data into the standard model.

Please try to be as complete and accurate as possible. This may mean that you will need to collect data for areas outside of your area of responsibility should some of the IS function belong to a different group.

In some cases, you will be asked for information that either you do not collect or that is extremely difficult to obtain. In either of these cases, we ask that you use your best judgement and estimate the appropriate number.

You may want to contact your Agency Consultant for assistance. Any time that you estimate a number (other than when it is a future projection), please circle the entry on the form so that during the review session and during analysis, we will know that the number is an estimate.

2.1.1 General client information explanations

1. **Agency Name:**

   The full name of the agency.

2. **Agency Location (Main):**

   The location of the main office of the agency.

3. **Other Agency Locations:**

   The locations of branch offices of the agency.

4. **Date Completed:**

   The date that this profile was completed.

2.1.2 General client information questions:

Agency Name: ______________________________

Agency Location (Main): ______________________

Other Agency Locations: ______________________

____
____
____

Date Completed: ____________________________

Comments

____
____
____
____

2.2 IS/Customer information

Agency Contact

The name of the person at the agency that IS contacts.

Agency Contact Title

The title of the person listed above.

Agency Contact Phone Number

The telephone number of the person listed above.

Agency Contact Fax Number

The fax number of the person listed above.

Agency Back-up Contact

The name of the person at the agency that IS should contact when the primary contact is not available.

Agency Back-up Contact Title

The title of the person listed as the Agency Back-up Contact.

Agency Back-up Contact Phone Number

The telephone number of the person listed as the Agency Back-up Contact.

Agency Back-up Contact Fax Number

The fax number of the person listed as the Agency Back-up Contact.

IS Agency Consultant

The agency consultant from IS representing this account.

IS Agency Consultant Phone Number

The agency consultant's telephone number.

IS Agency Consultant Fax Number

The agency consultant's fax number.

 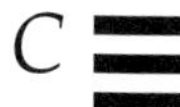

2.2.2 IS/Customer information questions

Agency Contact: ______________________________

Agency Contact Title: ___________________________

Agency Contact Phone Number: ____________________

Agency Contact Fax Number: ______________________

Agency Back-up Contact: ________________________

Agency Back-up Contact Title: ____________________

Agency Back-up Contact Phone Number: _____________

Agency Back-up Contact Fax Number: ______________

IS Agency Consultant: __________________________

IS Agency Consultant Phone Number: ______________

IS Agency Consultant Fax Number: ________________

Comments

____

____

____

____

____

____

2.3 Financial overview

IS operating expense for reporting year

Actual operating expense associated with IS for the reporting year. "Data Networks" includes all data communication costs associated with communications processors, modems, multiplexors, etc. "Voice Networks" includes all switches, phones, and voice software.

End-user/distributed systems includes all terminals, PC's, minicomputers, LANs, LAN servers, associated software costs and wiring, etc. Provide an estimate of costs if they are not known. These costs should include all annual expenses associated with IS, whether or not they were in the IS budget.

IS personnel for reporting year

Quantity of personnel resources associated with IS at the end of the Reporting Year in terms of Full Time Equivalents (FTE's). Estimate for end-user/distributed systems.

IS operating expense

Using the above definition of IS operating expense, provide annual IS expense for the two previous fiscal years (Reporting Yr-2 and Reporting Yr-1), the current Reporting Year (Reporting Year) and an estimate for the upcoming fiscal year (Reporting Year + 1).

IS personnel (FTE's)

Using the above definition of IS personnel, provide historical quantities of personnel resources associated with IS for Reporting Year - 2, Reporting Year - 1, Reporting Year, and an estimate for the upcoming fiscal year (Reporting Year + 1).

Number of users with system access

Number of people internal and external to the agency who have access to information processing systems (e.g., a user with three user IDs is counted once). Estimate for year-end of the Reporting Year (Reporting Year).

2.3.2 Financial overview questions

	IS Operating Expense for Reporting Year	IS Personnel (FTE's) for Reporting Year
Data Center:	__________	__________
Data Networks:	__________	__________
Voice Networks:	__________	__________
Applications:	__________	__________
End-User/Distributed Systems:	__________	__________
Other*:	__________	__________
Total IS:	__________	__________

*Other, please specify

____

____

____

Reporting Year –2Reporting Year - 1Reporting Year Reporting Year + 1

IS Operating

Expense:__________ __________ __________ __________

IS Personnel:__________ ____________________ __________

Number of users with system access: __________

Comments

____

____

____

____

____

____

____

____

____

3.0 General network information

Attended operation

Indicate the total number of hours per week that this network is attended (e.g. 7 days, 24 hours = 168).

End-user stations

Average number of end-user devices (e.g. PC's, workstations, terminals, and printers) at all local and remote locations connected to this network during the Reporting Year. Include devices connected through local controllers as well as those connected via multi-user machines (e.g. mini-computers). Exclude LAN attached devices. For dial-up lines, include the maximum possible simultaneous connections.

Number of remote agency locations

Total number of remote agency locations having end-user stations supported by this network during the Reporting Year. Do not include locations located with the data center providing their primary support. Also, provide the average number of non-LAN end-user devices (e.g. PC's, workstations, and terminals) connected through this network per remote location.

Help desks

Number of help desks directly and indirectly supporting this network during the Reporting Year. Include all levels of support for the network.

Average help desk calls per month

Average monthly number of help desk calls received by the help desks during the Reporting Year.

Help desk inquiries resolved on first call

Percent of network help desk calls that did not require any additional actions and were resolved during the initial conversation during the Reporting Year.

Rate of change

Expressed as a percent of change (during the Reporting Year) to the installed network devices or circuits.

3.1.2 General network information questions

Number of hours of attended operation per week: ________________

Number of end-user stations serviced by this network: ___________

Number of end-user connections added during the reporting year: ________

Number of remote agency locations supported by this network: ______

Average number of end-user devices per remote locations: _______

Number of helps desks supporting this network: ____________

Average number of help desk calls per month for this network: _______

Network help desk inquiries resolved on first call: __________________%

What is the rate of change to the network?: _______________________%

Comments

____

____

____

____

____

____

____

____

____

3.2 Network volume

Network volume monitoring

Indicate whether network traffic is measured, estimated, or not tracked and indicate what percent.

Number of characters transmitted

Average total number of characters transmitted per second from one user location to another over backbone and/or secondary network links during the Reporting Year (Reporting Year), the prior year (Reporting Year -1), two years prior to the Reporting Year (Reporting Year - 2), and an estimate of the year after the Reporting Year (Reporting Year + 1). Include "overhead" characters.

Percentages

Estimate the percentage of network traffic in the reporting year and in the following year that is image and video conferencing data.

3.2.2 Network volume questions:

Are volumes of transmitted characters (Check only one):

- Measured: _____
- Estimated: _____
- Not tracked: _____

What percent of the network traffic is measured or estimated?: ___%

Reporting Year - 2Reporting Year - 1 Reporting YearReporting Year + 1

Characters

Transmitted Per

Second: ________________________________

% of Network Traffic From

Imaging: ________________

% of Network Traffic from Video

Conferencing:________________

3.3 Network monitoring

Line availability

Indicate whether network availability is monitored and what tools (hardware and/or software) are used.

Line utilization

Indicate whether network utilization is monitored and what tools (hardware and/or software) are used.

Line response time

Indicate whether network response time is monitored and what tools (hardware and/or software) are used.

Mean time to failure

Indicate whether mean time to failure is calculated and measured.

Mean time to repair

Indicate whether mean time to repair is calculated and measured.

3.3.2 Network monitoring questions

Is line availability monitored? (Y/N) _____

What availability monitoring tools are used? ______________

____

Is line utilization measured? (Y/N) _____

What utilization monitoring tools are used? ____

Is line response time measured? (Y/N) _____

What response monitoring tools are used? ________________

____

Do you calculate and measure:

Mean time to failure? (Y/N) ___ Mean time to repair? (Y/N) ___

3.4 Backbone and secondary monitoring

Backbone/secondary

Indicate if the responses apply to the backbone or secondary data networks.

Physical lines

Indicate the number of physical lines in the backbone and secondary networks.

Availability

Indicate the average availability of the lines in the backbone and secondary networks.

Utilization

Indicate the average percent utilization of the lines.

Response Time

Indicate the average network response time (in seconds).

3.4.2 Backbone and secondary monitoring questions

	Backbone	Secondary
Number of physical lines:	________	________
Availability:	________	________
Utilization:	________	________
Response Time:	________	________

Comments

____

____

____

____

____

____

3.5 Network technologies

Technologies

Indicate (Yes or No) whether or not the network employs the technologies listed.

Line failure recovery

Provide the percent of lines that have automatic line recovery capabilities.

Line failure backup

Provide the percent of circuits that are equipped with redundant automatic switching.

Dynamic circuit rerouting

Provide the percent of circuits that are automatically rerouted on detection of primary link failure.

3.5.2 Network technologies questions

Does the network employ the following technologies? (Y/N):

	Rapt. Year	Planned For	Reporting Year + 1
Radio	______	______	______
Cellular	______	______	______
Satellite	______	______	______
Microwave	______	______	______

Indicate the percentage of physical lines for which the following features have been automated:

Line Failure Recovery: ______%

Line Failure Backup: ______%

Dynamic Circuit Rerouting: ______%

Comments

____

____

____

____

3.6 Network financial

Data networking expense

Provide the cost for data network(s) under study for the Reporting Year (Reporting Year), the prior year (Reporting Year - 1), and two years prior to the Reporting Year (Reporting Year - 2). Provide the amount budgeted for data networks for the next Reporting Year (Reporting Year + 1).

Assets

Total data network assets reported by the company for the Reporting Year.

3.6.2 Network financial questions

Reporting Year - 2Reporting Year - 1Reporting Year Reporting_Year + 1

Data networking expense:____________________________________

Assets (Current book value):__________

Comments

____

____

____

____

____

____

____

____

____

____

____

3.7 Network personnel function

Indicate organization responsible for the following (may be a combination — if in-house or IS, check the appropriate column — if outsourced, enter vendor).

	In-House	IS	Other
Network Operations-Procedures:			
Performance Monitoring:			
Security Administration:			
Problem Management:			
Change Management:			
Business Recovery:			
Vendor Management:			
Asset Management:			
Configuration Management:			
Help Desk Support:			
Systems Operation-Maintenance:			
Service Requests:			
Hardware & Software Support:			
Backups:			
Inventory Control:			
Training:			
Documentation:			
Network Design & Modeling:			
Capacity-Technology Planning:			
Strategic Planning:			
Billing:			
Reporting:			
Other Financial:			
Staff Support:			
Server Administration:			

Comments

4.0 Data facility review

Complete this form for each server, identify the following:

Number of Nodes:________________________________

Agency Department ______________________________

Network Operating System: _________________________

Access Method: ______________________________
Method:____

Function: ______________________________________

For each server, identify the following:

Server Name: ___________________________________

Server Type: ____________________________________

Server Address: __________________________________

Server Operating System: ____________ Version: ________

Server License Count: _____________________________

Total Connections: ________________________________

Server Location: _______ Floor: _______ Room: _______

Make/Model: __________ CPUs: _______ RAM: ________

Disk space: ____ Raid Level: ___

Server Administration: _____________________________

Trained Personnel ________________________________

Tape Format: ___________________________________

NIC Model: _____________________________________

Frame Type: ____________________________________

IPX Net Number: _________________________________

Backup Hardware: ________________________________

Backup Software: ________________________________

Optional/Other Features (Indicate Option, Model, S/W, Quantity):

____

Comments

____

____

____

4.2 Workstation breakdown

Current:	Planned FY_____
286:_____	286: _____
386: _____	386: _____
486:_____	486: _____
Pentium: _____	Pentium _____
Pentium II: _____	Pentium II: _____
Mac:_____	Mac _____
Unix:_____	Unix: _____
Other:_____	Other: _____

Desktop Licensed Applications:

Application	Version	License Count
______________	_____	_________
______________	_____	_________
______________	_____	_________
______________	_____	_________
______________	_____	_________
______________	_____	_________
______________	_____	_________
______________	_____	_________
______________	_____	_________
______________	_____	_________
______________	_____	_________
______________	_____	_________
______________	_____	_________
______________	_____	_________

Comments

____

____

____

4.3 Applications by server summary

Summarize the existing application deployment and relate the application to the operating system or Host connectivity. This information will serve as a master sheet for problem determination and network management. *Provide data for each server.*

App name	Database	Network protocol	Access Device/OS	Critical app?	Vendor or internal?	App owner

Table 14-9 *Please use additional copies as required to represent the entire application population.*

4.4 Hardware inventory by location

Current Equipment and Software as of ____________ (Date of Survey)

Survey Completed By: ______________________________

Include those items that have been purchased as of the Survey Date. This survey must be done per agency location.

Equipment	Quantity Loc 1	Loc 2	Loc 3
	_____	_____	_____
Computers:	_____	_____	_____
286:	_____	_____	_____
386:	_____	_____	_____
486:	_____	_____	_____

	Pentium:	____	____	____
	Pentium II	____	____	____
	Laptop:	____	____	____
	Fax:	____	____	____
	VRU:	____	____	____
	Wireless:	____	____	____
	Other (List):			
	________	____	____	____
	________	____	____	____
	________	____	____	____

Database	Application	Loc 1	Loc 2	Loc 3
________	____________	____	____	____
________	____________	____	____	____
________	____________	____	____	____
________	____________	____	____	____
________	____________	____	____	____
________	____________	____	____	____
________	____________	____	____	____

Comments

____

____

____

____

____

____

____

____

____

Use additional sheets to reflect entire inventory

4.5 Peripheral equipment by location:

Equipment	Quantity				
	Loc 1	Loc 2	Loc 3	Loc 4	Loc 5
	______	______	______	______	______
Modems - Type:					
__________	______	______	______	______	______
__________	______	______	______	______	______
__________	______	______	______	______	______
__________	______	______	______	______	______
CD-ROM:					
__________	______	______	______	______	______
__________	______	______	______	______	______
__________	______	______	______	______	______
__________	______	______	______	______	______
Printers - Type	Color Y/N				
__________	______	______	______	______	______
__________	______	______	______	______	______
__________	______	______	______	______	______
__________	______	______	______	______	______
__________	______	______	______	______	______
Other Equipment. - Specify:					
__________	______	______	______	______	______
__________	______	______	______	______	______
__________	______	______	______	______	______
__________	______	______	______	______	______
__________	______	______	______	______	______

Use additional sheets to complete the inventory, if required

Comments

____

____

____

5.0 Applications review

5.1 Application software: Generic — server

For this portion of the application software survey, indicate only generic software packages used by the agency (i.e. Windows, WordPerfect — not direct business-related packages). Enter the software name and version (if applicable).

Server ____________________ Location __________________

Software Name __________________ Version ________________________

QuantityLoc 1 __________ Loc 2 __________

Loc 3 __________ Loc 4 __________

Comment ____

Software Name __________________ Version ________________________

QuantityLoc 1 __________ Loc 2 __________

Loc 3 __________ Loc 4 __________

Comment ____

Software Name __________________ Version ________________________

QuantityLoc 1 __________ Loc 2 __________

Loc 3 __________ Loc 4 __________

Comment ____

Software Name __________________ Version ________________________

QuantityLoc 1 __________ Loc 2 __________

Loc 3 __________ Loc 4 __________

Comment ____

Software Name __________________ Version ________________________

QuantityLoc 1 __________ Loc 2 __________

Loc 3 __________ Loc 4 __________

Comment ____

Please use additional sheets to fully reflect the generic software

Comments

____

____

5.2 Application software: Generic — desktop

For this portion of the application software survey, indicate only generic software packages used by the agency (i.e., Windows, WordPerfect - not direct business-related packages). Enter the software name and version (if applicable).

Server ____________________Location __________________

Software Name __________________ Version ________________________

QuantityLoc 1 __________Loc 2 __________

Loc 3 __________Loc 4 __________

Comment ____

Software Name __________________ Version ________________________

QuantityLoc 1 __________Loc 2 __________

Loc 3 __________Loc 4 __________

Comment ____

Software Name __________________ Version ________________________

QuantityLoc 1 __________Loc 2 __________

Loc 3 __________Loc 4 __________

Comment ____

Software Name __________________ Version ________________________

QuantityLoc 1 __________Loc 2 __________

Loc 3 __________Loc 4 __________

Comment ____

Software Name __________________ Version ________________________

QuantityLoc 1 __________Loc 2 __________

Loc 3 __________Loc 4 __________

Comment ____

Please use additional sheets to fully reflect the generic software

Comments

____

____

____

5.3 Application software: Business — server

For this portion of the application software survey, indicate only ***direct business-related software packages***. Enter the software name and version number (if applicable). Ensure all in-house systems are entered. Use abbreviations where applicable, and provide a brief explanation.

Server ____________________ Location __________________

Software Name __________________ Version ________________________

QuantityLoc 1 __________ Loc 2 __________

Loc 3 __________ Loc 4 __________

Comment ____

Software Name __________________ Version ________________________

QuantityLoc 1 __________ Loc 2 __________

Loc 3 __________ Loc 4 __________

Comment ____

Software Name __________________ Version ________________________

QuantityLoc 1 __________ Loc 2 __________

Loc 3 __________ Loc 4 __________

Comment ____

Software Name __________________ Version ________________________

QuantityLoc 1 __________ Loc 2 __________

Loc 3 __________ Loc 4 __________

Comment ____

Software Name __________________ Version ________________________

QuantityLoc 1 __________ Loc 2 __________

Loc 3 __________ Loc 4 __________

Comment ____

Please use additional sheets to fully reflect the generic software

Comments

____

____

5.4 Application software: Business — desktop

For this portion of the application software survey, indicate only ***direct business-related software packages***. Enter the software name and version number (if applicable). Ensure all in-house systems are entered. Use abbreviations where applicable, and provide a brief explanation.

Server ____________________ Location __________________

Software Name __________________ Version ________________________

QuantityLoc 1 __________ Loc 2 __________

Loc 3 __________ Loc 4 __________

Comment ____

Software Name __________________ Version ________________________

QuantityLoc 1 __________ Loc 2 __________

Loc 3 __________ Loc 4 __________

Comment ____

Software Name __________________ Version ________________________

QuantityLoc 1 __________ Loc 2 __________

Loc 3 __________ Loc 4 __________

Comment ____

Software Name __________________ Version ________________________

QuantityLoc 1 __________ Loc 2 __________

Loc 3 __________ Loc 4 __________

Comment ____

Software Name __________________ Version ________________________

QuantityLoc 1 __________ Loc 2 __________

Loc 3 __________ Loc 4 __________

Comment ____

Please use additional sheets to fully reflect the generic software

Comments

____

____

5.5 Strategic or critical applications — server

For this portion of the Application Software Survey, indicate the appropriate applications that are considered Strategic or Critical. Of these applications, indicate ongoing support, disaster recovery, and date/year sensitivity (Y2K).

Strategic or critical applications — server ____________

Location __________

Application Name ____

Supplier (Owner) ____

Platform ____

Language ____

Disaster Backup ____

Date/Year ____

Comment: ____

Strategic or critical applications — Server __________

Location ________

Application Name ____

Supplier (Owner) ____

Platform ____

Language ____

Disaster Backup ____

Date/Year ____

Comment: ____

Strategic or critical applications — Server __________

Location ________

Application Name ____

Supplier (Owner) ____

Platform ____

Language ____

Disaster Backup ____

Date/Year ____

 C

Strategic or critical applications — Server __________

Location ________

Application Name ____

Supplier (Owner) ____

Platform ____

Language ____

Disaster Backup ____

Date/Year ____

Comment: ____

Strategic or critical applications — Server __________

Location ________

Application Name ____

Supplier (Owner) ____

Platform ____

Language ____

Disaster Backup ____

Date/Year ____

Comment: ____

Comment

____

____

____

____

Use additional sheets to complete the strategic — critical summary.

5.6 Strategic or critical applications — desktop

For this portion of the Application Software Survey, indicate the appropriate applications that are considered Strategic or Critical. Of these applications, indicate ongoing support, disaster recovery, and date/year sensitivity (Y2K).

Strategic or critical applications — desktop ____________

Location __________

Application Name ____

Supplier (Owner) ____

Platform ____

Language ____

Disaster Backup ____

Date/Year ____

Comment: ____

Strategic or critical applications — desktop __________

Location ________

Application Name ____

Supplier (Owner) ____

Platform ____

Language ____

Disaster Backup ____

Date/Year ____

Comment: ____

Strategic or critical applications — desktop __________

Location ________

Application Name ____

Supplier (Owner) ____

Platform ____

Language ____

Disaster Backup ____

Date/Year ____

Strategic or critical applications — desktop __________

Location ________

Application Name ____

Supplier (Owner) ____

Platform ____

Language ____

Disaster Backup ____

Date/Year ____

Comment: ____

Strategic or critical applications — desktop __________

Location ________

Application Name ____

Supplier (Owner) ____

Platform ____

Language ____

Disaster Backup ____

Date/Year ____

Comment: ____

Comment

____

____

____

____

Use additional sheets to complete the strategic — critical summary.

6.0 Staff review

A technical staff review will be done for all IS personnel. This review consists of several parts: a questionnaire on technical skills, an interview of each staff member, and then recommendations as to training skills needed.

On the questionnaire, each staff member will be required to provide the following:

1. **Languages, databases, applications, operating systems and hardware**
   - Indicate (from a selection menu) all of the items above that the staff has experience with, as well as the level of experience.
2. **Functional network experience**
   - Indicate the level of experience with network functions (i.e., add NetWare users, add LAN workplace users, configure file servers, etc.).
3. **Indicate the level of experience in:**
   - Project Management
   - Network Operating Systems
   - Network Components
   - Network Management
   - Standards
   - Protocols
   - Network Infrastructure
   - Wiring Schemes
   - Network Monitoring
   - Backup
   - Topologies
   - Certifications
   - Methodologies
   - Development Tools

7.0 Glossary of terms

Application Software

Examples are word processing software, spreadsheet software, and e-mail.

Chameleon

Name of software that enables users to access Enterprise Parallel Server resources and services via TCP/IP protocol. Alternative to gateway. Also able to directly transfer files from one IP address (PC/Printer/Server) to another via TCP/IP protocol.

Client/Server Network

A computing environment where end user workstations (clients) are connected to a LAN server(s) and possibly to mainframe superservers.

Enterprise Parallel Server

More efficient, smaller and cost effective replacement for the IBM 3090 Mainframe. Provides resources and services to end user (PROFS, LGFS, and HRMS).

Gateway

Alternative method to access mainframe (instead of Chameleon).

GUI

Graphical User Interface — Pictures and boxes to make it easy for a user to do tasks (e.g. icons in Windows).

Hardware

Physical equipment (printers, modems, etc.) as opposed to software (computer programs or applications using code).

IP Address

Specific address that allows data to be sent and received from another IP address.

LAN

Local Area Network — A communications network that typically connects computers, terminals, and other computerized devices within a limited physical areas such as an office, building or other worksite.

Network

An interconnected system of computers, terminals and communications channels and devices. A backbone network is defined as the data network nodes and the connections between them. The secondary network consists of those lines linking backbone data network nodes to remote sites.

Node

Your PC. A terminal point in a communications network.

Server

A computer that supports telecommunications in a local area network, as well as the sharing of peripheral devices, software and databases among the workstations in the network.

TCP/IP

The method by which data is communicated throughout the wide area network.

WAN

Wide Area Network — A data communications network covering a large geographic area.

8.0 Sign-off of survey proposal

I have read the preceding IS Survey Proposal, and am in agreement with the scope and deliverables as outlined in this proposal.

____

Name

____

Title

____

Agency

____

Date

Appendix: Sample service-level agreement

D 

The move to chargeback is gaining momentum. Chargeback provides the internal economics to match supply and demand. Chargeback also empowers customers and provides service metrics for IS departments. Chargeback requires a Service Level Agreement (SLA) to act as a contract between IS and its customers. We enclose this SLA as an example of how one IS organization defines its relationship with it's customers.

Enterprise costs

Enterprise costs are fixed costs to sustain general operations. These charges provide for the support of connectivity, operation and maintenance of the County's Enterprise network.

Enterprise Servers provide services to more that one customer. Enterprise Servers are those servers registered as of the fiscal year when the budget is approved. Servers not registered are defined as departmental servers and their support is billable at the standard Professional Services rate.

New equipment purchases planned for FY 96/97 will need to be projected on the SLA. This will provide ISS with information for staffing. New equipment that is not presented in the SLA will be charged a professional services fee to cover all cabling, hardware, software, and installation costs. In addition, a 1% per month charge for the value of equipment to cover the cost of non-budgeted resources will be assessed.

Professional services

Professional Services costs are charges that are incurred for services provided by ISS such as application services, training, desktop support, etc. ISS charges a competitive cost recovery rate, approved by the ISS Board, of $40 per hour for services.

Service level agreement

ISS services for *CUSTOMER NAME*

fiscal year 199x/199y

This Agreement made as of the First day of *MONTH, 199X*, by and among County, a Political Subdivision of the State of Florida, by and through its Board of County Commissioners, the ISS Board, and ***CUSTOMER NAME*** , a [pick one of the following. Constitutional Officer, Agency of the State of Florida, or other appropriate identification].

Whereas the County Board of County Commissioners (the County) by resolution No. 92-324 established the Information Systems Services Department (ISS) and the ISS Board, under which information systems services are being provided to those departments of County responsible to the Board of County Commissioners and to various other Governmental Officers and Agencies (hereinafter sometimes referred to as the "Customer" or "Customers"); and

Whereas the County has directed ISS to establish written Agreements with each Customer in order to better define the relationships between ISS and each of its Customers,

Therefore, the parties mutually agree to the following:

1. The ISS Services to be provided to the Customer and respective obligations of the parties shall be in accordance with the terms of the ISS Service Level Agreement for Governmental Customers thereto dated for fiscal years 1996/97 which has been prepared specifically for this Customer and which are incorporated herein.
2. This agreement shall be in effect for the one year period beginning October 1, 1996 and ending the following September 30, 1997. Customer may terminate this Agreement upon nine months written notice to the ISS Board.
3. Changes to this Agreement can be made by written Amendment signed by all parties.
4. The parties agree to conduct negotiations for a successor agreement for the following fiscal year 1997/1998 in sufficient time to meet County and Customer budgeting schedules.
5. The Customer will appoint an Information Services Officer in accordance with the Governance Policies. The Information Services Officer title is a working title. An individual performing this function will collaborate with ISS representatives to ensure the success of all projects. The Information Services Officer does not need to have an information systems background. It is imperative that this individual has extensive knowledge of the

customer's information needs and business practices. The Information Services Officer will be the primary liaison with the Agency Consultant. The Information Services Officer will maintain a list of critical applications and prioritize other applications for service by ISS.

6. All Customer hardware and software interfacing with the county-wide enterprise network shall be compatible with the system and operating standards established for the county wide network in accordance with the Palm Beach County ISS Governance Policies thereto dated July 22, 1995. Software, database management, and operating systems installed on servers owned by the customers, must be kept at the version levels specified by ISS.
7. The Customer will pay the County in two budget cost categories; Enterprise and Professional Services for a total sum of $ ***ANNUAL BUDGET***. These costs are:
   a. Enterprise Services cost for the amount of $ ***ENTERPRISE BUDGET***. Payments shall be due and made monthly in twelve equal installments of $ *** 1/12 of ENTERPRISE BUDGET***.
   b. The Professional Services cost for the amount of $ ***PROFESSIONAL BUDGET***. Payments shall be due and made monthly for services rendered. Interest charges incurred by ISS to fund its operation as a result of delinquent Customer payments will be billed directly to the Customer.

This Agreement shall become effective, as of the date written above upon execution by all of the parties.

(Signatures)

I. Purpose

The purpose of this Agreement is to define the services provided to the Customer by County Information Systems Services (ISS). These services are provided at the rates approved by the ISS Board.

II. Customer service requests

ISS uses a Customer Service Request (CSR) system to manage requests for services from its customers. This is an automated system available through the Enterprise network.

ISS customers enter all requests for services into the CSR tracking system. Once entered, a production date and project schedule are negotiated between the customer and ISS.

III. Status reporting

Project status is communicated through ISS Consulting Services. This occurs through meetings, telephone conversations, memorandums, E-mail, etc. On a monthly basis, ISS provides management reports to assist in tracking project activity. These reports detail both activity status and their associated costs.

IV. Solution Center

ISS Solution Center services is the first line customer support for the reporting of hardware and software problems. Problems are recorded in a Problem and Change Management system to facilitate problem resolution. The Solution Center telephone number is 355-HELP.

ISS Solution Center escalation and notification matrix — Severity level

1. Failure of server/router/cabling that effects more that one department.
   Response: Immediate
   60 minutes - first escalation
   4 hours - second escalation
2. Failure of server/hub/cabling/that effects entire department of more than three users.
   Response: Immediate
   2 hours - first escalation
   8 hours - second escalation
3. Failure of PC/cable segment that effects three or fewer users.
   Response: Immediate
   24 hours - first escalation
   48 hours - second escalation
4. Non-priority issues.
   Response: Immediate
   7 days - first escalation

V. Services

ISS offers a complete range of information system services. These services are customer business driven and are matched to the appropriate technology. Listed below are some of the Enterprise and Professional Services offered by ISS.

Enterprise services

Enterprise services encompass the countywide network, servers, and services.

- Documents on demand (one-time setup charge)
- Production application processing
- Problem and change management

- Business recovery services
- Enterprise printing
- Price agreement checking
- Printing and post processing services
- Purchase requisition reviews
- Public data access
- Microfilm / Microfiche (one-time set-up charge)
- Network software license registration (Chameleon, Oracle, NetWare, Unix, NT, etc.)
- Network software distribution
- Enterprise On-line data storage
- Support for GroupWise, cc:Mail[1] and PROFS E-mail
- Report distribution bundling
- System performance
- System monitoring
- Security
- Integration into the County's wide area network (WAN)
- Wide area network performance monitoring and tuning
- Internet access

Professional services

Professional Services costs are charges that are incurred for services provided by ISS over and above the Enterprise countywide services. Services may be selected from the following:

- Project management
- Planning, research, and technical review services
- Enterprise modeling
- Strategic planning
    - Business analysis
    - Software recommendation

1. * PROFS and cc:Mail will be phased out by September 30, 1997.

- Requests for proposal (RFP)
- Systems analysis, design and development
- Implementation of purchase/package software
- Software training
- Off-site data storage
- Installation and support of office automation services
- Application development
- Application maintenance after warranty period expires
- Form design and maintenance
- Server installation and administrative support (non Enterprise)
- System and network analysis, capacity and performance planning
- GIS support (scope defined by each customer)
- Installation of direct or remote devices
- Paper reduction services (i.e., Documents on Demand (DOD), report archival and retrieval)
- Document imaging (scope defined by each customer)
- Unplanned integration into the County's wide area network (WAN)
- Internet Web page design and integration

VI. Professional services

Based on a Professional Services annual budget of **$XXXXXX.XX**; billing for these allocated ISS resources is monthly on an "as-consumed" basis.

VII. Software portfolio

ISS will provide the Customer with an inventory of current applications that are supported. Support for applications that are not on the currently supported inventory will be negotiated. The Customer's information manager will identify any maintenance needs, upgrades, and re-engineering for these applications to be included in the budget for the fiscal year.

VIII. Inventory list

ISS will use an inventory list of terminals, PCs, and peripherals provided by the County's Asset Management System.

IX. Servers

Servers that are attached to the Enterprise Network will be maintained at the same software version levels specified by ISS. Database software must be maintained at the appropriate level to be compatible with the Enterprise network. A system management plan will be established to identify the system manager and the database administrator responsibilities, for each server. It will be the responsibility of the information manager to prepare the plan for servers that are controlled by the customer.

X. Millennium

Any applications that are not scheduled for completion of migration by 1998 will need to be reviewed for two digit year and algorithm issues occurring due to the change of century. Each customer will allocate the needed budget dollars to complete one-half of the required year 2000 changes during fiscal cycle 1996-1997.

XI. Area code

Because of the recent area code change (407 to 561), applications may have to be modified. Applications needing modification must be completed by April 30, 1997.

XII. GroupWise

GroupWise is the product selected by a countywide committee to be the electronic mail standard. Customers will need to budget for this product. It is intended that PROFS and cc:Mail will be shut down by September 30, 1997. Those Customers remaining on PROFS after October 1, 1997 will be billed directly for its operation in addition to their Enterprise charges.

XIII. Training

ISS publishes a list of training courses that are offered by Customer Services. The customer will need to identify their training needs for the fiscal year.

XIV. Performance measurements

Customer Service Request (CSR) completion dates will be negotiated among the Customer, Service Manager, staff member actually performing the work, and the Agency Consultant.

Once the completion date is established, the staff member performing the work will be responsible for completing the work. In the event that circumstances beyond the control of the employee or ISS result in a delay, the staff member and the Agency Consultant will meet and discuss the situation with the customer. ISS will maintain an appropriate level of response and system up time for the Enterprise network. Performance will be measured against industry standards. Additional performance measures requested by a customer will be submitted to the ISS Policy Board for review and approval.

XV. Projected purchase of PC's, printers, etc.

The customer will provide a projection of new hardware and software. Anything in addition to this list will be subject to additional costs for installation service and support.

XVI. Projected requirements for network connectivity.

The customer will identify in their SLA any new locations that will need to be connected to the Enterprise network. New equipment that is not presented in the SLA will be charged a professional services fee to cover all cabling, hardware, software, and installation costs. In addition, a 1% per month charge for the value of new equipment to cover the cost of non-budgeted resources will be assessed.

XVII. Products supported by ISS

ISS publishes a list of products supported and services offered as part of the Enterprise network.

XVIII. Professional services options (attachment)

The following attachment provides a list of planned activities for the upcoming fiscal year. It is intended that ISS act on these projects during the year and in the periods specified for each project. Customer projects noted below will be initiated as directed by the Information Services Officer, with available funding and available ISS resources.

Appendix: Sample security standards & guidelines manual

The ability of the County to deliver services to its citizens has grown enormously using computers. The County has significant investments in information resources. While the value of equipment such as computer hardware is easily appreciated, we must not overlook the larger investment that the County and taxpayers have in less tangible information assets such as data, software, and automated processes.

Information resources are vital County assets that require protection. Data, whether stored in central computers accessible through remote terminals, processed locally on microcomputers, or generated by word processing systems, is vulnerable to a variety of threats and must be afforded adequate safeguards.

Employees need to be aware of the value of these resources and the means of protecting them. User awareness through education is the first line of defense in maintaining confidentiality, reliability, availability, and integrity of County information resources.

The Information Resource Security Standards and Guidelines were developed to assist in the education of employees in the need for and means of protecting the County's information resources. This document should be useful in ongoing departmental security programs for security awareness and training.

The security standards and guidelines in this document specify management and administrative controls adopted by the Information Systems and Services Board and Board of County Commissioners. This document will define County security procedures as addressed in the Governance Policies, which should be applicable to most departments.

Departments requiring information security assistance should contact their departmental business unit Information Officer or the Consulting Services staff of Information Systems Services (ISS).

1.0 General policies, applicability, and responsibilities

1.1 Background and purpose

(a) The County has relied on the application of computer-based systems for the efficient and effective management of complex governmental operations. Rapid and continuing technical advances in information processing have increased the dependence of County departments on information and automated systems. The value of County data and software, in terms of restoration costs or losses due to unauthorized disclosure, far exceeds the value of its associated hardware. For that reason, information processed by computers must be recognized as a major County asset and be protected accordingly.

(b) The purpose of the Countywide Information Resource Security Standards and Guidelines is to:

1. Promulgate the County's Governance Policies regarding the security of data and information technology resources. The policies that are established in this document are broad principles, generic to all platforms and form the basis of the County's information security program.
2. Define minimum-security standards for the protection of County information resources. Standards presented are required administrative procedures or management controls, which are to be implemented, communicated and monitored.
3. Provide optional guidelines to assist County departments in the implementation and interpretation of standards, and to recommend effective security practices, which should be consideration for implementation by departmental management.
4. Provide a compilation of information security material in support of departmental security awareness and training programs.

1.2 Policy

It is the policy of the County that:

(a) County data is a valuable asset and must be protected from unauthorized modification, destruction, or disclosure, whether accidental or intentional. The protection of assets is a function of all information technology users.

(b) Access to County information resources must be strictly controlled. County information resources must be used only for official County purposes, including public access per the Public Records Act.

(c) Information that, by law, is sensitive or confidential must be protected from unauthorized access or modification. Data that is essential to critical County functions must be protected from loss, contamination, or destruction.

(d) Risks to information resources must be managed. The expense of security safeguards must be appropriate to the value of the assets being protected, considering value to both the County and a potential intruder.

(e) The integrity of data, its source, its destination, and processes applied to it must be assured. Data must change only in authorized, predictable, and acceptable ways.

(f) In the event a disruption of information processing or related telecommunication functions, the ability to continue critical governmental services must be assured. Information resources must be available when needed, or an alternate operational business plan must be developed by departments.

(g) Security needs must be considered and addressed in all phases of development or acquisition of new information processing systems.

(h) Security awareness and training of employees is one of the most effective means of reducing vulnerability to errors and fraud and must be continually emphasized and reinforced at all staff levels. Management must insure that each individual be accountable for his/her actions relating to information resources.

(I) County departmental information security programs must be reviewed to insure responsiveness and adaptable to changing vulnerabilities and technologies affecting County information resources.

(j) The County should support and uphold the legitimate proprietary interests of intellectual property holders. The copyright laws of all information technology will be observed by all County personnel.

(k) All County data shall be backed up to tape storage or an equivalent.

1.3 Applicability

(a) Information security policies and standards apply to all County departments. They apply to County automated information systems which access, process, or have custody of data. They apply to mainframe, minicomputer, microcomputer, distributed processing, and client/server networking environments of the County. They apply equally to all levels of management and to the personnel they supervise.

(b) County information security policies and standards apply to information resources owned by others, such as political subdivisions of the County, elected officials, or departments of the state and federal government. This includes cases where the County has a contractual or fiduciary duty to protect the resources while in the custody of the County.

1.4 Definitions

Access

To approach, view, instruct, communicate with, store data in, retrieve data from, or otherwise make use of computers or information resources.

Access control

The enforcement of specified authorization rules based on positive identification of users and the systems or data they are permitted to access, per the Public Record Act.

Access password

A password used to authorize access to data and distributed to all those who are authorized similar access.

Authentication

The process that verifies the claimed identity of a station, originator, or individual as established by an identification process.

Authorization

A positive determination by the owner of an information resource that a specific individual may access that information resource, or validation that a positively identified user has the need and the owner's permission to access the resource.

Business Unit(s)

An agency, department, division, group, unit or organization under the control of the Board of County Commissioners.

Central Computer Room

A facility dedicated to housing significant computing resources, such as parallel computers and facilities; commonly referred to as a data center.

Confidential information

See sensitive information.

County

Includes all departments under the the County Board of Commissioners, elected officials and anyone using their information resources.

Confidentiality

The state that exists when sensitive information is held in confidence and available only to a limited set of authorized individuals.

Critical information resource

That resource determined by department management to be essential to the department's critical mission and functions, the loss of which would have an unacceptable impact.

Custodian of an information resource

Guardian or caretaker, the holder of data; the agent charged with the resource owner's requirements for processing, telecommunications, protection controls, and output distribution for the resource. The custodian is normally a provider of services.

Data

A representation of facts or concepts in an organized manner in order that it may be stored, communicated, interpreted, or processed by automated means.

DAS

Database Administration Services.

DBMS

Data Base Management Systems.

Data integrity

The state that exists when computerized information is predictably related to its source and has been subjected to only those processes that have been authorized by the appropriate personnel.

Data security or computer security

Those measures, procedures, or controls which provide an acceptable degree of safety of information resources from accidental or intentional disclosure, modification, or destruction.

Data security administrator, or security officer

The person charged with monitoring and implementing security controls and procedures for a system. Whereas each County department and constitutional organization (business unit) shall appoint a business unit information officer with responsibility for that department's information management security, department management may designate a number of data security administrators.

Department(s)

Individual business units, divisions, groups and organizations under the control of the the County Board of Commissioners, agencies and elected officials.

Disclosure

Unauthorized access to confidential or sensitive information.

Elected Officials

Such as the Tax Collector, Property Appraiser, etc.

ECS

ISS Enterprise Center Services.

Encryption

The process of cryptographically converting plain text electronic data into a form unintelligible to anyone except the intended recipient.

Exposure

Vulnerability to loss resulting from accidental or intentional disclosure, modification, or destruction of information resources.

FIPS PUB

Federal Information Processing Standard Publication, a federal standard issued by the National Institute of Science and Technology (formerly the National Bureau of Standards).

Governance Policies

Policies directing the consistent and cohesive approach to the acquisition, implementation and support of information technology in the County.

Information resources

Data, automated applications, and information technology resources.

Information Officer (business unit)

A responsibility designated by the department head to administer the department's information security program in accordance with County policies, and the department's internal and external point of contact for all information security matters.

ISS

Information Systems Services.

Information Resources

Information processing hardware, software, and services, supplies, personnel, facility resources, maintenance, training, or other related resources.

NAS

Network Administration Services.

Owner of an information resource

The manager or agent responsible for the function that is supported by the County information resources.

Password

A protected word or string of characters which serves as authentication of a person's identity (personal password), or which may be used to grant or deny access to private or shared data (access password).

Personal identifier or user identification code

A data item associated with a specific individual which represents the identity of that individual and may be known by other individuals.

Personal password

A password that is known by only one person and is used to authenticate that person's identity.

Public Records Act

Section 119.07(l), Florida Statutes.

Risk

The likelihood or probability that a loss of information resources or breach of security will occur.

Risk analysis

An evaluation of system assets and their vulnerabilities to threats. Risk analysis estimates potential losses that may result from threats.

Risk management

Decisions to accept exposure or to reduce vulnerabilities by either mitigating the risks or applying cost effective controls.

Security controls

Hardware, programs, procedures, policies, and physical safeguards which are put in place to assure the integrity and protection of information and the means of processing it.

Security incident or breach

An event that results in loss, disclosure, unauthorized modification, or unauthorized destruction of information resources whether accidental or deliberate.

Security officer

See data information officer.

Security standard

A required procedure or management control.

Sensitive information

Information which is confidential by law; information that requires protection from unauthorized access by virtue of its legal exemption from the Public Records Act.

Sensitive software

Those portions of data processing software, including the specifications and documentation used to collect, process, store, and retrieve information which is exempt from the Public Records Act; collect, process, store, and retrieve financial management information of the department, such as payroll and accounting records; or control and direct access authorizations and security measures for automated systems.

SAS

Server Administration Services.

System control data

Data files such as programs, password files, security tables, authorization tables, etc., which, if not adequately protected, could permit unauthorized access to information resources.

User of an information resource

An individual or automated application that is authorized access to the resource by the owner, in accordance with the owner's procedures and rules.

1.5 Departmental security programs

The purpose of departmental security programs is to ensure that the security of the information and communication processing resources of the department are sufficient to reduce the risk of loss, modification, or disclosure of those assets to an acceptable level.

(a) Standard. Each department shall document and maintain an up-to-date internal information security program. The departmental security program shall include internal policies and procedures for the protection of information resources, and will be an instrument implementing County information security policies and standards.

(b) Guidelines.

1. Departmental security programs should include the following objectives:

a. To identify sensitive data and take steps to protect such data from disclosure or unauthorized modification.

b. To identify which information resources are essential to the continued operation of critical County functions and take steps to ensure their controlled availability.

c.To apply additional security safeguards that can be cost justified, considering the exposure.

d.To ensure the accuracy and integrity of data and automated processes.

e. To educate employees and contractor personnel concerning their responsibilities for maintaining the security of information resources.

2. Security practices described as guidelines should be considered for applicability within each department and incorporated internally in the department's policy and procedures manual.

3. See section 1.9.

1.6 Responsibility

Each department head is responsible for establishing security standards for the department's information resources and for establishing information security requirements on a department-wide basis. To assist management in carrying out security responsibilities, the department head must explicitly assign the duties and functions determined to be appropriate for the department.

(a) Standard. Each department head shall 1) appoint a business unit information officer to administer the departmental information security program, 2) maintain the department security policies and procedures manual and 3) manage the duties and responsibilities of the function.

(b) Guidelines. The security duties and functions below should be assigned to the business unit information officer tasked with overseeing the department security effort, she/he should:

1. Report directly to the manager responsible for the resources to be protected.

2. Keep management aware of legal and regulatory changes affecting information privacy and computer crime.

3. Develop departmental information security policies and standards and the departmental security awareness and training program.

4. Provide department-wide security consulting services; serve as the department's internal and external point of contact on information security matters.

5. Ensure that the department's critical and sensitive information resources are identified, that all information resources are assigned ownership, and that the duties of owners are prescribed.

6. Ensure that valid user lists are current and auditable.

7. Develop, implement, and maintain the department risk analysis program.

8. Manage the development, implementation, and testing of security controls and methods for their evaluation; direct efforts for including security safeguards in the development or acquisition stages of new automated information systems.

9. Ensure that a data security administrator is assigned to each system and that the duties of the function are defined.

10. Report to management periodically on departmental security posture and progress, including problem areas with recommended enhancements.

11. Oversee procedures for department password control and for secure distribution of encryption keys.

1.7 Owner, custodian, & user responsibilities

The major objective of computer and information security is to provide cost-effective controls to ensure that information is not subject to unauthorized modification, disclosure, or destruction. To achieve this objective, procedures that govern access to each collection of related information systems must be in place. The effectiveness of access rules depends largely on the correct identification of the owners, custodians, and users of information.

(a) Standard. Owners, custodians, and users of data and software shall be identified and documented, and their responsibilities shall be defined. All data and software shall be assigned an owner. In cases where data or software is aggregated for purposes of ownership, the aggregation shall be at a level that assures individual accountability. The duties and responsibilities of the custodian must be assigned by the owner of the data.

(b) Guidelines. The following distinctions among owner, custodian, and user responsibilities should guide determination of these roles:

1. The owner of information resources is the designated individual upon whom responsibility rests for carrying out the program that uses the resources. The owner is responsible and authorized to:

a. Approve access and formally assign custody of the asset.

b. Judge the asset's value.

c. Specify data control requirements and convey them to users and custodians.

d. Ensure compliance with applicable controls.

2. The custodian of information resources is the individual assigned the responsibility to:

a. Implement the controls specified by the owner.

b. Provide physical and procedural safeguards for the information resources in his/her possession or in his/her facility.

c. Administer access to the information resources.

d. Make provisions for timely detection, reporting, and analysis of unauthorized attempts to gain access to information resources.

e. Assist owners in evaluating the cost-effectiveness of controls.

f. Not approve access to any County access without the written approval of the owner.

3. The users of information resources have the responsibility to:

a. Use the resource only for the purposes specified by its owner.

b. Comply with controls established by the owner.

c. Prevent disclosure of sensitive information.

1.8 Risk management

Absolute security that assures protection against all threats is unachievable. Therefore, a means of weighing losses that may be expected to occur in the absence of an effective security control against the costs of implementing the control is required. Risk analysis is a systematic process of evaluating vulnerabilities of a processing system and its data to the threats facing it in its environment.

(a) Standard. Departments shall perform or update a comprehensive risk analysis of all critical and sensitive information processing systems at least annually. Risk analysis results shall be presented to the owner of the information resource for risk management

(b) Standard. Departments shall implement appropriate security controls determined through risk analysis to be cost effective in the reduction or elimination of identified risks to information resources. Any delegation by the department head of authority for risk management decisions shall be documented.

(c) Guidelines.

1. Risk analysis will assist management in the identification of controls appropriate for department standards or system standards that amplify or supplement the County minimum requirements.

2. Departments should appoint a risk analysis team to analyze the department's vulnerabilities to potential losses and to recommend cost-effective safeguards. The risk analysis team should consist of representatives of:

a. The resource owner, users, and custodians,

b. Application and system programmers,

c. Computer operations,

d. Internal auditors,

e. Physical security organization,

f. Business unit information officer or data security administrator(s), and

g. Communications network manager.

3. See section 1.9.

1.9 Confidentiality of departmental security programs and data

(a) The Florida Public Records Act, section 119.07, Florida Statutes, and the Open Meetings Law, section 286.011, Florida Statutes, apply to governmental records and meetings and presume that all records and meetings are open to the public, absent a specific statutory exemption from the Public Records Act or the Open Meetings Law. Sections 119.07 and 282.318, Florida Statutes, provide the following exemptions from these laws:

1. Departmental internal policies and procedures which, if disclosed, could facilitate the unauthorized modification, disclosure, or destruction of data or information technology resources.

2. Risk analysis information.

3. Results of internal audits of departmental computer security programs.

4. Data processing software obtained by a department under a licensing agreement which prohibits its disclosure and which software is a trade secret.

5. Departmental developed computer software, including the specifications and documentation, used to collect, process, store, and retrieve information which is exempt from the Public Records Act; financial management information of the department, such as payroll and accounting records; or software/data which is used to control and direct access authorizations and security measures for automated systems.

(b) In addition to these specific exemptions, section 281.301, Florida Statutes, provides a general exemption relating to the security systems for any property owned by or leased to the County or any of its political subdivisions, all records or portions thereof relating directly to or revealing such systems, and all meetings relating directly to or would reveal such systems.

(c) Guideline. Departments should review the following types of reports and documentation to determine if County security systems could be revealed if these records were made public:

1. Documentation related to risk management decisions, including documentation of decisions made to accept or assume identified risks.

2. Contingency plans.

3. Incident reports, as required by these standards.

4. Those portions of departmental Strategic Plans for Information Resources Management that identify needed or planned security controls.

5. Annual certifications by departments of their computer and data security programs.

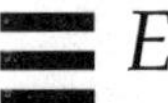

2.0 Control of computers and information resources

Information resources are valuable County assets. The willful and knowing unauthorized use, alteration, or destruction of these assets is a computer-related crime, punishable under Chapter 815, Florida Statutes.

2.1 Use of county information resources

(a) Standard. All information and telecommunication resources leased or owned by the County and all time-sharing services billed to the County shall be used only to conduct official County business. Access to data files and programs shall be limited to those individuals authorized to view, process, or maintain particular systems.

(b) Guidelines. The principles of least access, separation of functions, and need to know should be applied in the determination of user authorizations.

1. A user should be allowed to manipulate data only in constrained ways that are designed to preserve or ensure the integrity of the data and the process.

2. Functions involving sensitive or financial information should be under dual control. For example, the clerk who enters payment instructions must not be permitted to verify his or her own work.

3. Evidence, such as signatures, should be required to show individual accountability for transaction origination, authorization, and approval. All transactions should be auditable.

4. Task and transaction subsets should be defined during the system development process and reviewed by internal auditors as to transaction integrity, adequate separation of duties, and auditability of controls.

2.2 Ownership of software

(a) Standard. All computer software developed by County employees or contract personnel on behalf of the County or purchased for the use of the County is County property and shall be protected as such, unless the contract under which the software is developed specifically provides otherwise.

(b) Guidelines.

1. Departmental employment agreements with employees who write or modify County-owned software should specify ownership rights in the software, with the County retaining ownership in all programs written or modified by its employees.

2. Contracts for programming work by outside personnel should spell out the ownership of all rights to the software and associated documentation.

2.3 Access to and handling of sensitive information

(a) Standard. Sensitive information shall be accessible only to personnel who are authorized by the owner on a strict "need to know" in the performance of their duties. Data containing any sensitive information shall be readily identifiable and treated as sensitive in its entirety.

(b) Standard. An auditable, continuous chain of custody shall record the transfer of sensitive information. When sensitive information from a department is received by another department concerning the transaction of official business, the receiving department shall maintain the confidentiality of the information in accordance with the conditions imposed by the providing department.

(c) Guidelines.

1. The principles of least access, separation of functions, and need to know should guide the determination of user authorizations, rather than rank, position or precedent. Group level authorizations should be avoided.

2. Sensitive data, files, and software should be marked, or flagged as "Sensitive," "Confidential," or other designation which clearly distinguishes them from non-sensitive material. Data or files containing sensitive information need not be considered sensitive if the information is encrypted (see section 7.4) with encryption keys properly controlled.

3. Sensitive data in magnetic or electronic form should contain the markings in a manner appropriate to the media such that special protection requirements will be apparent to anyone accessing the data.

4. Sensitive hardcopy data should have markings on each page. Physical markings should also be applied to the exterior of all input/output media such as diskettes, tapes, and volumes that contain sensitive information.

5. Electronic media and/or paper copy data which has contained sensitive information should not be disposed of or removed from County security controls without assurance that sensitive information has been deleted and cannot be recovered. Processes to delete information from electronic media include complete degaussing, electronic overwriting, and physical destruction. Media that has been subjected to a deletion process should be tested periodically as a separate function to validate continued effectiveness of the process.

6. Departments may elect to establish more than one level or category of sensitivity, considering the vulnerabilities associated with the number of employees who would otherwise have access to more sensitive information than required by their duties. In such event, the different sets of sensitive information must be distinguishable and the controls for each must be defined.

7. Procedures for removal of sensitive information from records should be devised such that the desensitized version may be available to the public in accordance with the Public Records Act. Any collection of automated information or data that the owner has determined to contain no sensitive information is, by definition, public information.

8. While controls that limit access to sensitive information must normally be more restrictive than controls for the protection of non-sensitive information, the exposure associated with broad access to non-sensitive information must also be recognized.

2.4 Audit trails

(a) Standard. Audit trails shall be maintained to provide accountability for all accesses to sensitive and critical information and to sensitive software, for all modifications to records which control movement of funds or fixed assets, and for all changes to automated security or access rules.

2.5 End user computing workstations

(a) Standard. All software utilized on an end-use workstation shall be purchased license software, owned by the County. Any software copied from a bulletin board service shall be pre-approved by department managers for use and scanned for computer viruses.

(a) Guidelines. Unless extraordinary steps are taken to ensure control, the use of end-user computing workstations for sensitive or critical tasks should be avoided. Absent the types of controls ordinarily found in larger processing environments (e.g., backing up, access restrictions, and individual accountability for changes to data), end-user computing workstations are highly vulnerable to risks associated with data integrity, disclosure, and loss. The use of end-user computing workstations for sensitive or critical tasks should be strictly reviewed and only permitted where adequate controls are in place to provide continued data confidentiality, integrity, and availability.

Particular emphasis should be placed on training and awareness of end users responsible for data integrity and availability for sensitive or critical systems. Physical access to workstations should be limited to the degree necessary to provide data confidentiality, integrity, and availability, particularly where meaningful logical controls are not available or not used. Department management must recognize that the use of end-user computing workstations for sensitive or critical tasks implies a lack of centralized control and administration over information resources.

3.0 Physical security and access to data processing facilities

All County information processing areas must be protected by physical controls appropriate for the size and complexity of the operations and the criticality or sensitivity of the systems operated at those locations.

3.1 Centralized computer rooms

(a) Standard. Physical access to central computer rooms shall be restricted to only authorized personnel Authorized visitors shall be recorded and supervised.

(b) Guidelines.

1. Access to the computer operations area should be restricted to those responsible for operation and maintenance. Users and vendor service personnel should be subject to the same controls as visitors.

2. Access to tape storage areas should be restricted to ISS Enterprise Center Services staff.

3. Measures should be implemented to prevent and detect attempts to disrupt operations or to enter or depart from restricted areas in an unauthorized manner. Responsibility should be clearly assigned for timely and effective response to such attempts.

4. Entrances to areas of the highest sensitivity or criticality should be monitored using closed circuit television or automated systems or should be protected by guard. Some combination of these is preferable to relying wholly on one technique.

5. Card or badge-access systems and people traps should be installed in large central computer rooms. Some card or badge-access control systems have a feature that prevents their sharing such as requiring an exit before reentry.

6. Identification badges should contain only photographs, badge numbers, and sufficient information to associate them with their owner. Badges should contain no facility identification or address to which the badges will permit access. Procedures should require that they be worn at all times in computer operations areas.

7. Computer operations personnel should be instructed in actions to be taken upon discovery of an individual without a badge.

8. Physical access controls may be enhanced by biometric verification systems, such as those designed for palm print recognition, fingerprint matching, or retinal scanning. Systems that automatically test an individual's signature dynamics are also gaining acceptance.

9. Guards or alarmed doors, or both, should be used to protect facilities during off-hours.

10. A manager should notify the appropriate security section immediately when a person is no longer allowed access to the computer facility or when such action is impending.

11. Controls applicable to central computer rooms should be considered for facilities containing other sizeable collections of information resources, such as minicomputers or large concentrations of microcomputers.

3.2 Distributed computer rooms

(a) Standard. While handled or processed by workstations/terminals, communication switches, and network components outside the central computer room, critical or sensitive information shall receive the level of protection necessary to ensure its integrity and confidentiality. The required protection may be achieved by physical or logical controls, or a mix thereof.

(b) Guidelines.

1. As many system components as possible should be located contiguous to the computer room and accorded the same physical controls. Those components that must be located beyond the computer room controls should be provided the degree of protection appropriate to prevent tamping with the components.

2. Insufficient physical controls for remote system components may be compensated for by strengthened logical controls for gaining access to the information handled by the remote components.

3. Workstations/terminals, while unattended, should be protected from unauthorized use. Terminal devices should never be left logged-on while unattended.

4. Workstations/terminals should be installed where they are not readily accessible to personnel not authorized to use them and should be positioned in such a manner that minimizes unauthorized viewing of the screen. Facing the screen away from doorways and windows will enhance visual protection.

5. Minicomputer systems and distributed processing system CPUs should be maintained in locked spaces when authorized users are not present and capable of monitoring access to the system processor.

6. Except when in large concentrations (see section 3. 1 (b) 1 1.), single-user systems such as stand-alone microcomputers need not be installed in highly controlled areas provided they are secured against theft and unauthorized use, and the data and software are adequately protected.

3.3 Environmental controls

One of the major causes of computer downtime is the failure to maintain proper controls over temperature, humidity, air movement, cleanliness, and power. Environmental controls must also provide for safety of personnel.

(a) Standard. Employees and information resources shall be protected from environmental hazards. Designated employees shall be trained to monitor environmental control procedures and equipment and shall be trained in desired response in case of emergencies or equipment problems.

(b) Guidelines.

1. Personnel safety should be of paramount concern in the design of environmental controls.

2. Critical loads should be provided an alternate source of power independent from the primary source. Alternate power should be immediately switchable to all environmental units essential to continued operation of critical loads.

3. A power management analysis will aid in selecting appropriate power technology. The need for isolation and regulating transformers, line conditioners, motor generators, or uninterrupted power supplies should be explored. Single points of failure should be avoided.

4. The temperature and humidity within a computer facility should be monitored and controlled to ensure that the operational environment conforms to the manufacturer's specifications.

5. Air handler filters should be changed or cleaned on a regular basis.

6. Personal computer equipment should be protected as specified by the system manufacturer.

3.4 Fire prevention and protection

(a) National Fire Protection Association Standard 75 (NFPA 75), "Standard for the Protection of Electronic Computer/Data Processing Equipment" (reference section 10. 1 (g)), adopted by State Fire Marshal's Rule 4A-3.012, Florida Administrative Code, sets forth minimum requirements for the protection of electronic computer/data processing equipment from damage by fire or its associated effects, i.e., smoke, corrosion, heat, water. The standard covers the requirements for installations of electronic computer/data processing equipment where either:

1. Special building construction, rooms, areas, or operating environment are required, or

2. Fire protection for the equipment is required.

(b) Pursuant to State Fire Marshal's Rule 4A-3.012, Florida Administrative Code, for purposes of the rules in Title 4A, all appendices to all NFPA Standards adopted in this rule which appendices prescribe recommended operating procedures and sound practices are mandatory.

(c) Guideline. Although NFPA 75 does not cover installations of electronic computer/data processing equipment that do not require special construction or protection, it will be useful as a management guide for the protection of other information resources.

3.5 Water damage prevention and protection

(a) Standard. Controls to prevent or minimize water damage to information resources in case of a water leak or rising water shall be established and enforced.

(b) Guidelines.

1. As noted in section 3.4 above, NRFPA 75 sets forth minimum requirements for the protection of electronic computer/data processing equipment from damage by fire or its associated effects, i.e., smoke, heat, water. Measures instituted for the protection against fire-associated effects of water will satisfy most protection needs against leaks or flooding unrelated to fire protection.

2. Central computer rooms should be installed above flood level. Provision should be made for drainage.

3. Water cutoff valves should be clearly marked and easily accessible. The risk of falling water can be compensated for, in part, by having plastic sheeting material readily available.

4.0 Logical and data access controls

Information handled by processing systems and associated telecommunications networks must be adequately protected against unauthorized modification, disclosure, or destruction. Effective controls for logical access to information resources minimizes inadvertent employee error and negligence, and reduces opportunities for computer crime.

4.1 Personal identification, authentication, & access

Properly implemented and managed, access control systems will improve the likelihood that users are who they purport to be and that a user's access can be controlled effectively. Access control systems are an important deterrent to intrusion.

(a) Standard. Except for public users of systems where such access is authorized, or for situations where risk analysis demonstrates no need for individual accountability of users, each user of a multiple-user automated system shall be assigned a unique personal identifier or user identification. User identification shall be authenticated before the system may grant that user access to automated information.

(b) Standard. A user's access authorization shall be removed from the system when the user's employment is terminated or the user transfers to a position where access to the system is no longer required.

(c) Guidelines. (See section 4.2 for password controls.)

1. Users' access rights should be established based on validated identification. The user identification code should be traceable to the user for the lifetime of the records and reports in which they appear.

2. The user should be required to provide unique authentication (e.g., a password) with something that is known or possessed only by that user.

3. Each user should agree in writing to only use the identification code for the purpose for which it was intended, to not disclose a password to any other person, and to change the password promptly if he or she suspects it has been disclosed to anyone else. A copy of the agreement should be retained in the user's personnel file.

4. An automatic terminal/workstation time-out should occur after a certain period of inactivity. The user should be forced to authenticate his or her identity before resuming activity.

5. Users must be trained to log-off or secure workstations/terminals when not in use.

6. Inadequate physical controls for remote system components may be compensated for by strengthened logical access controls.

7. Consultants and contractors should have their access rights carefully controlled. Automatic expiration of access authorization is one effective technique.

8. Authentication need not be required for a personal computing system if all users of the system have authorization to all of the information on the system and the computer and files are physically secured when not in use.

9. In situations where an employee's system access is terminated under adverse conditions (such as forced termination of employment or forced reassignment), it is particularly important that the employee be denied any further opportunity for unsupervised access to the system once he/she is so notified.

10. Systems authorized for public use need not require individual user identification as long as the class identification as public is retained and public access functions are prescribed and controlled.

4.2 Password controls

Personal passwords are used to authenticate a user's identity and to establish accountability. Access passwords are used to grant access to data and may be used where individual accountability is not required. Federal Information Processing Standard Publication 112 (FIPS PUB 112) (reference section 11.1[b]) specifies basic security criteria in the use of passwords to authenticate personal identity and data access authorization.

(a) Standard. Systems that use passwords shall conform to the federal standard contained in FIPS PUB 112, sections 1, 2, and 3. A current Password Standard Compliance Document that specifies the criteria to be met for the ten factors contained in the standard shall be maintained for each system that uses passwords.

(b) Guidelines.

1. The adequacy of a password system should be established through risk analysis.

2. Appendices to FIPS PUB 112 provide guidance on meeting the minimum criteria, reasons for exceeding them, and examples of password compliance documents.

3. Passwords stored on a computer should be encrypted in storage.

4. System operators and administrators should not have unlimited access to super passwords. Such passwords should be carefully controlled by user management; monitoring the use of privileged passwords is critical and should be documented.

5. Consideration should be given to the use of one-time passwords (Appendix E.5, FIPS PUB 112) when there is a high threat of password compromise or for very sensitive applications.

4.3 Access to software and data

(a) Standard. Controls shall ensure that legitimate users of the computer cannot access stored software or system control data unless they have been authorized to do so.

(b) Guidelines.

1. If software is inadequate to control access to segregated parts of information within the computer, access to the entire computer system should be restricted to those with permission to access all the information.

2. Violations of access controls should be reviewed by both the owner and the user's manager.

3. If access control software is incapable of preventing programmed attacks on the information, all program compilers or assemblers and all general-purpose utilities capable of reading or updating files should be partitioned or removed from the system.

4. County information resources are County property. Thus, software that relates to or reveals security systems for information resources are included under section 1.9 above.

5. See section 2.5.

5.0 Data and system integrity

A major goal of County data processing is to ensure the integrity of information processes on all platforms to prevent fraud and errors. No user of a County system, even if authorized, may be permitted to modify data items in such a way that assets or accounting records of the County are lost or corrupted.

5.1 Data integrity

In terms of volume, the problem of errors and omissions is the greatest cause of incorrect information processing.

(a) Standard. Controls shall be established to ensure the accuracy and completeness of data. User management shall ensure that data comes from the appropriate source for the intended use.

(b) Standard. All systems that contain data must maintain a periodic archival of that data to either tape or other preapproved storage medium.

(c) Guidelines.

1. Redundant data, parity checks, control totals, etc., and should be used to guard against errors in entry and transmission.

2. Selected fields should be verified. Programmed edit checks, feedback, confirmations, and reconciliation should be employed as appropriate.

3. Time stamps and sequence numbers should be employed to ensure completeness of data and to relate data across files and transactions.

4. Once it has been processed, each collection of source material should be canceled or specially marked, either manually or under control of validated software, to prevent duplications or omissions.

5. User management should reconcile data submitted against data processed and returned.

6. The user organizational unit should maintain a log of the batches submitted for processing. The data input organizational unit should generate a log, by user organizational unit, of the batches received and processed.

7. The integrity of information against undetected corruption during transmission or while in storage may be enhanced by encryption (see section 7.4). Although encryption alone may not prevent modification or destruction, any unauthorized alteration of encrypted information should be readily detected since decrypting will produce unintelligible garbles.

5.2 Separation of functions

Segregation of duties is a fundamental element of internal control and an effective risk reduction technique. For tasks that are susceptible to fraudulent or other unauthorized activity, the likelihood of such activity successfully occurring is reduced when it requires collusion between employees. The purpose of separation of functions is to minimize the opportunity for any one person to subvert or damage the system.

(a) Standard. For tasks that are susceptible to fraudulent or other unauthorized activity, departments shall ensure adequate separation of functions for controlled execution.

(b) Guidelines.

1.Tasks related to the design, implementation, operation, maintenance, and use of information systems should be structured such that each acts as a check upon the others.

2.Access rights to data and programs should be based on specific job requirements in user as well as data processing organizations.

3. Personnel duties should not overlap and should be separated so that a single individual cannot independently perform all of the steps necessary to violate the protection mechanisms of the system.

4. Information processing personnel should record and process data, but they should not originate or authenticate transactions, perform final reconciliation of input and output, correct reconciliation differences, or have unchecked access to assets.

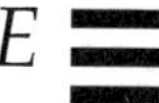

5.Responsibilities for day-to-day production processing should be separate from system development, testing, and maintenance.

6. Programmers and analysts should not have unrestricted access to programs and data files used for production runs.

7. Those who can authorize and approve must not be able to originate and record.

8. Personnel policies that enhance separation by enforced practices such as required vacations, job rotation, and restrictions on overtime should be instituted.

9. No individual should be allowed to have exclusive control of any automated system.

5.3 Testing controls and program maintenance

(a) Standard. The test functions shall be kept either physically or logically separate from the production functions. Copies of production data shall not be used for testing unless the data has been desensitized or unless all personnel involved in testing are otherwise authorized access to the data.

(b) Standard. After a new system has been placed in operation, all program changes shall be approved before implementation to determine whether they have been authorized, tested, and documented.

(c) Guidelines.

1.System testing should be a joint effort of users and information processing organizations and should include both the manual and automated phases of the system.

2.A naming standard should be in effect to distinguish between test jobs and production jobs, test data sets and production data sets.

3. Change control procedures should ensure that all moves between the test and production environments have been authorized in writing by the appropriate manager.

4.Parallel or acceptance tests should be considered production work and therefore run by production personnel.

5.Program development personnel should only access production data to resolve emergencies. Only those authorized by the supervisor of production operations should authorize and log this access.

6. All programs should be installed into production from the source code (i.e., programs will be recompiled by a change control or comparable group).

7. Software generally referred to as "public domain" software (such as might be acquired through software exchanges or electronic bulletin boards) or software not acquired under license or contract should never be used for processing sensitive or critical information.

8. For non-sensitive or noncritical applications, public domain software should not be used unless it has been thoroughly tested in a non-operational, isolated environment and validated to be free of contaminants or software viruses.

9. Requested program changes should be documented and signed by both the initiator of the request and the system owner. Changes should also be approved by the programming manager.

10. Independent peer review (whereby programmers examine each other's program code) will reduce program maintenance exposure.

11. Acceptance testing of modified programs should be performed by a quality assurance (or independent) function using control test files.

12. Only quality assurance (or independent) personnel should be authorized to apply program changes, catalog and copy newly updated programs to production libraries.

13. See section 2.5.

5.4 Transaction history

Automated chronological or systematic records of changes to data are important in the reconstruction of previous versions of the data, in case of corruption. Such records, sometimes referred to as journals, are useful in establishing normal activity, in identifying unusual activity, and in the assignment of responsibility for corrupted data.

(a) Standard. A sufficiently complete history of transactions shall be maintained for each session involving access to critical and sensitive information to permit an audit of the system by tracing the activities of individuals through the system.

(b) Guidelines.

1.In addition to system start-up and shutdown times, transaction histories should log the following information, at a minimum:

- Update transactions,
- Date, time of activity,
- User identification,
- Sign-on and sign-off activity, and

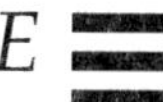

- Sensitive display transactions.

2.Departments should prescribe the analysis required of transaction histories and the person or function designated to perform the analysis. Only designated personnel should have access to the transaction histories and to the results of the analyses.

3. An analysis of transaction histories for detecting variances from the norm should be conducted regularly. In addition to checks against authorizations, particular attention should be paid to unusual times, frequency, and length of accesses, as well as anomalies that could indicate potential violations.

4. See section 2.5.

6.0 Database controls

All applications development will use the contained standards to ensure the security and auditability of data maintained by the County. Existing applications should be modified to conform to the database access standards when possible. The standard will require that roles are assigned to customers and development personnel commensurate with the access required to do job-related tasks.

6.1 Database access

Data security policy for information maintained by the County will be based on needs within job function. Information Resource developers and customer personnel will have individual user IDs authenticated by the operating system when possible. Connections to relational databases through the network will be authenticated by the database management system (DBMS). Individual users will be grouped (assigned secondary IDs) by job function and assigned to roles. These roles will be granted specific access to specific data. Users will ultimately be assigned either system-type or customer-type access.

(a) System access.

System-type access is defined as Database Administration or Server Administration personnel whose job functions require their access to DBMS internal structures.

(b) Customer access.

Customer-type access will be used for customers of County Database Administration Services. In the case of three-tier application systems, the middleware will be considered a separate customer and assigned appropriately.

6.2 User authentication

Two options exist for authenticating individuals' access to a database:

1. Authentication by the operating system
2. Authentication by the DBMS

User authentication by the operating system is preferred for the following reasons:

1. Users can connect to the database faster and more conveniently (without specifying a user name or password).

2. Centralized control over user authentication in the operating system. The database need not store or manage user passwords and user names if the operating system and the database correspond.

3. User entries in the database and operating system audit trails correspond.

6.3 Group assignment

(a) Standard. Development staff and customers requiring database access will be categorized based on job-function. Categories of users, (groups or secondary IDs), will be granted database privileges appropriate to job responsibilities.

6.4 Role assignment

(a) Standard. Individual database access and resource usage privileges will be grouped together and assigned to roles. Database access will be controlled at the group level. This will standardize the authorization process and limit exposure to errors and omissions. Individuals requiring access beyond that granted by the role will be evaluated on case-by-case basis.

(b) Standard. The addition or deletion of an individual's access will be accomplished by assigning that person to or deleting that person from a predefined group with predefined privileges in place. This procedure allows the privilege granting process to be centrally administered and closely monitored. The adding or deleting of users can then be delegated to authorized non-DBA staff (e.g., ISS Customer Service, customer staff, etc.) while centralized control is maintained.

(c) Standard. This philosophy is applicable to DB2, Oracle, and other relational database management systems (RDBMS). The following explains it concisely.

"If the database is large with many users, the [database] security administrator can decide what groups of users can be categorized, create user roles for these user groups, grant the necessary privileges or application roles to each user role, and assign the user roles to end users. To account for exceptions, the security administrator must also decide what privileges must be granted to individual users."[1]

6.5 Separation of duties and privilege standards

(a) Standard. Separation of duties.

As persons with like job functions are grouped together, so also will be those groups. Groups will have different access privileges to maintain a separation of duties. Samples of some more prominent roles and privileges follow.

Note: The privileges are presented here in plain text. Expanded descriptions will vary by database.

(b) Standard. Developer duties.

Application developers have broad access to development databases and tables. Persons assigned to this role can create, alter and delete database clusters, stored procedures, synonyms, tables and views of tables. Developers have complete access to all data in development databases. The developer role is subdivided into project-related or focus-related subroles (e.g., MRTS_DEVELOPER, BT_DEVELOPER). Application developers will not be allowed on production databases. By imposing this restriction:

1. Application programmers do not compete with end-users for database resources.

2. Application developers cannot detrimentally affect a production database.

When required, developers may obtain access to modify data in production databases. This will be accomplished by use of a specific ID associated with problem resolution (e.g., MRTSEMER, BTEMER, etc.). Accordingly, these IDs are heavily audited.

(c) Standard. General user.

General users can create, alter, and delete tables and views for only their own ID.

(d) Standard. End user.

End users are customer personnel accessing and updating database files associated with a specific application or applications.

(e) Standard. Server Administration Services (SAS).

---

1. Oracle7 Server Administrator's Guide pg. 10-4

Has responsibility for doing business recovery of all production and test data base file using commands and utilities appropriate to the particular DBMS. ISS Enterprise Center Services (ECS) will provide support staff to provide services to backup servers as requested by ISS Server Administration Services.

(f) Standard. DBA.

ISS Database Administration Services (DAS) staff has DBA privilege. DBA privilege is encompassing. Individuals assigned to the DBA role define stored procedures, database links, views, and remote connections in distributed environments. DBAs are responsible for performing data base recovery operations after files have been restored by SAS and ECS personnel.

Production databases will be secured from update or alteration from all but DBA staff connected as the owner of the data as INTERNAL, SYSTEM or Operating System Data Base Management System (OSDBA). DAS personnel logged on with their personal ID will not alter production databases. This will reduce unintentional errors. The data owner ID will normally not be correctable except when connection is required for modifications.

7.0 Network security

Networking, including distributed processing, concerns the transfer of data among users, hosts, applications, and intermediate facilities. During transfer, data is particularly vulnerable to unintended access or alteration.

7.1 Network controls, general

(a) Standard. Network, resources participating in the access of sensitive information shall assume the sensitivity level of that information for the duration of the session. Controls shall be implemented commensurate with the highest risk.

(b) Standard. All network components under County control must be identifiable and restricted to their intended use.

(c) Guidelines.

1. Workstations/terminals should be selected with a lock and key option so that access can be controlled by locking the terminal while it is unattended. This is particularly important at locations where access to the network during non-business hours is not tightly controlled.

2. All line junction points (cable and line facilities) should be located in secure areas or under lock and key.

3. Control units, concentrators, multiplexors and front-end processors should be protected from unauthorized physical access. The sophistication and extent of this control will depend on the sensitivity of the systems involved

4. Procedures should be implemented which ensure that the County's access to data or information is not dependent on any individual. There must be more than one person with authorized access.

5. Techniques to achieve verification include message counts, character counts, error detection and correction (protocols), and dual transmissions.

6. Eliminating removable media, e.g., diskette, capability from Local Area Network workstations reduces vulnerability of LANs to unauthorized copying. This approach requires that workstations be equipped without diskette drives, and that all data and programs be stored on the network.

7. Some types of network protocol analyzers and test equipment are capable of monitoring (and some, of altering) data passed over the network. Use of such equipment should be tightly controlled since they can emulate workstations/terminals, monitor and modify sensitive information, or contaminate both encrypted and unencrypted data.

7.2 Security at network and server entry

County-owned or leased network facilities and host systems are County assets. Their use must be restricted to authorized users and purposes. Where public users are authorized access to networks or host systems, these public users as a class must be clearly identifiable and restricted to only services approved for public functions. County employees who have not been assigned a user identification code and means of authenticating their identity to the system are not distinguishable from public users and must not be afforded broader access.

(a) Standard. Owners of information resources served by networks shall prescribe sufficient controls to ensure that access to network services and host services and subsystems is restricted to authorized users and uses only. These controls shall selectively limit services based upon:

1. User identification and authentication (e.g., password) or,

2. Designation of other users, including the public, where authorized, as a class (e.g., public access through dial-up or public switched networks) for the duration of a session.

3. All network devices, including, but not limited to terminals, printer, hubs, routers, bridges, control units, repeaters etc., shall not be connected with or activated to the the County wide area network unless approved by the ISS Manager of Network Administration Services.

(b) Guidelines.

1. Authorization at network entry on the basis of valid user identification code and authentication (e.g., password) should be provided under the framework of network Server Administration Services and controlled by the a minimum of one or all of the following including server, data bases and/or applications access.

2. Network access should be controlled as close to the physical point of network entry as possible.

3. Connections between users on a network should be authorized by the server, or the network node security manager program as appropriate.

4. The designated manager of an internal server independent network serves the dual role as owner of the network system and as custodian of data under another's ownership while the data is being transported by the network.

5. The host security management program should maintain current user-application activity authorizations through which each request must pass before a connection is made or a session is initiated.

7.3 Security at the application

(a) Standard. Network access to an application containing critical or sensitive data, and data sharing between applications, shall be as authorized by the application owners and shall require authentication.

(b) Guidelines.

1. The owner of applications containing noncritical or non-sensitive data should likewise establish criteria for access and user validation, particularly on systems authorized for public use.

2. Additional protection, such as might be applicable to especially sensitive data, is afforded by a two-person password procedure; each person's password validates user authorization for either host or application access, exclusively. Neither person alone can gain combined host-application access.

7.4 Data and file encryption

The most cost-effective means of protecting the confidentiality of information against disclosure during transfer is using a properly implemented and validated encryption methodology. Properly implemented, an encryption system virtually eliminates risks of disclosure of sensitive information at network nodes and facilities that are not under County control, such as the public switched network. Encryption also protects against undetected modification of data and thus enhances integrity as well as confidentiality. Depending on the value of information to an unauthorized recipient, interception or modification of unencrypted information must be recognized as a significant threat.

(a) Security through encryption depends upon both of the following:

1. Proper use of an approved encryption methodology, and

2. Only the intended recipients holding the encryption key-variable (key) for that data set or transmission.

(b) Standard. While in transit, information which is sensitive or information which in and of itself is sufficient to authorize disbursement of County funds shall be encrypted if sending stations, receiving stations, workstations/terminals, and relay points are not all under positive County control, or if any are operated by or accessible to personnel who have not been authorized access to the information, except under the following conditions:

1. The requirement to transfer such information has been validated and cannot be satisfied with information which has been desensitized, and

2. The department head, or the designated official if the department head has delegated authority for risk management decisions, has documented acceptance of the risks of not encrypting the information based on evaluation of the costs of encryption against exposures to all relevant risks.

(c) Standard. For systems employing encryption as required by section 7.4 [b], procedures shall be prescribed for secure handling, distribution, storage, and construction of Data Encryption Standard (DES) key variables used for encryption and decryption. Protection of the key shall be at least as stringent as the protection required for the information encrypted with the key.

(d) Standard. Encryption of data or files for transmission or storage as required by section 7.4 [b] shall conform to the federal DES defined in Federal Information Processing Standard Publication 46-1 (FIPS PUB 46-1) (reference section 11.1 [a]).

(e) Guidelines.

1. In making the determination required by section 7.4 [b] 2., the following risks should be reviewed for relevancy:

a. Personal injury or loss of life,

b. Loss of County funds,

c. Violation of individual expectations of privacy,

d. Violation of County or federal law,

e. Civil liability on the part of the County,

f. Compromise of County legal, investigative, regulatory, fiduciary, or educational efforts,

g. Loss of business opportunities for affected persons, and

h. Undue advantage to any person in County competitive business relations.

2. The need for encryption, other than the requirements of section 7.4 [b], should be determined based on risk analysis.

3. Interception of unencrypted information may not be readily detectable. It should be assumed that unencrypted information is available to any determined intruder.

4. Proprietary algorithms and software implementations of the DES algorithm do not conform to the FIPS PUB 46-1 standard and, therefore, do not conform to Florida standards.

5. When encrypted data is transferred interdepartmental, the respective business unit information officer shall devise a mutually agreeable procedure for secure essential management. In the case of conflict, the data owner department should establish the criteria.

6. Keys should be communicated separately from the encrypted information, preferably through different channels.

7. Passwords and dial-up terminal identifiers should be encrypted during transmission and in storage. They should be encrypted during session logon if the information to be exchanged requires encryption.

8. Encryption and decryption devices should be located as near the using devices (connected workstations/terminals and processors) as possible to minimize the need for other safeguards on the unencrypted segments of the link.

9. Sensitive or critical information should be stored in encrypted form if physical controls are not sufficient. Volumes or files where all sensitive information is encrypted may be controlled as though the information is not sensitive as long as encryption keys are appropriately controlled.

10. Security through encryption may be enhanced by requiring that two trusted individuals control the key; each having custody of half the key.

11. FIPS PUB 81 (reference section 11.1 (c)) describes four different modes for using the DES algorithm.

12. Information concerning encryption devices that have been tested and validated by the National Institute of Science and Technology may be obtained directly from the NIST, Gaithersburg, MD 20899.

7.5 Remote dial-up access

Systems accessible from dial-up workstations/terminals are particularly vulnerable to unauthorized access since the call can be initiated from virtually any telephone instrument. Official users of dial-up facilities must be distinguishable from public users if they are to be given access rights greater than those given public users.

(a) Standard. For services other than those authorized for the public, users of dial-up workstations/terminals shall be positively and uniquely identifiable and their identity authenticated (e.g., by password) to the systems being accessed.

(b) Guidelines. For dial-up services other than those authorized for public use:

1. Dial-up numbers should be unlisted.

2. At a minimum, dial-up facilities should be provided automatic hang-up and callback feature, with callback to only pre-authorized numbers.

3. A port protection device (PPD) connected to communications ports of a host computer is typically capable of providing:

- authentication and access control decisions,
- automatic hang-up and callback to originator, and
- attack signaling and event logging.

4. A high level of dial-up security combines the callback feature with password authentication (an encryption key entered by the individual) and terminal identification (an encryption key embedded in the hardware), with all data exchanged online being encrypted.

(c) Guidelines. For dial-up facilities authorized for public use.

1. Systems that allow public access to the host computer require strengthened security at the operating system and application to reduce the likelihood of public intrusion into non-public applications. Such systems also should have the capability to monitor activity levels to ensure public usage does not unacceptably degrade system responsiveness for official functions.

2. Systems which identify public users based on communications port usage provide only minimal security since they are highly vulnerable to mistakes through erroneous hardware connections.

8.0 Backup and business recovery

It is prudent to anticipate and prepare for the loss of information processing capabilities. Plans and actions to recover from losses range from routine backing up of data and software in the event of minor losses or temporary outages to comprehensive disaster recovery planning in preparation for catastrophic losses of information resources.

8.1 Backing up of data

On-site backup is employed to have readily available current data in machine-readable form in the production area in the event operating data is lost, damaged, or corrupted, without having to resort to re-entry from source material. Off-site backup or storage embodies the same principle but is designed for longer term protection in a more sterile environment, requires less frequent updating, and is provided additional protection against threats potentially damaging to the primary site and data.

(a) Standard. Data and software essential to the continued operation of critical department functions shall be backed up. The security controls over the backup resources shall be as stringent as the protection required of the primary resources.

(b) Guidelines.

1. In backing up information, all supporting material (e.g., programs, control files, and operating system software) which is required to process the information must also be backed up, though not necessarily during each backup cycle.

2. The owner should determine what information must be backed up, in what form, and how often. The custodian, familiar with the processing environment, should provide valuable counsel to the owner regarding on-site threats and effective backup options.

3. Operational information which would otherwise be critical but which has been properly backed up in a secure, controlled environment need not be considered critical if the backup version (which would then be critical) is separately protected and readily available.

4. Because of particular vulnerabilities of microcomputer data to loss or damage, removable and fixed disks containing critical County information should be backed up after each significant change.

5. A new backup copy should be made whenever the original has been changed significantly. Updated information that is not backed up by the end of the specified period should be retained until the new backup copy is made.

6. Off-site backup and production material should not be subject to the same destructive event.

7. Receipt of a new copy of the backup material should be confirmed before the old copy is destroyed.

8. The backing up of non-critical data and software is recommended as an effective practice to minimize the expense of reconstruction.

9. Contracts for software should include provisions for use of the software in testing and implementation of disaster recovery plans.

10. See section 2.5.

8.2 Contingency planning

Contingency Business plans, or disaster control plans, specify actions management has approved in advance to achieve each of three objectives. The emergency plan assists management in identifying and responding to disasters to protect personnel and systems and limit damage. The backup plan specifies how to accomplish critical portions of the mission in the absence of a critical resource such as a computer. The recovery plan directs recovery of full mission capability.

(a) Standard. All information resource owners, all departments operating computer rooms, and all automated user functions identified as critical to the continuity of governmental operations shall have a written and cost effective contingency plan that will provide for the prompt and effective continuation of critical County missions in the event of a disaster.

(b) Standard. Contingency plans as required by section 8.2[a] shall be tested at least annually.

(c) Guidelines.

1. Contingency plans should be reviewed or tested when there are significant system or mission changes, and upon the replacement of essential personnel.

2. See section 1.9.

9.0 Personnel security and security awareness

In any organization, people represent the greatest possible assets in maintaining an effective level of security. At the same time, people represent the greatest threats to information security. No security program can be effective without maintaining employee awareness and motivation.

9.1 Employee requirements, general

(a) Standard. Every employee shall be held responsible for systems security to the degree that his/her job requires the use of information and associated systems. Fulfillment of security responsibilities shall be mandatory, and violations of security requirements may be cause for disciplinary action, up to and including dismissal, civil penalties, and criminal penalties under chapters 119, 812, 815, 817, 839, or 877, Florida Statutes, or similar laws.

9.2 Positions of special trust or responsibility or in sensitive locations

Individual positions must be analyzed to determine the potential vulnerabilities associated with work in those positions. In some cases, it may be appropriate for departments, with the approval of the County Administration, ISS, and/or passwords to designate classes of employment as being positions of special trust or responsibility. It may also be appropriate to designate locations as sensitive and require appropriate procedures and safeguards for all employees whose duties include access to those areas.

(a) Standard. Each department shall establish procedures for reviewing data processing positions to determine which positions require special trust or responsibilities or are in sensitive locations.

(b) Guidelines. The review procedures should be based on risk analysis and should consider the following criteria:

1. Whether the assigned duties bring the person occupying the position into contact with information that is, or may reasonably be expected to be:

a. Required by law to be kept confidential.

b. Related to security systems, procedures, or reports, or other information that may reveal County security systems.

c. Valuable to persons outside the organizational unit employing the individual.

d. Readily convertible to a form this is valuable to persons outside the organizational unit employing the individual

e. Required by the County to continue its critical information processing activities, whether such information is confidential or public.

f. Entrusted to the County under a licensing agreement or by similar means, and which remains proprietary to others and, therefore, may be subject to laws protecting copyrights, patents, or trade secrets.

2. Whether the assigned duties bring the person occupying the position into contact with information resources that are necessary for the continued operation of critical information processing activities.

3. The degree of independence of the position, and whether the individual occupying the position is capable, by acting alone and without further review or approval, to direct or influence the disposition of County assets.

9.3 Nondisclosure agreements

Nondisclosure agreements document the acceptance by employees and contractors of special information security requirements.

(a) Guidelines.

1. All persons occupying positions of special trust or responsibility, or occupying positions in sensitive locations should:

a. Acknowledge, by signing a nondisclosure agreement, that their duties will bring them into contact with information or information resources that are of value to the County and that require protection.

b. Be required to uphold the policies and procedures adopted to safeguard the information and associated resources that may be entrusted to them or that they may meet.

c. Be required to agree to report violations of policies or procedures to their supervisor, their business unit information officer, or other person designated by the department head.

2. Copies of non-disclosure agreements should be maintained in employee or contract files, and the agreements should be updated at least annually. A discussion of the terms of the agreement should be conducted with new employees upon hiring, and with terminating employees.

3. In addition to persons occupying positions of special trust or responsibility or occupying positions in sensitive locations, departmental management may require other information processing users to sign non-disclosure agreements in accordance with this requirement.

9.4 Security awareness and training

An effective level of awareness and training is essential to a viable information security program. Employees who are not informed of risks or of management's policies and interest in security are not likely to take steps to prevent the occurrence of violations.

(a) Standard. Departments shall provide an ongoing awareness and training program in information security and in the protection of County information resources for all personnel whose duties bring them into contact with critical or sensitive County information resources. Security training sessions for these personnel shall be held at least annually.

(b) Standard. Awareness and training in security shall not be limited to formal training sessions, but shall include periodic briefings and continual reinforcement of the value of security consciousness in all employees whose duties bring them into contact with critical or sensitive County information resources.

(c) Guidelines.

1. The annual training should be comprehensive and include, at a minimum, emergency procedures, departmental policies for information security and integrity, authorized uses of County information processing resources, and procedures for handling sensitive information and reporting potential violations.

2. Employee security education should not include detailed instructions on how to commit a fraud. Examples of security incidents that have occurred is an effective training technique, but specific details could encourage attempts by others.

3. Departments may incorporate into their procedures for personnel evaluations a means of documenting information security consciousness and awareness as an element of employee performance ratings.

9.5 Hiring and termination procedures

County departments should take advantage of opportunities arising through hiring and termination of employees and contractors to reinforce security awareness and to indoctrinate them regarding their obligations in departmental security policies and procedures.

(a) Guidelines.

1. Upon the voluntary or involuntary termination of a person occupying a position of special trust or responsibility or working in a sensitive area, or upon notification to the employee of impending involuntary termination, department management should revoke all access authorizations and should take custody or ensure the safe return, modification, or destruction of all of the following items assigned or relating to the terminating or notified person:

- keys, lock combinations, and identification badges
- passwords
- sensitive data and documentation
- operator procedures
- program documentation
- County-owned equipment and tools
- documentation on uncompleted tasks
- on-line files
- active files and libraries
- archive files and libraries
- distribution lists

- control lists

2. Security awareness training should be a part of the indoctrination for all new employees whether or not they are assigned specific security responsibilities.

3. Departments should specify procedures to safeguard County property upon the voluntary or involuntary termination of persons occupying positions in which they may have been in contact with valuable County information or related resources.

10.0 Systems acquisition, auditing, and reporting

10.1 Systems acquisition

The addition of security controls after a system has been acquired is normally more expensive and less effective than when security needs are included in the system design. Major system development decisions must be based on consideration of security and audit requirements during each phase of life cycle development.

(a) Standard. Appropriate information security and audit controls shall be incorporated into new systems. Each phase of systems acquisition shall incorporate corresponding development or assurances of security and auditability controls.

(b) Guidelines. The following security (including audit) activities should be addressed at the appropriate phase in acquiring new information processing systems:

1. Determine sensitivity and criticality of the system information and define security objectives; assess the threats, vulnerabilities, and risks to the system.

2. Identify security alternatives and basic security framework in the selected system architecture.

3. Define security requirements and select appropriate controls.

4. Develop security test plans.

5. Design contracts to include security requirements.

6. Include approved security requirements and specifications in the development baselines.

7. Conduct tests of security in the configured components and in the integrated system.

8. Prepare documentation of security controls and assign to the documentation the appropriate level of sensitivity.

9. Conduct acceptance test and evaluation of system security.

10.2 Audits

The establishment and maintenance of a system of internal control is an important management function. Internal audits of information resource management functions, including security of data and information technology resources, are an integral part of an overall security program. The frequency, scope, and assignment of internal audits for security of data and information technology resources should be established to ensure that departmental management has timely and accurate information concerning functions management is responsible to perform.

(a) Standard. An audit of the department information security function shall be performed annually, when there are major system changes, or as directed by the head of the department.

(b) Guidelines.

1. At a minimum, the audit should evaluate the following attributes of the department's internal information security program, its effectiveness, its compliance with the County policies and standards, and the degree to which it is implemented.

10.3 Incident reporting

Any event that results in loss, disclosure, unauthorized modification, or unauthorized destruction of information resources constitutes a security incident or breach. The analysis of trends and types of security breaches is important to the integrity of the County's security program. Security incident reporting provides a basis for a continuing evaluation of the County information security posture. The objective of such analysis is to refine County security policies, standards, and guidelines to assure their continued effectiveness and applicability.

(a) Standard. Security breaches shall be promptly investigated.

(b) Standard. The business unit information officer shall provide analysis and centralized reporting of trends and incidents to Information Systems Services, and shall initiate appropriate changes of County policies, standards, guidelines, or statutes.

(c) Guidelines.

1. An incident report should include recommendations for changes in County policy, standards, or guidelines that may serve to strengthen the security program County wide.

2. Risk Management, Audit and security functions should participate in incident investigations and reporting.

3. Since the objective of incident reporting is to strengthen information security County wide, the detection of potential insecurities arising from the absence of effective controls (whether or not an incident or violation has occurred) should be the subject of an incident report.

4. See section 1.9.

10.4 Compliance

(a) Standard. Each department shall provide a general description of its existing information security program and its plans for assuring the security of information resources.

(b) Standard. Commencing in January 1996, and annually thereafter, each department shall certify to Internal Auditing the extent to which it has implemented the County information security policies and standards. A department is in conformance with a security policy or standard when its principles have been effectively embodied in the departmental information security program or the required procedure or management control has been implemented.

(c) Guidelines.

1. Properly performed risk analyses should provide indication of greatest exposures and potential losses. Thus, risk analysis should be an essential factor in determining departmental priorities for implementing information security standards.

2. See section 1.9.

11.0 References

Publications referred to in this document and their sources are described below.

11.1 Publications

(a) Federal Information Processing Standard Publication (FIPS PUB) Nr. 46-1; Title: Data Encryption Standard; dated January 22, 1988.

(b) Federal Information Processing Standard Publication (FIPS PUB) Nr. 112; Title: Password Usage; dated May 30, 1985.

(c) Federal Information Processing Standard Publication (FIPS PUB) Nr.8 1; Title: DES Modes of Operation; dated December 2, 1980.

(d) Information Resource Commission (IRC) memorandum dated May 31, 1985; Subject: Guidelines for conducting Risk Analysis.

(e) Information Resource Commission (IRC) document dated August 14, 1986; Subject: Florida Information Technology Resources Contingency Planning Guidelines.

(f) Information Resource Commission (IRC) document dated August 28, 1990; Subject: Florida Information Resources Security Standards and Guidelines.

(g) "Security Checklist for Computer Center Self-Audits," published by the American Federation of Information Processing Societies, Inc. (AFIPS), 1979.

(h) "Standard for the Protection of Electronic Computer/Data Processing Equipment," National Fire Protection Association Standard Nr. 75 (1987 edition).

(i) Oracle7 Server Administration Guide

11.2 References

(a) Federal Information Processing Standard Publications (FIPS PUB):
National Technical Information Service (NTIS)
5285 Port Royal Road
U.S. Department of Commerce
Springfield, VA 22161

(b) Information Resource Commission (IRC) documents:
Information Resource Commission
Executive Office of the Governor
The Capitol
Tallahassee, FL.32399-0001

(c) American Federation of Information Processing Societies (AFIPS) documents:
AFIPS Press
1899 Preston White Drive
Reston, VA 22091

(d) Standards published by the National Fire Protection Association (NFPA):
NFPA
Batterymarch Park
Quincy, MA 02260

(e) Governance Policies published by Information Systems Services
Information Systems Services
301 North Olive Ave.
West Palm Beach, FL 33401

Appendix: Sample marketing materials

This material is used by Palm Beach County ISS for marketing to departmental customers to ensure they are aware of the scope and quality of IS services.

Enterprise Center

The IS Enterprise Center is a state-of-the-art automated operations center for around-the-clock processing of data and reports needed for your business operations. Our enterprise data operations are behind closed doors with the highest security system to protect the county's valuable equipment and data storage under all circumstances.

Systems management

To efficiently support your processing workloads, IS focuses on your business-driven technologies for both the legacy and client/server environments. We are changing to add value by incorporating many technologies and deployment styles.

Quality assurance

The IS Enterprise Center functions to initiate and maintain programs that provide a high level of computer availability with high-quality production jobs for you, our customer. The scheduling and production of accurate and timely data and reports is accomplished by control standards for all processes, procedures, and equipment.

Through a continuous-improvement quality-assurance program, our services are designed to ensure that we meet your expectations. With our business processes, our efforts are focused on availability, security, recoverability, stability, predictability, and scalability. Your changing operational demands are primary in directing us to provide the quality performance levels to meet your business needs.

Customized reports

The Enterprise Center has customized reports for each customer's needs, which can be either manually printed or electronically routed to a person at your location. The ability to dynamically create electronic versions gives you the flexibility to get reports as needed and can be more economical with reduced paper costs.

Data storage

Information data is considered one of the enterprises most valued assets. The IS Enterprise Center manages this data as a primary and most important priority, in both your daily operations or in case of a disaster.

Mission

The mission of the Enterprise Center is to be a dynamic and progressive, state-of-the-art information provider. Our investment in automation propels us to new levels of ability and achievement with our customer to become the preferred information provider.

Enterprise Center tours

If you are interested in a tour of our facility, please call your agency consultant to arrange your request. IS can demonstrate to you those products that support your business operations.

High-tech equipment

The storage of data has made with efficient equipment, software, and a specially trained staff that is available 24 hours a day.

High-tech equipment that automates these processes, such as our robotics tape library, improve the efficiency of the operations process of backing up your critical information. These tapes are sent off-site in a secured vault for the highest protection standards and procedures.

Our Enterprise Center is a computing environment that includes the latest servers from various vendors, such as IBM and Sun, support the diverse software, processes, and procedures for the diverse needs of our many government customers.

Information technology survey

Imagine the convenience of having a comprehensive document detailing your current information systems environment. Having this valuable information available assists you in managing hardware, software, and personnel issues.

IS invites you to participate in a unique service that provides management and staff with the right information at the right time.

The service, "Information Technology Survey," is available now at all Palm Beach County Agencies and Departments. Highlights of the Information Technology Survey include:

1. Client information review
2. Transport and presentation review
3. Applications review
4. Staff review

Combined with a comprehensive project management control utility built into the service, IS will perform the service in an expedient and professional manner, with as little interruption as possible to your management and staff personnel. Use this information in strategic planning, problem determination, network design, desktop management, resource planning, and many more ways that are valuable. When it comes to managing networks, you need accurate reliable data, not opinions and estimates. Contact your IS Agency Consultant at xxx-xxxx to obtain a complete overview of this valuable service offering.

Consulting services

A trusting relationship

It is the basic ingredient for a successful business partnership. At IS, we know that and prove ourselves to you every day. We need to understand your business, where you are going and help you plan how to get there.

You need a strong technical advisor, someone who understands how information system technology can make your agency succeed.

That is what IS Consulting Services is all about. Our agency consultants are there with you to help define requirements based on your business needs, formulate a solution and lead you through a successful implementation.

Strategic vision

When it come to developing a strategic vision for your information systems, you are putting the future of your agency or department on the line. It is imperative that you have expert counsel.

Alignment of you information systems plan with your business strategies is essential. Maximizing the return on your current information technology investment is a requirement.

IS Consulting Services is uniquely positioned to advise you on today's technology and to help you plan for your future systems and applications.

Requirements

Within IS, our expertise ranges from project management to software installation from application and database design through development and delivery.

You benefit from that experience every time you rely on us. IS stands by you every step of the way. Whether you want us to do the entire job or just supplement your staff, you can count on us for quality results.

With IS on your team, you can concentrate on your team, you can concentrate on your business objectives while we assume much of the risk for your projects.

We will deliver totally integrated systems, ensuring that deadlines are met and budgets are adhered to. Fewer risks and less hassle for you, our valued clients.

Shared vision

IS Consulting Services, in concert with the Agency Information Officer can tailor a solution that's just right for you. We have the skills, resources, and experience to deliver precisely what you are looking for. For more information please contact IS Consulting Services at xxx-xxxx.

Appendix: Frequently asked questions

Johnson and Kern speak with thousands of IS professionals each year, and hear the same questions almost everywhere they go. In no particular order...

People issues

1. How do I transition my legacy staff without impacting my infrastructure? How do I support a heterogeneous world of UNIX, NT, mainframe, PC, and Macintosh?

It can be done but it is not going to be easy. You need initiative and drive, not to mention a quality training curriculum. See *Working with limited resources* on page 31 for the complete details. It took time and lots of hand-holding (not in a negative connotation) by management. Management has to be involved, even as far as grading homework, tracking metrics i.e., projects and classes completed, etc. Many of your staff is scared and intimidated by the flood of this technology. It may sound corny but they need to see that you care. We will tell you one more time—this stuff is not easy but it can be done and *should* be!

2. I have no people trained in these new technologies. I am stuck. What can I do?

People love training, so be sure to move your people into training opportunities as you move toward your preferred architectures. If you need short-term help, use consultants. Do not keep a mixed environment of high-paid freelancers and lower-paid employees. That is a recipe for long-term brain-drain and internal friction.

3. If I have people trained in one version of UNIX how long will it take to get them up to speed on another?

About a week of formal training and you should expect them to be up to speed in about a month. All UNIX systems use the same kernel (AT&T System V) and the commands are mostly common. The various UNIX "flavors" (Solaris, IRIX, AIX, HP/UX) are mostly differentiated by various OS services and administration procedures. The shift should not take long.

4. What are some of the most common organizational issues/problems facing IS?

It all starts here. We have performed hundreds of Infrastructure reviews providing analysis on people, process, and technology issues over the past few years with the outcome always having recommendations to re-structure the organization.

You would think that after decades of biannual reorganizations, IS would possibly get this one right. Guess again! See *IS's unlucky 13 organizational problems* on page 38 for a long list of ailments awaiting the hapless.

5. Where in the organization do you fit in the Internet and intranet function?

Although these functions are the latest/greatest and the hottest stuff going on in the industry at this time it does not mean you should build a separate organization to support it. Technologies are continuously changing. There is no reason why it could not fit into an existing organization with a project leader/staff focusing on this particular technology. Because client/server is so complicated especially the support functions when dealing with everyone's support roles and responsibilities, trust us it's best to keep the organization as simple as possible.

6. What percentage of legacy staff will be able to transition into a newer technology such as Unix or NT?

Perhaps eight out of ten will change. The remainder will probably want to retire with the mainframe, or they simply don't possess the initiative and drive to put in the effort. See *Transitioning/training/mentoring staff* on page 34 for more.

7. Why do organizations continue to organize by technology?

Many IS shops are organized by technology or will be in the near future. Their concern is if they do not keep legacy staff focused on the bread and butter of the company everyone will abandon ship to work on the fun client/server stuff and RAS will deteriorate. We beg to differ, if you be up-front with your entire staff and communicate the priorities you will not have this problem also let it be known that training must be done on their own time and RAS should not be measured for a particular technology.

The following issues arise when organizing by technology:

- Communication between groups is poor at best.
- Barriers and walls come up.
- Cross-training is difficult.
- Resource constraints.

- Morale issues surface.
- Politics drives technology decisions.

Never organize by technology. The best way to organize is by function and mentor your staff that a production system is a production system is a production system regardless of platform.

8. How do you improve communication within IS and external to IS?

One of the biggest client/server killers in the land today—communication. This is due to several reasons:

- Technology is moving so quickly that no one has the time to address it.
- Corporations are more global—support staffs are more decentralized than ever.
- Applications are running wild throughout your network.
- Corporations are trying to do more with less.
- Organization structure inhibits good communication.

There is only one way to battle communication problems. Every company has them but some worse off than the others. On page 61 we talk about the Client/Server Production Acceptance process (CSPA), which is the single most important process for Network Computing. This process promotes and instills communication practices throughout the IS organization. You cannot just talk about improving communication and having quarterly departmental picnics do not cut it. You need a process that forces communication *each* and *every day.*

9. How do you get your existing staff to learn and support multiple platforms without burning them out?

You must do more with less and unfortunately with technology moving as quickly as it is you cannot force the staff. The ones with initiative and drive will do whatever it takes to learn this new enterprise the others will need some hand-holding. In *Transitioning/training/mentoring staff* on page 34, we describe the curricula in detail. However, hand-holding is critical. Management must be involved with the curricula (i.e., grading homework, curriculum progress discussed in each staff meeting, working in training lab with staff) unfortunately we all need a personal life and have family obligations. Nevertheless, if you want your staff to succeed and put in extra effort on their own time—periodically show presence—not all the time just enough to show them you are sincere.

10. Why is it so difficult to define everyone's roles and responsibilities in the New Enterprise?

Network computing has caused much confusion for IS. Who does what is not as clear as it was back in the olden days? A Systems Programmer knew where their responsibilities started and ended, it is the same with the DBA. That was a very predictable and easy to support paradigm. Things have changed considerably.

You still need those time-tested job descriptions — you will probably need to take the dust off them and revise them a bit. Please make them as generic as possible for supporting any technology. Job descriptions alone will not cut it. You will still need to define everyone's roles and responsibilities during the deployment of any new application using the CSPA process. Each application will have different requirements and IS will need to adapt to these new guidelines. The CSPA will allow you to define who does what to who and when for supporting the companies mission critical distributed systems.

11. We are losing our best staff. How can we keep them?

The pressures of changing IS has produced a serious shortage of trained IS professionals. In this environment, if you do not stay close to your people and the job market, you will lose your people, and the best always seem to go first. Here are some suggestions:

Do not count on HR. The typical salary surveys and averaging processes done by most corporate HR departments will never produce competitive price-outs. Read the salary surveys published on the web or in the trade press. (You should do it for yourself too).

Remember what motivates good IS professionals — doing cool work and growing in their careers. Make sure your staff has a good work environment, provide the best equipment and ample opportunities for them to take classes, work on interesting projects, and showcase their work and grow professionally. People will often stay for less money if they feel valued.

12. Salaries are out of control. What do I do?

Yes they are. The job market is changing fast with all the pressures for year 2000 and the rapid move to client server systems. Salary surveys more than 6 months old are obsolete. We suggest this simple rule of thumb — try to be within 15% of the market. Leading edge salaries are not necessary — if you are providing a good professional environment for your staff.

13. How many operations staff will I need?

Hard to say specifically since so many variables are involved. Ask if you are using best practices in your environment. Best practices include more automated server room environments, managing servers on second and third shifts from home using auto-paging, the ability to have your data centers back each other up using remote management tools, automated backup and storage management, and automated job scheduling.

When best practices are employed, operations staff can be more fully integrated into other departments. Data center staff should not be watching monitors or performing routine functions and can become more involved in higher level functions of support, design, and development. Production Control is a good career path for Computer Operators.

14. There are not enough hours in the day. How can I keep up?

IS Management is becoming ever more demanding and the time pressures are high. Basic time management principles apply. There are structural reasons for time demands that you should think about how much of your time is reacting to situations instead of moving forward. We realize this is easy for us to talk about but things will only get worse. Technology will not slow down—if anything it will speed up. Start by implementing the type of processes that we talk about throughout all of our books. Processes that will help you become more active. The CSPA is the one to start with.

15. I am being blindsided by customer concerns and demands.

Customers want more than ever before and rightly so. If we were customers we would want to get as much as possible from our vendor. You, as the vendor, need to listen. We recommend having a set of business consultants that report into IS but reside with the customer — and report dotted-line into the business unit. These people should be directors and above. Their job is to schmooze with the customer to acquire have an in-depth knowledge of the business and secondly to provide process/technology solutions to their business issues. A job description of this individual is provided in *Appendix: IS job descriptions* on page 133.

We also recommend that you had better implement a very simple to use charge-back system. First, you had better have your house in order. See page *Cost-of-service* on page 74, for details of implementing a complete cost-of-service methodology.

16. We have done good work but we do not get any credit for it. How can we get the customer to appreciate us?

You have a serious problem. If customers do not understand the value of what you do or how hard you work, you are not managing their expectations properly. A huge problem for IS is still that perception where IS is just a bunch of costly bureaucrats. Hopefully this is no longer true at your shop. If it is then you would better get all three of our previous books and start reading. If you do have your house in order then we suggest you start marketing and selling your services. This is extremely time consuming but this is necessary for the 21st century.

17. How can you use vendors appropriately?

The competition is fierce out there. Hopefully you are getting the most out of your vendor. Relationships need constant work just like a marriage. This is very time consuming but needs to be done. You have scarce resources and need all the help you can get. Building the right client/server infrastructure will take everything your organization does not have—bandwidth.

18. How can I improve customer satisfaction while cutting my IS support costs?

First, you have to change the way you were doing this in the past. Survey forms do not cut it. You were doing great if you received 40 percent feedback. If you think about it that is horrible. These metrics are more critical than any other. You need to receive 100 percent feedback. All it takes is one bad incident getting to the wrong VP and your toast. Tracking every request for service should not be that difficult.

Your help desk process tracks each problem (or at least that is the intent). It should also track customer satisfaction for all problems and work-related requests.

We recommend something as simple as point and click. Why not have a tool delivered online that lets users quickly and easily rate the quality and timeliness of the service performed. How about something as silly as three faces; smiley, frown, and neutral. An icon is automatically e-mailed to the user that opened the trouble call, they open it, point, click, and IS will have a metric on gauging customer satisfaction.

We recommend tracking on the frown faces — do not worry about the smileys and neutral response — the frowns will kill you. Set departmental goals. If you beat the number bonus the staff. Also you will need to follow-up and visit each customer that logged a frown so it does not occur again. Your organization should be able to market and sell this very simple concept with their customers if they cannot maybe you have the wrong people in front of your customers.

The only way to control costs is to first understand what your actual expenditures are — that should be easy to achieve. Then you will need to document the services provided to your users and put those costs next to those services. Now get out there and benchmark with vendors that provide some of these services (i.e., system administration services). Now you have a good understanding of how cost-efficient your services are. If they are not then you will need to follow our methodologies, purchase our three books, and do it right.

19. Is selective outsourcing recommended (i.e., help desk)?

Yes but again only if the department is already running efficiently. PC installation/maintenance is another area but also remember that you will need to manage your vendor. Nothing works that easily. If you turnover a mess to them, what makes you think they will do a better job than you will? We do not think so. Outsourcing garbage will only buy you double the headaches—because now you'll need to focus on not only managing your customer expectations but this newly acquired vendor. If you turn something over to them that's already running efficiently then.

20. What can IS do to cut support costs?

IS needs to continually benchmark itself to become more efficient than the competition. That competition is outsourcing vendors or other companies providing these types of services. See *The economics of client/server and process engineering* on page 67 for details.

Process issues

1. How does IS implement charge back for this new network environment?

Good luck! Who likes to get a new bill? It can be done. We recommend keeping it very simple. In the mainframe world, we charged for everything (disk space, CPU utilization, etc.). It was so complicated that no one could understand the bill, the cost was outrageous, and they did not have a say in the manner. The bottom line is that it angered people.

It is always best to keep things simple, even in charge back methodology. We have spent time identifying new ways to deal with capital and expense budgets; now let us look at a simple method of charge back. For networking, determine the network charge. This consists of all network-related expenses such as: labor, leased lines, equipment, software, etc. Divide the total network charge by the number of employees.

This becomes the "network charge" (and can be monthly or quarterly). Do the same for desktop, telephone, voice mail, etc. Add these figures together for the 'total' desktop charge. Bill the using department this charge times the total number of employees in the department/division. For the data center, define the total data center charge including hardware, labor, software licensing, maintenance, etc. Divide the total data center charge by the number of applications/servers supported to obtain a per application charge. Bill the business unit an application/server charge for each of their owned applications. See *Charge back* on page 78 for more details.

2. What are the most common process issues/problems?

The lack thereof! OK lets be a bit more specific:

- Lack of a complete Problem Management solution?
- Lack of a centrally owned enterprise-wide Change Management process.
- Lack of a formalized application deployment methodology from an operational support perspective.
- With all the talk of security — very little is being done.

3. What are the top disciplines (problem management, disaster recovery, security, etc.) that are required to effectively support mission critical production applications?

After providing client/server infrastructure analysis to hundreds of fortune 500 companies the Top 3 disciplines that are lacking from most IS shops are:

- Production Acceptance
- Problem Management
- Change Management

In that order! Production Acceptance is by far leading the pack. As we have discussed earlier in the book applications are being developed at an accelerated pace and development has this nasty habit of throwing these applications over the wall to Operations. There needs to be an effective deployment methodology that provides RAS into newly developed applications. Operations need to be involved from the beginning.

See *Client/Server Production Acceptance (CSPA)* on page 61 for a detailed explanation. The CSPA concept is new to most of you but change and problem management should not be. Guess again. For the hundreds of infrastructure reviews we have performed each one of them had problems in implementing an effective enterprise-wide problem and change management process.

Technology issues

1. Which system management tools do I use? Do I need to purchase CA Unicenter or Tivoli?

Be very careful here — both are expensive. Are you really getting what the sales rep promises? Frameworks are fine if you want one look-and-feel for all your management tools i.e., asset management, software distribution, scheduling, etc. That is the positive side of buying a framework with all the components. On the negative side — if you buy 10 components — a few might be good, a few might be so-so, and a few might not meet your requirements.

If possible, we highly recommend you look at point solutions. Remember what we used to go through on the mainframe. We documented the system management process, extensively tested the top two or three products, then implementation. Sure this route takes much more resource but at least you know what you are purchasing and you will be implementing the possible tool for managing the enterprise.

2. What is less costly to implement, operate, and maintain NT or UNIX?

This always comes up in discussions. It is quite simple. We have been telling you for years that it has nothing to do with technology. If you implement processes (problem management, software distribution, asset management, configuration management, and so on. that are streamlined and non-bureaucratic you will achieve a cost-effective infrastructure regardless of the technology.

3. How does IS win its customers back to regain control of technology?

You thought World War II was difficult. That was nothing compared to this challenge of the nineties and the next millennium. It is going to be an uphill battle. Your customers have tasted freedom in a big way the past 10 years. With the sins of the past you've dug yourself a hole and your about 6 feet under — digging out will not be easy. Do not go back on your hands and knees asking for mercy. It will not help. You have to get your house in order first. Implement the right products (cost efficient process) then market and sell your goods.

4. Do I treat my server like a mainframe? Multiple applications on one server? On the other hand, do I size the application to the server?

Today you have a choice. The hardware is there. What would you like flexibility or to control costs? If you decide to have multiple applications on one box you lose flexibility, suddenly things are slowly but surely reverting to the mainframe days. If you size the application to a server then you retain flexibility for your end-user but the cost of support goes way up. See page *Technology infrastructure* on page 103 for a detailed explanation.

5. Middleware — Which tools to manage production scheduling etc.?

This is a very complex question and *Technology infrastructure* on page 103 and *Technology: Design & hardware* on page 87 for suggestions on architecture and tools. The good news is the tools to manage client server systems are rapidly evolving and there are many vendors who offer tools for system management functions.

- How long is the design life of the system and how often do you expect to change it?
- Does the system interface with other systems, or is it relatively stand-alone?

- What are the consequences of not being able to get information from the system moved to other systems?
- What happens if the vendor fails with a new release, or suffers financial problems?
- Are there accepted standards for the system or interface with multivendor support and standards setting organizations?

6. We bought a system from a leading company a few years ago and now they are no longer the leaders. How can I avoid this problem?

Many IS managers we work with seem to feel their job would be easy if only they could pick winning vendors and have them solve all the problems.

There are two issues here. First to be sure the vendors you are working with have a reputation for understanding their installed base, and have a clear technology vision, and migration plans to move you forward with evolving technology. Looking at financial statements is not helpful in picking quality vendors. Second, ask about the consequences of vendor failure. Are there substitutes for the application, and is the architecture sufficiently open to be able to get other products connected to it, or to be able to get the data out of it if needed?

7. Management expects our new system to last 5-10 years minimum. How do I pick a system that will last that long? You need to ask the following questions:

- Is the software and hardware architecture open or Closed?
- If you had to change to an alternative system in case of a vendor collapse, how would you do it?
- What is the depth of support for the platform in the market?

That is a tough challenge in rapidly changing times. We often doubt that the design life for new systems shouldn't be that long, since customers are often asking for changes more frequently, but for long lived production systems ask the following questions: How long will the vendor support their hardware after end of life, what is the migration path to new hardware and software what is the backwards compatibility plan?

Enterprise packaged systems (Businessware)

1. How do I select a vendor for our new accounting package?

We discuss the issues surrounding this process in detail in *Technology: Software* on page 95, but remember that in package selection, process is everything. Ask whether you need highly integrated packages, or whether specific "best-of-breed" solutions are appropriate. What do your customers want, not only immediately, but also into the future. Consider how you are going to support the installation and sustaining of the package you select.

A bit of all three

1. How do you build a world-class infrastructure?

It took decades and millions of dollars and more importantly, time to develop those processes which surround those big blue boxes. It was not the box. Below we outline our 10 IS commandments (methodologies) in building a world-class infrastructure. See *Ten commandments of a world-class IS infrastructure* on page 1 for details.

1. The network becomes the data center
2. Modified mainframe disciplines
3. Minimum and sufficient architectures
4. Centralized control with decentralized operations
5. Communicate, communicate, and over communicate
6. A production system is a production system is a production system
7. If you cannot measure it you cannot manage it
8. If you build it they will come
9. Market and sell your services
10. Success is equal to the amount of change you can manage

2. How does corporate IS regain respect and credibility—something which was lost with the advent of client/server?

It is really all about re-engineering IS in a major way! You need to build that world-class infrastructure and they will come back! Once you build it, you need to market and sell it in a big way. Marketing and selling is an art today. IS needs to embrace it and incorporate it into everyone's job. Yes we know you do not have the time but you need to make the time.

3. How do you define "infrastructure"?

Quite simple People, Process and Technology. Everything and anything as it relates to supporting your corporations business systems from the desktop to the network. From the people that provide 24-hour support to the processes required to maintain RAS.

4. What would be the success factors for implementing a world-class production environment?

Success or building that elusive world-class infrastructure is attainable but the effort will be enormous. Below is what it will take.

- Up front planning
- Define and communicate the architecture
- Follow our 10 commandments (see *Ten commandments of a world-class IS infrastructure* on page 1)
- Transition/mentor your staff

No one said it would be easy. It took decades to get it right on the mainframe but unfortunately, that luxury is no longer available. In the 1970s the infrastructure came first even before developing new systems — IBM was paid before anyone else. Now the tide has turned, 100 percent is development and developing quickly the infrastructure can wait. Right? Wrong BIGTIME wrong! No one can slowdown the development of new systems but because of this crazy world we refer to as client/server you need to focus on your infrastructure more than ever before.

5. What are the risk factors involved when deploying network computing?

The risk factors are:

Staff burnout as they still maintain legacy environments while deploying Network Computing. There's enormous training requirements, designing and implementing a new infrastructure, keeping up with the accelerated pace of developing/deploying distributed systems.

Implementing an infrastructure that is not cost-effective.

Implementing processes without resolving people issues first.

Focusing on technology first. You cannot effectively implement technology without fixing people and process issues first. We'll say it over and over again until some of those CIOs out there will start listening to the cries from the trenches.

6. What are the most critical issues that need to be resolved before you can effectively support network computing?

It would be nice to say you need to have all the People, Process, and Technology issues resolved before you can support networking computing in the most cost efficient manner. That is asking a bit much. Let us prioritize them for you:

- Organizational structure
- Implement the CSPA process

- Mentor and train staff in implementing streamlined processes.
- Implement an enterprise-wide problem management solution.
- Implement an enterprise-wide change management solution.

These are the minimum set of issues to address.

7. How do you know when you have implemented a cost-effective and flexible infrastructure?

A very simple non-technical answer. "Build it and they will come," referring to your customers. When they start requesting your services instead of you attempting to dictate services then you know you have done a good job. The alternative is building it and they *do not* come.

8. How do you support global infrastructures?

By deploying the same processes organization-wide. These processes should be flexible enough to adapt to regional or divisional facilities. Consistent architectures, standards, and processes are necessary. It is also important to have only one person in charge of your global infrastructure. Multiple owners cause major political conflict and duplication of efforts in regards to System Management processes and tools. The focus is no longer towards having an enterprise solution but more of a region. It should be an equal mix.

9. We have too many servers. How do I consolidate them?

This question is too detailed to be answered quickly, but first ask why you have too many and how you know you have too many. The most important question is to understand whether you have a server proliferation problem, or a systems management problem. Since servers are often inexpensive, it may be more cost effective to have more servers that are lightly used than a more highly consolidated server suite.

10. I do not know how many servers we have. What do I do?

The bad news is that you are really out of control. The good news is that you are not alone. We see IS shops all the time that do not know how their operating environment works. You must find all your servers, by hand if need be, and build a comprehensive system diagram before you can begin to organize your environment.

Once organized all future servers need to be deployed via the CSPA process. Configuration standards must be consistent as possible throughout your enterprise.

11. What can I do to fix my mail system?

Many organizations have allowed their mail and messaging systems to grow in an unplanned way, and are now finding high administrative costs and poor service plague their systems. We suggest building a messaging system from the enterprise down. Ask what services you want to provide all your employees, and where they are located and then begin working with vendors to build a system to meet those needs. We believe there is much to be gained by a centralized mail system instead of hundreds (literally) of small mail servers for each department.

12. Are other IS organizations having the same problems?

Count on it. We are always amazed at hearing managers say their problems are unique. The bottom line is that everyone is frustrated managing client/server. Your problems are not unique. We have been advising IS professionals for years that it is only a matter of time until the People, Process, and Technology problems with client/server causes major heartburn.

13. How can I learn more about what other organizations are doing to address their problems?

Read our books regardless of whatever the time pressures, every IS manager needs to set aside some time to read the trade journals and participate in professional interactions with colleagues. We suggest joining professional societies like the Society for Information Management, which often sponsor excellent meetings, and reading journals including *Information Week* and *CIO*. Consulting organizations such as Gartner Group and Forrester Research can also be valuable clearinghouses for product information and industry trends.

We will inform you that the most common problems are:

- Development throws new C/S applications over the wall to operations.
- Ineffective enterprise-wide problem management process.
- Help desk not effective:
- Perception is that the help desk is not as responsive as it could be
- Lack of root cause analysis
- Lack of close loop feedback
- Level-2 analysts not putting in detailed description of how they resolved the problem.
- Staff has very little authority.
- Lack of training
- Many of the groups provide no feedback on problems being worked on.
- Acts more like a dispatch center.

- Sometimes you cannot get through the telephone. If you get through they take the problem — sometime written incorrectly.
- Very little exposure to new systems when deployed.
- Ineffective enterprise-wide change management process.
- Organization structured to support technology.
- Communication is worse than ever throughout IS.
- Training staff to support the enterprise.

14. What am I supposed to do when management asks me to implement a 'lights-out' production environment?

Tell him that the authors of this book said there is no such thing as "lights-out."In our third book, *Networking the New Enterprise,* Chapter 1, tables 1-7 we define what lights-out really means.

Outsourcing

1. Should I consider outsourcing my IS organization?

Watch out for this one. Those service bureaus have some slick sales people and they are trained to sell to the CFO. They will schmooze them, wine and dine them, show them pretty charts on cost savings. So why shouldn't the CFO outsource that entire headache — after all it's probably not your company's core competency and besides you know what the perception of IS is throughout the company — money continuously flushing down the drain.

We have seen very few outsourcing partnerships work. We have been asked to come in and resolve conflict between these vendors and their customers throughout the world — we mention no names but they are some of the biggest in the industry. Let us get a fact out on the table right now. Service bureaus are not less costly. They will definitely cost your company more in the long haul. So what good are they? If you have a perfectly stable and efficient legacy infrastructure — they can handle that and let you focus on other technology i.e., client/server. Can they manage this client/server world? They do not have a clue as those sales reps say they do. It has taken them decades to manage that mainframe and that is straightforward — servers all over the net? We do not think so.

To summarize; if you turnover a perfectly tuned legacy environment then that is okay — but if you turnover your unmanageable new enterprise then you will get twice the trouble in return.

 G

Metrics

1. What metrics should we track to ensure RAS?

In the New Enterprise metrics are more important than ever before. When things were simple — your entire company's computing infrastructure was under one roof or shall we say one glass house. In the legacy world we used to track and measure everything and then some including:

- Availability
- Response times
- Abends
- Reports not printed by 08:00
- Batch jobs not completed by 08:00
- # users: High-water mark
- # users: throughout the day
- # of application transactions
    - <1 second Response
    - >3 second response
- Total # of production jobs
- # of production reports
- CPU utilization
- Network availability

We managed to those numbers. Our former vice president used to tell us that if you didn't know the numbers in your area then who does? You must know those numbers! You need to measure everything! How can you improve unless you benchmark? You need them more than ever. The only way to improve service and customer satisfaction is to benchmark.

We have been telling people for years that the reason mainframe computing was so reliable was not because of the box but because of the surrounding disciplines. Metrics is a major part of disciplines.

2. We cannot measure how we are doing — the mainframe is up, but customers are not happy.

The old adage applies — if you cannot measure it, you cannot manage it.

Inappropriate metrics are devastating, because it makes it impossible for customers and service providers to align on service goals and standards. Be sure your metrics are customer-centric not system-centric. We see situations all the time where the operations staff believes they are doing a good job, but customers are not happy because metrics do not reflect customer concerns and perceptions.

Service-level agreements

1. How do you establish effective service-level agreements (SLA)?

We recommend that you do not have separate SLA. We are not saying to trash the SLAs only to incorporate them into the CSPA. Remember automate, automate, automate, and streamline as many of the processes as possible. See *Service levels* on page 77 for more details.

The CSPA is an SLA for each application. Each application has different users with different requirements. You do not need a separate document but you do need the process.

Budgets and planning

1. How can I get more money from management? They want us to be more cost-efficient, but demands are always increasing.

Everyone faces budget pressures. The key is establishing value with management. We are continually amazed at IS departments that are doing work that is critical to the success of the organization, that are viewed as non-strategic cost centers that are spending too much. If you are in this position, you need to help management understand the business value of your efforts.

2. Why can't we afford my client/server system?

Poorly managed client/server systems are expensive to operate. Unraveling the confusion surrounding this problem is a major theme throughout this book. See *Principles of organizational design* on page 11 and *The politics of people, process, and technology* on page 23 for suggestions on how to plan and reign in an uncontrolled client/server environment.

3. We are about to be merged with another company. How do we plan for the transition?

This one is much in the hands of the company executives. Which IS shops swallows the other. Hopefully you followed our recommendations throughout the book, which is about all you can do now.

Bibliography

Boar, B., *Cost-Effective Strategies for Client/Server Systems*, John Wiley & Sons, Inc., 1996.

Brooks, Jr. Frederick P., *The Mythical Man Month*, Addison Wesley, 1975.

Coad and Yourdon, *Object Oriented Analysis*, Yourdon Press, 1990.

Computers and managerial choice, Peter G.W. Keen, "Organizational Dynamics," 14(2), 35-49. (1985, Autumn).

DeGrace and Stahl, *Wicked Problems, Righteous Solutions*, Yourdon Press, 1990.

Davenport, Thomas, *Process Innovation: Reengineering Work Through Information Technology*, Harvard Business School Press, 1993.

Fallon, Howard, *How to Implement Information Systems and Live to Tell About it*, John Wiley & Sons, 1995.

Hammer and Champy, *Reengineering The Corporation*, Harper Collins, 1993.

Keen, Peter G. W., *Every manager's guide to information technology: A glossary of key terms and concepts for today's business leader*, Harvard Business School Press, 1991.

Kern, Johnson, Hawkins, Law, *Managing The New Enterprise*, Prentice-Hall, 1996.

Kern, Johnson, Hawkins, Lyke, *Networking The New Enterprise*, Prentice-Hall, 1997.

Kern, Johnson, *Rightsizing The New Enterprise*, Prentice-Hall, 1994.

McGee and Pruzak, *Managing Information Strategically*, John Wiley & Sons, 1993.

Organization versus competitive advantage, Peter G.W. Keen, "Proceedings of the Eight International Conference on Information Systems," Pittsburgh PA. (1987, December)

Porter, M., *Competitive Advantage: Creating and Sustaining Superior Performance*, Macmillan Publishing, 1985.

Strassmann, Paul, *The Politics of Information Management: Policy Guidelines*, Information Economics Press, 1994

The coming of the new organization, Peter Drucker, "Harvard Business Review," 88(1), 45-53, (1988, January-February).

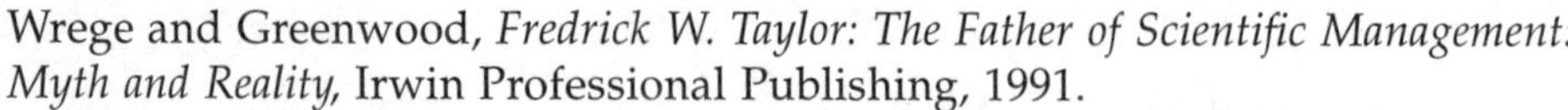

Wrege and Greenwood, *Fredrick W. Taylor: The Father of Scientific Management: Myth and Reality*, Irwin Professional Publishing, 1991.

Yourdon, Edward, *Death March*, Edward Yourdon, Prentice-Hall, 1997.

Yourdon, Edward, *Decline and Fall of the American Programmer*, Yourdon Press Computing Series, 1992.

Yourdon, Edward, *Techniques of Program Structure and Design*, Prentice-Hall, 1975.

Zmud, Robert W. *Information Systems in Organizations*, Scott Foresman & Co., 1983.

Glossary

abend

Abnormal end. A program condition on the IBM 370 when a program reaches an abnormal end. This is different from an abort.

application server

Server on a distributed network that provides access to an application.

architecture

The specific components of a computer system and the way they interact with one another.

3270

A type of device, like a terminal and printer, used to communicate with mainframes

APS

Application Services. One of the IS service areas.

Baan

Baan is a Dutch software company that competes with SAP, Oracle, and others in the enterprise software market.

BLOBS

Binary Large Objects — A database type that allows large binary files to be managed as fields of a database. Usually used for video, audio, or program files.

capacity planning

Active monitoring system for computer resources across multiple systems; includes system resources, such as CPU power, I/O transfer rate, memory size, disk storage, and network bandwidth.

centralized control

One central support group that serves to test for quality on a timely basis, decreases labor costs through the use of one location, simplifies problem determination, and implements and supports computing resources.

CGI

Common Gateway Interface — A technique to allow programmers to connect web interfaces to databases.

change control

A process that coordinates changes that can potentially impact the production environment.

client

A system on the network that requests a service from a server.

client/server model

A computing model where the processing of applications is distributed across different systems on a network. The systems are often front-end clients and back-end servers.

Client/Server Production Acceptance (CSPA)

A process comprising of guidelines and procedures developed to support and implement distributed mission-critical business systems with mainframe disciplines and central control.

Clist

A mainframe programming language which is often used for systems management.

configuration management

The actual process of changing and maintaining the release of objects: Hardware, System Software, Application Software, etc., between the staging and the production environments.

console management

A process to consolidate physical consoles in a centralized location.

Data Warehouse

A marketing term for a repository (typically large) of corporate data that can be accessed using specialized query tools. This technique separates the analysis of data from the recording of data, and often is used to combine data from different computing systems to make information access more convenient and coherent.

Disaster Recovery

A well planned, contingency system that will enable (business-defined) recovery in the event a disaster should render your daily operations incapable of performance.

DNS

Domain Name Service — A directory service that allows the naming of computers so that they can be integrated into a computer network.

Event Monitoring

A process which monitors an event on a system, a network, a database, an application (e.g. a fault, a threshold) sending an alert to a centralized location.

Extranet

An extranet is an Intranet that includes external organizations or individuals such as suppliers or customers.

GAAP

Generally accepted accounting principles — The basis for all accounting done by publicly traded companies.

GroupWare

A term applied to supercharged e-mail systems such as Lotus Notes or Microsoft Exchange. These systems allow for group collaboration on documents and manage workflow among workgroups.

HP Openview

An Enterprise system management tool developed and sold by Hewlett-Packard.

HTML

Hypertext Markup Language — The page description language used by browsers on the World Wide Web.

HTTP

Hypertext Transfer Protocol — The standard protocol for transferring information on the World Wide Web.

Infrastructure

The functions that perform utility services, such as networking, data center, and system administration. Each organization should have an architecture statement defining the organizational structure and operational procedures.

Internal Support Agreement

An understanding and agreement among the different IS groups. Its primary purpose is to clearly define support roles, responsibilities, and the set of expectations.

Intranet

An information system internal to an enterprise that follows the Internet Web based Metaphor. Intranets are most commonly used to provide on-line manuals and procedures, and as electronic bulletin boards to post internal information.

IPX

A network transport protocol developed by Novell Corp.

Java

A computer language introduced by Sun Microsystems in the spring of 1995. JAVA is a language specifically designed to allow the safe transfer of computer programs over computer networks.

JDBC

Java Database Connectivity — An analog of ODBC that will allow JAVA applications to connect to foreign databases.

JDK

Java Development Kit — A developers kit and libraries developed by Sun Microsystems and available for downloading from www.javasoft.com.

Middleware

A generic term for software that sits between the application and the operating system to provide services such as transaction control, reliability, security, inter-application information routing.

MVS

IBM's operating system for its mainframe computers.

Network administration

Tasks of the person who maintains a network, such as adding systems to a network or enabling sharing between systems.

Network architecture

Defines the structure of the network and how different network components and functions work together.

Network management

Refers to all the aspects of planning, implementing and operating the network to ensure it is reliable, available, and serviceable.

Network Router

A device to route packets of information throughout networks and translate different protocols between different subnets.

Network utilization

The capacity of a network that is actually used to transmit data.

NFS

Network File System — A system that allows computers to share files over networks. Originally developed by Sun Microsystems in 1983.

NIS

Network Information System — A directory system developed by Sun Microsystems.

ODBC

Open Database Connectivity — A database connection specification that allows Microsoft applications to connect to databases such as Oracle or Sybase.

OLAP

Online Analytical Process - a marketing term that refers to tools and techniques to allow the interactive analysis of database information.

Performance management

A global view of network and system resource utilization, which identify potential performance bottlenecks/problems

Performance monitoring
A process or program that appraises and records status information about various network or system devices and other processes.

PDA
Personal Digital Assistant

Port Concentrator
A device that allows multiple physical connections to be made to a single I/O slot.

Print Management
A process to decentralized printing by on-line viewing, and provides print spooling for required centralized printing.

Problem Management
A centralized process to manage and resolve user problems.

Production Acceptance
A methodology to implement and support mission critical client/server distributed systems.

RAS
Reliability, Availability, Serviceability — An acronym describing the set of hardware and software features that make a computer less likely to fail, more tolerant of component failure when it happens, and easier and faster to repair if it does fail.

Runbook
The support requirements for a batch process on the mainframe.

SAP
Systems, Applications, and Programs. SAP, AG is a German software company that has gained a substantial share of the market for enterprise business software.

Scheduling
A process to schedule jobs, perform job-restart and job-dependency checking in a computing environment.

Service Level Agreement
An agreement between the network users and the network operations. It describes the expected levels of network service.

Service Levels

The agreed upon specification that a customer of IS services will receive.

SKIP

Simple key management for the Internet protocol — A protocol for managing encryption keys on the Internet.

SLA

See *Service Level Agreement*.

Software Distribution

Workgroup software is "distributed" to user instead of being installed on the user's desktop.

SMTP

Simple Mail Transfer Protocol — The Internet standard way of transferring mail.

Storage Management

To keep back up and archive tapes off-site in a safe and controlled environment. A backup/restore, catalogue, and storage process to effectively manage disk and tape usage.

SunNet Manager

An enterprise system management tool developed and sold by Sun Microsystems. SunNet Manager allows for the remote administration of a network of computers. The product is no longer called SunNet Manager. It is referred to as Sun Domain Manager, Enterprise Manager, and Site Manager.

Symantec

A software development company.

System monitoring

Procedures by which IS monitors network computing systems across multiple platforms and details system availability.

URL

Universal Resource Locator — The address of World Wide Web resources.

Visual J++

A Java development product from Microsoft Corp.

VMS

Digital Equipment Company's operating system for its VAX family of machines.

VSAM

Virtual Sequential Access Method — A file management system introduced by IBM in 1973 to manage flat files on IBM mainframes.

Web top

A marketing and technical concept stolen from the metaphor of the "desktop" used by personal computers. The Web top metaphor replaces operating desktop look and feel by one evolved from a browser metaphor of the World Wide Web.

World Wide Web

A common interface and supporting protocols within the world of the Internet that allow content providers and users to display data in the form of text, graphics and sound, all combined to make the viewing navigation of information easy to use and pleasant to look at (and hear).

Index

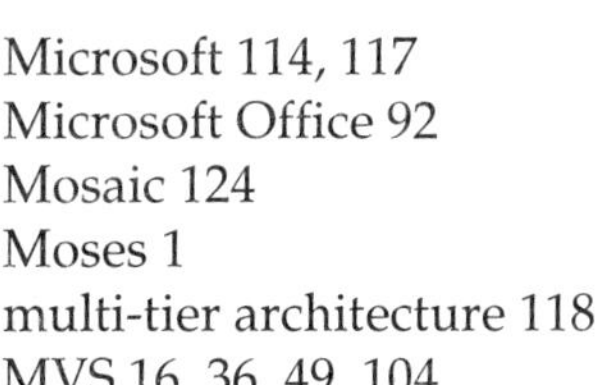

T

U

V

W

SUN MICROSYSTEMS PRESS BOOKS
Bringing Sun's Expertise to You!

PRENTICE HALL PTR is pleased to publish **SUN MICROSYSTEMS PRESS** books. This year's **SUN MICROSYSTEMS PRESS** catalog has unprecedented breadth and depth, covering not only the inner workings of Sun operating systems, but also guides to intranets, security, Java™, networking, and other topics important to anyone working with these technologies.

CORE JAVA 1.1
Volume I: Fundamentals

CAY S. HORSTMANN and GARY CORNELL

628 pages; (includes CD-ROM)
ISBN 0-13-766957-7

Now in its third revision, CORE JAVA is still the leading Java book for software developers who want to put Java to work on real problems. Written for experienced programmers with a solid background in languages ranging from Visual Basic to COBOL to C and C++, CORE JAVA 1.1, VOLUME 1 concentrates on the underlying Java 1.1 language along with the fundamentals of using the cross-platform graphics library supplied with the JDK™ 1.1.

This must-have reference features comprehensive coverage of the essentials for serious programmers:

- Encapsulation
- Classes and methods
- Inheritance
- The Java 1.1 event model
- Data structures
- Exception handling

The accompanying CD is packed with sample programs that demonstrate key language and library features — no toy code! The CD also includes the Windows 95/NT and Solaris™ versions of the JDK 1.1 and shareware versions of WinEdit, WinZip and TextPad for Windows95/NT.

CORE JAVA 1.1
Volume II: Advanced Features

CAY S. HORSTMANN and GARY CORNELL

630 pages; (includes CD-ROM)
ISBN 0-13-766965-8

For programmers already familiar with the core features of the JAVA 1.1 language, VOLUME 2: ADVANCED FEATURES includes detailed and up-to-date explanations of topics such as:

- Streams
- Multithreading
- Network programming
- JDBC, RMI, JavaBeans™
- Distributed objects

The accompanying CD includes useful sample programs (no toy code!), Windows 95/NT and Solaris™ versions of JDK 1.1, and shareware versions of WinEdit, TextPad, and WinZip.

"Cornell and Horstmann make the details of the powerful and expressive language understandable and they also furnish a conceptual model for its object-oriented foundations."

— GRADY BOOCH

...Also available from Sun Microsystems

INSIDE JAVA WORKSHOP 2.0, 2nd Edition

LYNN WEAVER

380 pages; ISBN 0-13-899584-2 (includes CD-ROM)

A guide for new and experienced Java WorkShop users, INSIDE JAVA WORKSHOP 2.0 provides a task-based tour of every tool in the Java development environment from Sun and also highlights how to use the significant new features in version 2.0.

You will quickly learn the basics of the development model, including setting development preferences, building Java projects interactively, analyzing Java program performance, editing code with the enhanced Source Editor,and debugging applets across the Internet. You'll also learn how to use advanced debugging and GUI building features, and how to create, import and deploy JavaBeans projects.

The CD-ROM includes a 30-day, full-functioning version of Java WorkShop along with project examples and sample programs, complete with source code. It also features links to Java resources on the Web.

JUMPING JAVASCRIPT

JANICE WINSOR and BRIAN FREEMAN

1200 pages; (includes CD-ROM) ISBN 0-13-841941-8

JUMPING JAVASCRIPT™ is a hands-on tutorial with loads of examples that will show both programmers and non-programmers how to use JavaScript to easily incorporate the interactivity of Java into their Web sites. It covers both basics such as scripting concepts, embedded Java applets, image maps, and buttons as well as advanced topics such as creating JavaScript objects and the cookies property. CD-ROM contains all the scripts discussed in the book.

WEB PAGE DESIGN
A Different Multimedia

MARY E. S. MORRIS and RANDY J. HINRICHS

200 pages; ISBN 0-13-239880-X

Everything you always wanted to know about practical Web page design! Anyone can design a web page, but it takes more than basic HTML skill to build a world-class Web site. Written for Web page authors, this hands-on guide covers the key aspects of designing a successful Web site and shows how to integrate traditional design techniques into Web sites. Contains sixteen full color examples of successful Web pages, and techniques for:

- Cognitive and content design
- Audience consideration
- Interactivity, organization, and navigational pathways
- Designing with VRML and Java
- Working with templates, style sheets, and Netscape™ Frames
- Evolving your design

HTML FOR FUN AND PROFIT, 3rd Edition

MARY E. S. MORRIS and JOHN E. SIMPSON

400 pages; ISBN 0-13-079672-7

The international best seller has been completely revised and updated to feature in-depth coverage of the fundamentals and all the hottest new HTML innovations. You will quickly master using tags, adding hyperlinks, graphics and multimedia, and creating clickable imagemaps. You will also learn the benefits of tables and frames and how to generate pages "on the fly." You will also find information on Dynamic

...Also available from Sun Microsystems

DEVELOPING VISUAL APPLICATIONS
XIL: An Imaging Foundation Library
WILLIAM K. PRATT

368 pages; ISBN 0-13-461948-X

A practical introduction to using imaging in new, innovative applications for desktop computing. DEVELOPING VISUAL APPLICATIONS breaks down the barriers that prevent developers from easily integrating imaging into their applications. It covers the basics of image processing, compression, and algorithm implementation and provides clear, real-world examples for developing applications using XIL™ a cross-platform imaging foundation library. More experienced imaging developers can also use this book as a reference to the architectural features and capabilities of XIL.

READ ME FIRST!
A Style Guide for the Computer Industry
SUN TECHNICAL PUBLICATIONS

256 pages; (includes CD-ROM)
ISBN 0-13-455347-0

User documentation should be an asset, not an afterthought. The READ ME FIRST! style guide can help technical publications groups outline, organize, and prepare high quality documentation for any type of computer product. Based on the award-winning Sun Microsystems documentation style guide, READ ME FIRST! includes complete guidelines—from style pointers to legal considerations, from writing for an international audience to forming a documentation department.

TOPICS INCLUDE:

- Grammar and punctuation guidelines
- Technical abbreviations, acronyms, and units of measurement
- How to set up your own documentation department

The CD-ROM includes ready-to-use FrameMaker templates for instant page design and the entire book in searchable FrameViewer and HTML format for easy reference.

INTRANET SECURITY:
Stories From the Trenches
LINDA McCARTHY

300 pages; ISBN 0-13-894759-7

Do you have response procedures for systems break-ins? Is your e-mail encrypted? Is your firewall protecting your company? Is your security staff properly trained? These are just a few of the security issues that are covered in INTRANET SECURITY: STORIES FROM THE TRENCHES. Author Linda McCarthy, who in her job as a worldwide security team leader at Sun broke into thousands of corporate intranets, presents detailed case studies of real-life break-ins that will help you make your systems safer. She explains how each breach occurred, describes what steps were taken to fix it, and then provides a practical and systematic solution for preventing similar problems from occurring on your network!

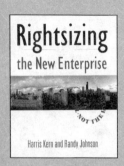

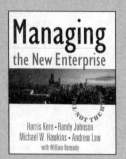

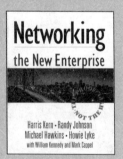

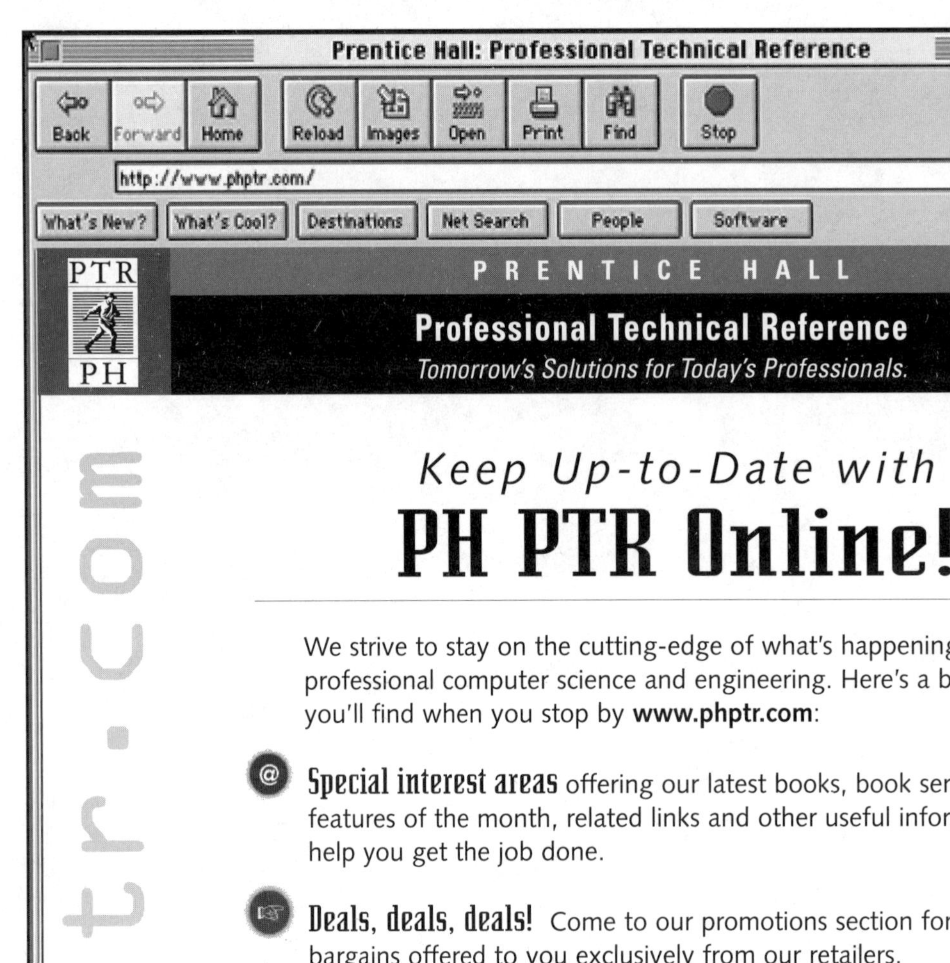
Prentice Hall: Professional Technical Reference
Back
Forward
Home
Reload
Images
Open
Print
Find
Stop
http://www.phptr.com/
What's New?
What's Cool?
Destinations
Net Search
People
Software
PTR
PH
PRENTICE HALL
Professional Technical Reference
Tomorrow's Solutions for Today's Professionals.
www.phptr.com